LIVING LANGUAGE®

COMPLETE
SPANISH
THE BASICS

Written by
Marisa Cid, Ph.D.

Edited by
Christopher A. Warnasch

Published in the United States by Living Language, an imprint of Random House, Inc.

www.livinglanguage.com

Editor: Christopher Warnasch
Production Editor: Carolyn Roth
Production Manager: Tom Marshall
Interior Design: Sophie Chin

First Edition

ISBN: 978-1-4000-2423-0

PRINTED IN THE UNITED STATES OF AMERICA

10 9 8 7 6 5 4 3 2 1

ACKNOWLEDGMENTS

Thanks to the Living Language team: Tom Russell, Nicole Benhabib, Christopher Warnasch, Zviezdana Verzich, Suzanne McQuade, Shaina Malkin, Elham Shabahat, Sophie Chin, Denise De Gennaro, Linda Schmidt, Alison Skrabek, Lisbeth Dyer, and Tom Marshall.

DEDICATION

To my precious Catherina.

COURSE OUTLINE

How to use this course .... *xi*

Language learning tips .... *xv*

Spanish spelling and pronunciation .... *xxv*

UNIT 1: Talking about yourself and making introductions *1*

Lesson 1 (words) *1*

        The numbers 0–10 .... *2*
        Gender *3*

Lesson 2 (phrases) *5*

        Subject pronouns *6*
        The numbers 11–20 .... *8*

Lesson 3 (sentences) *10*

        Ser (*to be*) in the singular *10*
        Ser (*to be*) in the plural *12*

Lesson 4 (conversations) *13*

        Countries and nationalities *15*
        Greetings *18*

UNIT 2: Talking about family *21*

Lesson 5 (words) *21*

        Indefinite articles and plurals *22*
        Definite articles *24*

Lesson 6 (phrases) 27

           Estar (*to be*) 27
           The numbers 20–100 29

Lesson 7 (sentences) 31

           Using **ser** and **estar** 31
           Using **estar** 33

Lesson 8 (conversations) 36

           Tener (*to have*) 37
           Hay (*there is/there are*) 40

UNIT 3: Everyday life 45

Lesson 9 (words) 45

           Numbers above 100 46
           Telling time 49

Lesson 10 (phrases) 53

           Adjective agreement 53
           More on adjective agreement 57

Lesson 11 (sentences) 60

           Question words 61
           More question words 63

Lesson 12 (conversations) 67

           Yes/no questions 69
           Saying what you like to do 72

UNIT 4: Health and the human body 79

Lesson 13 (words) 79

Possessive adjectives (singular) 80
Possessive adjectives (plural) 82

Lesson 14 (phrases) 84

Possession with **de** + pronoun 85
More possession with **de** 87

Lesson 15 (sentences) 89

Possessive pronouns 90
Conjugation of **-ar** verbs 94

Lesson 16 (conversations) 97

Conjugation of **-er** verbs and
ver (*to see*) 99
Conjugation of **-ir** verbs 104

UNIT 5: Using the telephone and making appointments 109

Lesson 17 (words) 109

Demonstrative adjectives 109
Demonstrative pronouns 112

Lesson 18 (phrases) 114

Negation 115
Indefinite pronouns 117

Lesson 19 (sentences) *120*

Irregular verbs: **Hacer** (*to make, to do*),
poner (*to put*), **traer** (*to bring*), and
caer (*to fall*) *121*
Irregular verbs: **salir** (*to go out*) and
decir (*to say*) *123*

Lesson 20 (conversations) *126*

Ir (*to go*) *128*
Querer (*to want, to love*) *131*

UNIT 6: Getting around town *135*

Lesson 21 (words) *135*

Saber and **conocer** (*to know*) *136*
Poder (*can*), **deber** (*must*), and
tener que (*to have to*) *139*

Lesson 22 (phrases) *142*

Ver (*to see*), **venir** (*to come*), and
dar (*to give*) *143*
The present progressive *146*

Lesson 23 (sentences) *148*

Common prepositions of location *149*
Common prepositions of time *152*

Lesson 24 (conversations) *156*

The imperative *158*
Para and **por** (*for*) *163*

UNIT 7: Shopping *167*

Lesson 25 (words) *167*

              Stem-changing verbs *167*
              More stem-changing verbs *171*

Lesson 26 (phrases) *175*

              Comparatives *175*
              Equal comparisons and superlatives ... *177*

Lesson 27 (sentences) *180*

              Direct object pronouns *180*
              The future with **ir a** (*going to*) *184*

Lesson 28 (conversations) *187*

              Reflexive verbs *189*
              Colors, patterns, and fabrics *194*

UNIT 8: Let's eat! *199*

Lesson 29 (words) *199*

              Indirect object pronouns *199*
              Adverbs *203*

Lesson 30 (phrases) *206*

              More on adverbs *207*
              The preterite of **-ar** verbs and **estar** ... *209*

Lesson 31 (sentences) 213

    The preterite of -er and -ir verbs 213
    The preterite of **ser, ir, tener,**
    and **hacer** 216

Lesson 32 (conversations) 218

    Spelling changes in the preterite 220
    Irregular verbs in the preterite 224

UNIT 9: School and work 229

Lesson 33 (words) 229

    More irregular verbs in the preterite . . . 230
    Double object pronouns 232

Lesson 34 (phrases) 234

    Expressing past actions with **hace**
    and **acabar de** 235
    Expressing obligation or necessity 237

Lesson 35 (sentences) 238

    The imperfect of -ar verbs 239
    The imperfect of -er and -ir verbs 240

Lesson 36 (conversations) 243

    Ir, ser, and **ver** in the imperfect 244
    Using the preterite and the imperfect . . 247

UNIT 10: Sports and hobbies 253

Lesson 37 (words) 253

        The conditional 253
        Impersonal **se** 256

Lesson 38 (phrases) 258

        The subjunctive 258
        Using the subjunctive 262

Lesson 39 (sentences) 264

        Irregular verbs in the subjunctive 265
        Verbs followed by the subjunctive 267

Lesson 40 (conversations) 270

        The subjunctive vs. the indicative 272
        Relative pronouns and clauses 276

Spanish in action 281

Supplemental vocabulary 289

Internet resources 308

Summary of Spanish grammar 311

Welcome to *Living Language Complete Spanish: The Basics*! We know you're ready to jump right in and start learning Spanish, but before you do, you may want to spend some time familiarizing yourself with the structure of this course. It will make it easier for you to find your way around, and will really help you get the most out of your studies.

UNITS AND LESSONS

Living Language Complete Spanish: The Basics includes ten *Units,* each of which focuses on a certain practical topic, from talking about yourself and making introductions to asking directions and going shopping. Each Unit is divided into *Lessons* that follow four simple steps:

1. *Words,* featuring the essential vocabulary you need to talk about the topic of the Unit;

2. *Phrases,* bringing words together into more complex structures and introducing a few idiomatic expressions;

3. *Sentences,* expanding on the vocabulary and phrases from previous lessons, using the grammar you've learned to form complete sentences; and,

4. *Conversations,* highlighting how everything works together in a realistic conversational dialogue that brings everything in the Unit together.

The lessons each comprise the following sections:

WORD LIST/PHRASE LIST/SENTENCE LIST/CONVERSATION
Every lesson begins with a list of words, phrases, or sentences, or a dialogue. The grammar and exercises will be based on these components, so it's important to spend as much time reading and rereading these as possible before getting into the heart of the lesson.

Notes

A brief section may appear after the list or dialogue to highlight any points of interest in the language or culture.

Nuts & bolts

This is the nitty-gritty of each lesson, where you'll learn the grammar of the language, the nuts and bolts that hold the pieces together. Pay close attention to these sections; this is where you'll get the most out of the language and learn what you need to learn to become truly proficient in Spanish.

Practice

It's important to practice what you've learned on a regular basis. You'll find practice sections throughout each lesson; take your time to complete these exercises before moving on to the next section. How well you do on each practice will determine whether or not you need to review a particular grammar point before you move on.

Tip!

In order to enhance your experience, you'll find several tips for learning Spanish throughout the course. This could be a tip on a specific grammar point, additional vocabulary related to the lesson topic, or a tip on language learning in general. For more practical advice, you can also refer to the *Language learning tips* section that follows this introduction.

Culture notes and language links

Becoming familiar with the culture of Spanish-speaking countries is nearly as essential to language learning as grammar. These sections allow you to get to know these cultures better through facts about Spanish-speaking countries and other bits of cultural information. You'll also find the links to various websites you can visit on the internet to learn more about a particular country or custom, or to find a language learning tool that may come in handy.

DISCOVERY ACTIVITY

Discovery activities are another chance for you to put your new language to use. They will often require you to go out into the world and interact with other Spanish speakers, or simply to use the resources around your own home to practice your Spanish.

UNIT ESSENTIALS

Finally, each Unit ends with a review of the most essential vocabulary and phrases. Make sure you're familiar with these phrases, as well as their structure, before moving on to the next Unit.

FURTHER REFERENCE

The coursebook also includes additional reference material to help you enhance your Spanish studies. *Spanish in action* offers more examples of Spanish in everyday use, featuring the vocabulary and grammar from all ten units. *Supplemental vocabulary* lists essential vocabulary by category, while the *Grammar summary* can be used for thorough review of key grammar points. Finally, the book contains a list of *Internet resources* where you can seek out more exposure to the language and information on Spanish-speaking countries.

LEARNER'S DICTIONARY

If you've purchased this book as a part of the complete audio package, you also received a Learner's Dictionary with more than 20,000 of the most frequently used Spanish words, phrases, and idiomatic expressions. Use it as a reference any time you're at a loss for words in the exercises and discovery activities, or as a supplemental study aid. This dictionary is ideal for beginner- or intermediate-level learners of Spanish.

AUDIO

This course works best when used along with the four audio CDs included in the complete course package. These CDs feature all the word lists, phrase lists, sentence lists, and conversations from each unit, as well as key examples from the *Nuts & bolts* sections. This audio can be used along with the book, or on the go for hands-free practice.

And it's as easy as that! To get even more out of *Living Language Complete Spanish: The Basics*, you may want to read the *Language learning tips* section that follows this introduction. If you're confident that you know all you need to know to get started and would prefer to head straight for Unit 1, you can always come back to this section for tips on getting more out of your learning experience.

Good luck!

If you're not sure about the best way to learn a new language, take a moment to read this section. It includes lots of helpful tips and practical advice on studying languages in general, improving vocabulary, mastering grammar, using audio, doing exercises, and expanding your learning experience. All of this will make learning more effective and more fun.

GENERAL TIPS
Let's start with some general points to keep in mind about learning a new language.

1. FIND YOUR PACE
The most important thing to keep in mind is that you should always proceed at your own pace. Don't feel pressured into thinking that you only have one chance to digest information before moving on to new material. Read and listen to parts of lessons or entire lessons as many times as it takes to make you feel comfortable with the material. Regular repetition is the key to learning any new language, so don't be afraid to cover material again, and again, and again!

2. TAKE NOTES
Use a notebook or start a language journal so you can have something to take with you. Each lesson contains material that you'll learn much more quickly and effectively if you write it down or rephrase it in your own words once you've understood it. That includes vocabulary, grammar points and examples, expressions from conversations, and anything else that you find noteworthy. Take your notes with you to review wherever you have time to kill—on the bus or train, waiting at the airport, while dinner is cooking, or whenever you can find the time. Remember—practice (and lots of review!) makes perfect when it comes to learning languages.

3. MAKE A REGULAR COMMITMENT

Make time for your new language. The concept of "hours of exposure" is key to learning a language. When you expose yourself to a new language frequently, you'll pick it up more easily. On the other hand, the longer the intervals between your exposure to a language, the more you'll forget. It's best to set time aside regularly for yourself. Imagine that you're enrolled in a class that takes place at certain regular times during the week, and set that time aside. Or use your lunch break. It's better to spend less time several days a week than a large chunk of time once or twice a week. In other words, spending thirty or forty minutes on Monday, Tuesday, Wednesday, Friday, and Sunday will be better than spending two and a half or three hours just on Saturday.

4. DON'T HAVE UNREALISTIC EXPECTATIONS

Don't expect to start speaking a new language as if it were your native language. It's certainly possible for adults to learn new languages with amazing fluency, but that's not a realistic immediate goal for most people. Instead, make a commitment to become "functional" in a new language, and start to set small goals: getting by in most daily activities, talking about yourself and asking about others, following TV and movies, reading a newspaper, expressing your ideas in basic language, and learning creative strategies for getting the most out of the language you know. Functional doesn't mean perfectly native fluent, but it's a great accomplishment!

5. DON'T GET HUNG UP ON PRONUNCIATION

"Losing the accent" is one of the most challenging parts of learning a language. If you think about celebrities, scientists, or political figures whose native language isn't English, they probably have a pretty recognizable accent. But that hasn't kept them from becoming celebrities, scientists, or political figures. Really young children are able to learn the sounds of any language in the world, and they can reproduce them perfectly. That's part of the process of learning a native language. In an adult, or even in an older child, this ability has diminished, so if you agonize over sounding like a native speaker in your new language, you're just setting yourself up for disappointment. That's not to say that you can't learn pronunciation well. Even adults can get pretty far through mimicking the sounds that they hear. So, listen carefully to the audio several times. Listening is a very important part of this process: you can't reproduce a sound until you learn to distinguish the sound. Then mimic what you hear. Don't be afraid of sounding strange. Just keep at it, and soon enough you'll develop good pronunciation.

6. DON'T BE SHY

Learning a new language inevitably involves speaking out loud, and it involves making mistakes before you get better. Don't be afraid of sounding strange, or awkward, or silly. You won't: you'll impress people with your attempts. The more you speak, and the more you interact, the faster you'll learn to correct the mistakes you do make.

TIPS ON LEARNING VOCABULARY

You obviously need to learn new words in order to speak a new language. Even though that may seem straightforward compared with learning how to actually put those words together in sentences, it's really not as simple as it appears. Memorizing words is difficult, even just memorizing words in the short term. But long term memorization takes a lot of practice and repetition. You won't learn vocabulary simply by reading through the vocabulary lists once or twice. You need to practice.

There are a few different ways to lodge a word in your memory, and some methods may work better for you than others. The best thing to do is to try a few different methods until you feel that one is right for you. Here are a few suggestions and pointers:

I. AUDIO REPETITION

Fix your eye on the written form of a word and listen to the audio several times. Remind yourself of the English translation as you do this.

2. Spoken repetition

Say a word several times aloud, keeping your eye on the written word as you hear yourself speak it. It's not a race—don't rush to blurt out the word over and over again so fast that you're distorting its pronunciation. Just repeat it, slowly and naturally, being careful to pronounce it as well as you can. And run your eye over the shape of the word each time you say it. You'll be stimulating two of your senses at once that way—hearing and sight—so you'll double the impact on your memory.

3. Written repetition

Write a word over and over again across a page, speaking it slowly and carefully each time you write it. Don't be afraid to fill up entire sheets of paper with your new vocabulary words.

4. Flash cards

They may seem childish, but they're effective. Cut out small pieces of paper (no need to spend a lot of money on index cards) and write the English word on one side and the new word on the other. Just this act alone will put a few words in your mind. Then read through your "deck" of cards. First go from the target (new) language into English—that's easier. Turn the target language side face-up, read each card, and guess at its meaning. Once you've guessed, turn the card over to see if you're right. If you are, set the card aside in your "learned" pile. If you're wrong, repeat the word and its meaning, and then put it at the bottom of your "to learn" pile. Continue through until you've moved all of the cards into your "learned" pile.

Once you've completed the whole deck from your target language into English, turn the deck over and try to go from English into your target language. You'll see that this is harder, but also a better test of whether or not you've really mastered a word.

5. Mnemonics

A mnemonic is a device or a trick to trigger your memory, like "King Phillip Came Over From Great Spain," which you may have learned in high school biology to remember that species are classified into kingdom, phylum, class, order, family, genus, and species. Mnemonics work well for vocabulary, too. When you hear and read a new word, look to see if it sounds like anything—a place, a name, a nonsense phrase. Then form an image of that place or person or even nonsense scenario in your head. Imagine it as you say and read the new word. Remember that the more sense triggers you have—hearing, reading, writing, speaking, imagining a crazy image—the better you'll remember.

6. GROUPS

Vocabulary should be learned in small and logically connected groups whenever possible. Most of the vocabulary lists in this course are already organized this way. Don't try to tackle a whole list at once. Choose your method—repeating a word out loud, writing it across a page, etc.—and practice with a small group.

7. PRACTICE

Don't just learn a word out of context and leave it hanging there. Go back and practice it in the context provided in this course. If the word appears in a conversation, read it in the full sentence and call to mind an image of that sentence. If possible, substitute other vocabulary words into the same sentence structure ("John goes to the *library*" instead of "John goes to the *store*"). As you advance through the course, try writing your own simple examples of words in context.

8. COME BACK TO IT

This is the key to learning vocabulary—not just holding it temporarily in your short term memory, but making it stick in your long term memory. Go back over old lists, old decks of flash cards you made, or old example sentences. Listen to vocabulary audio from previous lessons. Pull up crazy mnemonic devices you created at some point earlier in your studies. And always be on the lookout for old words appearing again throughout the course.

TIPS ON USING AUDIO

The audio in this course not only lets you hear how native speakers pronounce the words you're learning, but also serves as a second kind of input to your learning experience. The printed words serve as visual input, and the audio serves as *auditory* input. There are a few different strategies that you can use to get the most out of the audio. First, use the audio while you're looking at a word or sentence. Listen to it a few times along with the visual input of seeing the material. Then, look away and just listen to the audio on its own. You can also use the audio from previously studied lessons as a way to review. Put the audio on your computer or an MP3 player and take it along with you in your car, on the train, while you walk, while you jog, or anywhere you spend your free time. Remember that the more exposure you have to and contact you have with your target language, the better you'll learn.

TIPS ON USING CONVERSATIONS

Conversations are a great way to see language in action, as it's really used by people in realistic situations. To get the most out of each of the conversations in this book as a language student, think of it as a cycle rather than a linear passage. First read through the conversation once in the target language to get the gist. Don't agonize over the details just yet. Then, go back and read through it a second time, but focus on individual sentences. Look for new words or new constructions. Challenge yourself to figure out what they mean from the context of the conversation. After all, that's something you'll be doing a lot of in the real world, so it's a good skill to develop! Once you've worked out the details, read the conversation again from start to finish. Now that you're very familiar with the conversation, turn on the audio and listen to it as you read. Don't try to repeat yet; just listen and read along. This will build your listening comprehension. Then, go back and listen again, but this time, pause to repeat the phrases or sentences that you're hearing and reading. This will build your spoken proficiency and pronunciation. Now listen again without the aid of the printed conversation. By now you'll know many of the lines inside out, and any new vocabulary or constructions will be very familiar.

TIPS ON DOING EXERCISES

The exercises are meant to give you a chance to practice the vocabulary and structures that you learn in each lesson and, of course, to test yourself on retention. Take the time to write out the entire sentences to get the most out of the practice. Don't limit yourself to just reading and writing. Read the sentences and answers aloud, so you'll also be practicing pronunciation and spoken proficiency. As you gain more confidence, try to adapt the practice sentences by substituting different vocabulary or grammatical constructions, too. Be creative and push the practices as far as you can to get the most out of them.

TIPS ON LEARNING GRAMMAR

Each grammar point is designed to be as small and digestible as possible, while at the same time complete enough to teach you what you need to know. The explanations are intended to be simple and straightforward, but one of the best things you can do is to take notes on each grammar section, putting the explanations into your own words, and then copying the example sentences or tables slowly and carefully. This will do two things. It will give you a nice, clear notebook that you can take with you so you can review and practice, and it will also force you to take enough time with each section so that it's really driven home. Of course, a lot of grammar is memorization—verb endings, irregular forms, pronouns, and so on. So a lot of the vocabulary-learning tips will come in handy for learning grammar, too.

I. AUDIO REPETITION

Listen to the audio several times while you're looking at the words or sentences. For example, for a verb conjugation, listen to all of the forms several times, reading along to activate your visual memory as well.

2. SPOKEN REPETITION

Listen to the audio and repeat several times for practice. For example, to learn the conjugation of an irregular verb, repeat all of the forms of the verb until you're able to produce them without looking at the page. It's a little bit like memorizing lines for a play—practice until you can make it sound natural. Practice the example sentences that way as well, focusing, of course, on the grammar section at hand.

3. WRITTEN REPETITION

Write the new forms again and again, saying them slowly and carefully, as well. Do this until you're able to produce all of the forms without any help.

4. FLASH CARDS

Copy the grammar point, whether it's a list of pronouns, a conjugation, or a list of irregular forms, on a flash card. Stick the cards in your pocket so you can review them when you have time to kill. Glance over the cards, saying the forms to yourself several times, and when you're ready to test yourself, flip the cards over and see if you can produce all of the information.

5. GRAMMAR IN THE WILD

Do you want to see an amazing number of example sentences that use some particular grammatical form? Well, just type that form into a search engine. Pick a few of the examples you find at random, and copy them down into your notebook or language journal. Pick them apart, look up words you don't know, and try to figure out the other grammatical constructions. You may not get everything 100% correct, but you'll definitely learn and practice in the process.

6. COME BACK TO IT

Just like vocabulary, grammar is best learned through repetition and review. Go back over your notes, go back to previous lessons and read over the grammar sections, listen to the audio, or check out the relevant section in the grammar summary. Even after you've completed lessons, it's never a bad idea to go back and keep the "old" grammar fresh.

HOW TO EXPAND YOUR LEARNING EXPERIENCE
Your experience with your new language should not be limited to this course alone. Like anything, learning a language will be more enjoyable if you're able to make it a part of your life in some way. And you'd be surprised to know how easily you can do that these days!

1. USE THE INTERNET
The internet is an absolutely amazing resource for people learning new languages. You're never more than a few clicks away from on-line newspapers, magazines, reference material, cultural sites, travel and tourism sites, images, sounds, and so much more. Develop your own list of favorite sites that match your needs and interests, whether business, cooking, fashion, film, kayaking, rock climbing, or . . . well, you get the picture. Use search engines creatively to find examples of vocabulary or grammar "in the wild." Find a favorite blog or periodical and take the time to work your way through an article or entry. Think of what you use the internet for in English, and look for similar sites in your target language.

2. CHECK OUT COMMUNITY RESOURCES
Depending on where you live, there may be plenty of practice opportunities in your own community. There may be a cultural organization or social club where people meet. There may be a local college or university with a department that hosts cultural events, such as films or discussion groups. There may be a restaurant where you can go for a good meal and a chance to practice a bit of your target language. Of course, you can find a lot of this information online, and there are sites that allow groups of people to get organized and meet to pursue their interests.

3. FOREIGN FILMS
Films are a wonderful way to practice hearing and understanding a new language. With English subtitles and the pause and rewind

functions, foreign films are practically really long dialogues with pictures, not to mention the cultural insight and experience they provide! And nowadays it's simple to rent foreign DVDs online or even access films online. So, if you're starting to learn a new language today, go online and rent yourself some movies that you can watch over the next few weeks or months.

4. MUSIC

Even if you have a horrible singing voice, music is a great way to learn new vocabulary. After hearing a song just a few times, the lyrics somehow manage to plant themselves in the mind. And with the internet, it's often very easy to find the lyrics of a song online, print them out, and have them ready for whenever you're alone and feel like singing . . .

5. TELEVISION

If you have access to television programming in the language you're studying, including, of course, anything you can find on the internet, take advantage of that! You'll most likely hear very natural and colloquial language, including idiomatic expressions and rapid speech, all of which will be a healthy challenge for your comprehension skills. But the visual cues, including body language and gestures, will help. Plus, you'll get to see how the language interacts with the culture, which is also a very important part of learning a language.

6. FOOD

A great way to learn a language is through the cuisine. What could be better than going out and trying new dishes at a restaurant with the intention of practicing your newly acquired language? Go to a restaurant, and if the names of the dishes are printed in the target language, try to decipher them. Then try to order in the target language, provided, of course, that your server speaks the language! At the very least, you'll learn a few new vocabulary items, not to mention sample some wonderful new food.

If you've ever had trouble with English spelling, or if you've ever come across an unfamiliar word and had no idea how to pronounce it, you'll be happy to know that neither of these things is likely to be an issue in Spanish. Spanish spelling is phonetic, meaning that things are pronounced the way they're written. The rules for stress—which SYL-la-ble gets the EM-pha-sis—are very regular in Spanish, and any irregularities are marked in spelling with an accent mark. We'll cover all of that little by little, but let's get started with an overview of Spanish pronunciation.

1. Vowels

Each vowel in Spanish is pronounced clearly and distinctly, and each vowel has one and only one pronunciation. A vowel may be written with an accent, as in **sí** or **América**, but this never changes the pronunciation of that vowel. It may mark stress, as in **América**, or it may only serve to distinguish between two words, as in **sí** (*yes*) and **si** (*if*). Let's look at each vowel, starting with simple vowels.

a	like *a* in *father*	a, amigo, la, las, pan, habla, Santiago
e	like *ay* in *day*, but cut off before the *ee*	él, de, en, padre, tren, este, Mercedes
i	like *i* in *police*	mí, amiga, hiciste, cinco, Chile, Sevilla
o	like *o* in *no*, but cut off before the *oo*	no, dos, hombre, costar, ocho, teléfono, Colombia
u	like *u* in *rule*	uno, tú, mucho, azúcar, Honduras, puro

Vowels can also appear in pairs, which are called diphthongs. A diphthong is usually a combination of a weaker vowel (**i** or **u**) and a more prominent one.

ai, ay	like *i* in *bide*	aire, hay, traigo, ¡ay!
au	like *ou* in *house*	restaurante, autobús, automóvil, Mauricio
ei, ey	like *ay* in *day*	seis, ley, treinta, rey
ia, ya	like *ya* in *yard*	gracias, comercial, estudiar, ya
ie, ye	like *ye* in *yet*	pie, quiero, tiene, yerba, abyecto
io, yo	like *yo* in *yoga*	yo, acción, despacio, estudio
iu, yu	like *u* in *united*	ciudad, yuca, yugo, yunta
oi, oy	like *oy* in *toy*	estoy, hoy, oiga, voy
ua	like *wa* in *want*	cuatro, Juan, ¿cuál?, ¿cuánto?
ue	like *we* in *west*	nueve, fuego, puerta, cuesta, bueno
uo	like *wo* in *woe*	continuo, antiguo, mutuo, superfluo
ui, uy	like *we* in *week*	muy, ruido, cuidado, huir

2. CONSONANTS

b	like *b* in *boy* at the beginning of a word	**bueno, brazo, bajo, barca, bocadillo**
b	for some speakers, close to *v* in *very* between vowels	**Cuba, haber, beber, cobayo, deber, ubicar**
c	like *k* in *kite* before consonants, *a, o,* and *u*	**Cristóbal, cosa, casa, ¿cuánto?, ¿cuál?, truco**
c	like *s* in *sea* before *e* and *i*	**cerca, servicio, cierto, fácil, posición**
ch	like *ch* in *choose*	**charlar, chico, muchacho, ocho, mucho**
d	at the beginning of a word or after *n,* like *d* in *day,* but with the tongue touching the back of the teeth	**día, despegar, durante, ¿cuándo?, ¿dónde?, mando**
d	between vowels, like *th* in *thin*	**media, nada, todo, poder, freiduría, prometido**
f	like *f* in *father*	**familia, Francisco, Federico, formulario**

g	like *g* in *go* before consonants, *a, o,* and *u*	grande, Gloria, gustar, gusano, goloso, ganar, vengo
g	like the strong *h* in *hope* before *e* or *i*	general, Gibraltar, girar, rígido, urgente
gü	like *gw* in *Gwen*	vergüenza, lengüeta, cigüeña
h	silent	hablo, hay, hubo, ahora, hombre, deshonroso
j	like the strong *h* in *hope*	julio, jabón, mejor, José, tarjeta, jefe, trujar
ll	like *y* in *yes* or *j* in *jar*	llamo, pollo, llama, llover, allí, llaves, trulla
m	like *m* in *met*	mismo, Marco, mano, Manuel, pluma, mandar
n	like *n* in *not*	nunca, no, Nicaragua, Argentina, nombre
ñ	like *ni* in *onion*	español, mañana, muñeca, ñame, gañir
p	like *p* in *pear*	para, pueblo, postre, Panamá, Perú
qu	like *k* in *kite*	que, querer, paquete, saquen, quemar, quizás

r	at the beginning of a word, a trilled sound made with the tongue against the ridge behind the upper teeth	**rico, rubio, Ramón, Rosa, rincón, red, risa**
r	otherwise like the tapped *d* in *ladder*	**América, pero, quisiera, aire, libre, brazo, caro**
rr	like word-initial *r*, a trilled sound made with the tongue against the ridge behind the upper teeth	**perro, carro, tierra, horror, irritar, terrible**
s	like *s* in *see* (never like *z* in *zone*)	**casa, sucio, San Salvador, soltero, vasto, rosa**
t	like *t* in *take*, but with the tongue touching the back of the teeth	**tocar, fruta, tú, teclado, traje, tener**

v	like *b* in *boy* at the beginning of a word; for some speakers, close to *v* in *very* between vowels	**vaso, veinte, vivir, vivo, veramente**
y	like *y* in *yes*; on its own, like *ee* in *teen*	**ayer, ayudo, Bayamo, poyo**
z	like *s* in *see*	**zona, diez, luz, marzo, azul, azúcar**

3. STRESS

There are three simple rules to keep in mind when it comes to stress. First, if a word ends in any consonant other than -n or -s, the last syllable receives the stress.

ciudad, capaz, notabilidad, navegar, familiar, refrigerador

Second, if a word ends in a vowel or in -n or -s, the penultimate (second-to-last) syllable receives the stress.

amigo, hablan, derechos, cubierto, portorriqueño, examen, libros

Note that diphthongs with the weak vowels *i* or *u* count as one syllable, so the stress will regularly fall before them.

academia, continuo, manubrio, sanitario, justicia

Combinations with two strong vowels count as two syllables.

tarea, menudeo, banqueteo, barbacoa

Anytime stress doesn't follow these rules, an accent is used.

inglés, teléfono, tomó, práctico, drogaría, todavía, título, farmacéutico, petróleo

4. REGIONAL SPANISH PRONUNCIATION

The Spanish pronunciation that you'll learn in this course is standard Latin American Spanish. There are certainly some local differences in pronunciation that you will probably come across, the most commonly known being the difference between Latin American and Castilian, or European, Spanish. The major difference in pronunciation has to do with the sound *th*. In Latin America, *th* as in *this* is typically found in *d* when it comes between vowels or at the end of a word.

media, nada, todo, poder, puedo, pared, merced

These words are pronounced with the same *th* in Spain, too. But in Spain, *th* as in *thin* also exists. C before i or e and z is pronounced this way.

cerca, servicio, cierto, fácil, docena, diez, voz, luz, marzo, azul, razón

There are some noticeable differences in local varieties of Spanish found in Latin America, as well. You don't need to worry about imitating these differences; the standard pronunciation you'll learn in this course will serve you perfectly well. But you may notice, for example, that the combination ll is pronounced like the *lli* in *million,* the *j* in *juice,* the *sh* in *show,* or the *s* in *pleasure.* The semivowel y may have a similar range of pronunciation. In some countries, particularly in the Caribbean, final s may be dropped altogether, if not the entire last syllable! You may even hear r pronounced as something similar to l. There's certainly nothing wrong with any of these variations, although as a student, you'll probably find it useful to concentrate on the standard pronunciation offered in this course first.

UNIT 1
Talking about yourself and making introductions

¡Hola! In Unit 1, you'll learn how to introduce yourself and others, how to say where you're from, and how to ask other people for basic information. Naturally, you'll learn greetings and other essential courtesy expressions. You'll also be introduced to key structures so that you can begin to speak right away. Are you ready?

—————————— Lesson 1 (words) ——————————

WORD LIST 1
Each unit begins with a lesson that focuses on words. The words will be used throughout the unit, so familiarize yourself with them. For advice on learning new vocabulary, consult the *Language learning tips* section at the beginning of this program.

tarjeta	*card*
premio	*prize*
esta	*this*
también	*also*
nombre	*name*
nacionalidad	*nationality*
profesión	*profession*
su	*your*
cafetera	*coffeemaker*
abogado *(m.)*	*lawyer*
abogada *(f.)*	*lawyer*
España	*Spain*
Alemania	*Germany*

The following abbreviations will be used in this course: *(m.)* = masculine, *(f.)* = feminine, *(sg.)* = singular, *(pl.)* = plural, *(fml.)* = formal/polite, *(infml.)* = informal.

NUTS & BOLTS 1
THE NUMBERS 0–10

Let's look at the numbers zero through ten in Spanish.

cero	*zero*
uno	*one*
dos	*two*
tres	*three*
cuatro	*four*
cinco	*five*
seis	*six*
siete	*seven*
ocho	*eight*
nueve	*nine*
diez	*ten*

PRACTICE 1

Can you read the following telephone numbers out loud?

1. 958 9522
2. 662 7890
3. 440 7612

4. 780 1211
5. 670 7633

WORD LIST 2

disfrute	*enjoy*
español *(m.)*	*Spanish*
española *(f.)*	*Spanish*
casado/a *(m./f.)*	*married*
soltero/a *(m./f.)*	*single*
provisional	*temporary*
código	*code*
cuál	*which*
obtener	*to get*
necesito	*I need*
algunos	*some*
dónde	*where*
alemán *(m.)*	*German*
alemana *(f.)*	*German*

NUTS & BOLTS 2

GENDER

Did you know that in Spanish all nouns and adjectives indicate gender, either masculine or feminine? For nouns with natural gender, this is easy: **hombre** (*man*), **muchacho** (*boy*), and **abogado** (*male lawyer*) are all masculine, while **mujer** (*woman*), **muchacha** (*girl*), and **abogada** (*female lawyer*) are all feminine. In cases where there is no natural gender, masculine nouns and adjectives usually end in **-o,** and feminine in **-a.**

masculine	feminine
libro (*book*)	**tarjeta** (*card*)
bolígrafo (*pen*)	**carta** (*letter*)

Unfortunately, to every rule there is always an exception. Don't panic; there aren't too many exceptions, and they're easy to learn. As a general rule, nouns ending in -dad or -ción are feminine, and most nouns that end in -e are masculine. You can read more about gender in the grammar summary if you'd like. For now, the best thing to do is simply memorize the gender of each new word you learn. Let's look at the genders of some of the nouns and adjectives you've learned so far.

masculine	feminine
premio (*prize*)	tarjeta (*card*)
español (*Spanish*)	española (*Spanish*)
alemán (*German*)	alemana (*German*)
casado (*married*)	casada (*married*)
soltero (*single*)	soltera (*single*)
código (*code*)	cafetera (*coffeemaker*)
nombre (*name*)	nacionalidad (*nationality*)
cheque (*check*)	profesión (*profession*)

PRACTICE 2
Are these words feminine or masculine?

1. soltero
2. alemán
3. cheque
4. bolígrafo

5. profesión
6. casada
7. premio
8. nacionalidad

ANSWERS
PRACTICE 1: 1. nueve, cinco, ocho, nueve, cinco, dos dos;
2. seis, seis, dos, siete, ocho, nueve, cero; **3.** cuatro, cuatro, cero, siete, seis, uno, dos; **4.** siete, ocho, cero, uno, dos, uno, uno;
5. seis, siete, cero, siete, seis, tres, tres.

PRACTICE 2: 1. masculine; **2.** masculine; **3.** masculine;
4. masculine; **5.** feminine; **6.** feminine; **7.** masculine;
8. feminine.

--- Lesson 2 (phrases) ---

PHRASE LIST 1
The second lesson of each unit moves from words to phrases. The following is a list of phrases commonly used when greeting someone or saying goodbye.

Buenos días.	*Good morning.*
Buenas tardes.	*Good afternoon.*
Buenas noches.	*Good evening./Good night.*

¿Cómo está? *(fml.)*	*How are you?*
¿Cómo estás? *(infml.)*	*How are you?*
Bien, gracias, ¿y usted? *(fml.)*	*Fine, thank you, and you?*
Bien, gracias, ¿y tú? *(infml.)*	*Fine, thank you, and you?*
Adiós.	*Good-bye.*
Hasta luego.	*Till later.*
Hasta pronto.	*Till later.*
Hasta mañana.	*Till tomorrow.*
Mucho gusto.	*Nice to meet you.*

NUTS & BOLTS 1
SUBJECT PRONOUNS

Notice that there are two ways of asking *how are you?* in Spanish. One is a formal form, which you'd use with strangers and anyone to whom you want to show respect, and the other is an informal form, which you'd use with family, friends, and people who you know better and are more familiar with. Spanish actually even has different forms of the pronoun *you* to show this distinction. Let's take a look at subject pronouns that refer to only one person in Spanish.

yo	*I*
tú *(infml.)*	*you*
él	*he*
ella	*she*
usted *(fml.)*	*you*

As you can see, there are two forms of *you* in the table above. The **tú** form is the familiar or informal form. It's used to address people of the same age as you or younger, as well as family and friends. The formal form, **usted,** is used when talking to people who are older than you or not familiar to you. Now let's look at the personal pronouns that refer to more than one person.

nosotros	*we*
nosotras *(f.)*	*we*
vosotros *(infml.)*	*you, all of you*
vosotras *(infml. f.)*	*you, all of you*
ellos	*they*
ellas *(f.)*	*they*
ustedes *(fml.)*	*you, all of you*

Notice that **nosotros, vosotros,** and **ellos** also have feminine forms. The feminine forms (**nosotras, vosotras, ellas**) are used exclusively for women, while the masculine forms are used for men or for groups including both men and women.

PRACTICE 1
Which Spanish pronoun would you use in each of the following situations?

1. Talking to your best friend Roberto

2. Asking directions from an older stranger you see on the street

3. Talking about your brother

4. Talking about yourself

5. Talking about your boss, Señora Ramírez

6. Talking to you sister and your mother

7. Talking about your father and your uncle

8. Talking to your classmates (of both genders)

9. Talking about yourself and your friends (of both genders)

PHRASE LIST 2
Here are some more phrases we'll be using later on in this unit.

datos personales	*personal information*
felicitaciones	*congratulations*
mucha suerte	*lots of luck*
próximo sorteo	*next raffle, drawing*
muy bien	*very well*
número de teléfono	*telephone number*
No hay de qué.	*You're welcome.*
gerente de ventas	*sales manager*
muy contenta	*very happy*
Aquí tiene.	*Here you are.*
Firme aquí.	*Sign here.*
por favor	*please*
Gracias.	*Thank you.*

NUTS & BOLTS 2
THE NUMBERS 11–20
Now let's look at the numbers eleven through twenty in Spanish.

once	*eleven*
doce	*twelve*
trece	*thirteen*
catorce	*fourteen*
quince	*fifteen*

dieciséis	*sixteen*
diecisiete	*seventeen*
dieciocho	*eighteen*
diecinueve	*nineteen*
veinte	*twenty*

PRACTICE 2
Can you write the following series of numbers?

1. 0–12–3–18
2. 15–4–19–2
3. 9–11–17–5

4. 14–1–20–7
5. 8–13–16–6

Tip!
Maybe you're wondering why Spanish has a weird upside down question mark or exclamation point at the beginning of a question or an exclamation. Well, it was not always like that. In 1754, the **Real Academia Española,** the institution responsible for regulating the Spanish language, decided to adopt these symbols because in Spanish, in many cases, the reader has almost no way to determine at what moment a sentence in progress is a question or an exclamation. It's actually very practical and useful. As we go on, you will see why.

ANSWERS
PRACTICE 1: 1. tú; **2.** usted; **3.** él; **4.** yo; **5.** ella; **6.** ustedes or vosotras; **7.** ellos; **8.** ustedes or vosotros; **9.** nosotros.

PRACTICE 2: 1. cero, doce, tres, dieciocho; **2.** quince, cuatro, diecinueve, dos; **3.** nueve, once, diciesiete, cinco; **4.** catorce, uno, veinte, siete; **5.** ocho, trece, dieciséis, seis.

SENTENCE LIST 1
The third lesson of each unit moves on to sentences.

¿Cuál es su nombre?	*What's your name?*
Mi nombre es Juan.	*My name is Juan.*
¿Cuál es su nacionalidad?	*What's your nationality?*
Soy francés.	*I'm French. (male)*
Soy francesa.	*I'm French. (female)*
Soy de Venezuela.	*I'm from Venezuela.*
¿Cuál es su número de teléfono?	*What's your phone number?*
Soy casada.	*I'm married. (female)*
Soy soltero.	*I'm single. (male)*

NUTS & BOLTS 1
SER (*TO BE*) IN THE SINGULAR

Now let's look at one of the most important verbs in Spanish, **ser** (*to be*). The form **ser** is called the infinitive, which is like the English *to* form. When you change the forms of a verb to match different subjects, as in the English *I speak* but *she speaks*, it's called a conjugation. Here's the singular conjugation of **ser** (*to be*).

yo soy	*I am*
tú eres *(infml.)*	*you are*
él es	*he is*
ella es	*she is*
usted es *(fml.)*	*you are*

In Spanish, it's very common to drop the pronoun, because the conjugated form of the verb makes it clear who or what you're talking about.

Yo soy estadounidense/Soy estadounidense.
I'm an American.

Eres mi amigo.
You're my friend.

¿Es Marta de Madrid o de Barcelona?
Is Marta from Marid or from Barcelona?

PRACTICE 1
What pronoun has the speaker of each of these sentences dropped?

1. Eres casado.

2. Soy francés.

3. Es argentino.

4. Soy soltera.

5. Es colombiana.

6. Eres abogada.

SENTENCE LIST 2

¿Es usted también español?	*Are you also from Spain?*
Su premio es la cafetera para capuccino.	*Your prize is the cappuccino machine.*
¿Cuál es su profesión?	*What's your profession?*
Soy abogada.	*I'm a female lawyer.*
¿Sois de Argentina?	*Are you (pl.) from Argentina?*
No, somos colombianos.	*No, we're Colombian.*
Ustedes son artistas.	*You're artists.*
¿Cuál es su número de fax?	*What's your fax number?*
¿Cuál es su dirección de correo electrónico?	*What's your email address?*
Nosotros no somos de Brasil.	*We're not from Brazil.*

NUTS & BOLTS 2

SER (*TO BE*) IN THE PLURAL

Now let's look at the plural conjugation of **ser** (*to be*).

nosotros/as somos	*we are*
vosotros/as sois *(infml.)*	*(all of) you are*
ellos/as son	*they are*
ustedes son	*(all of) you are*

Somos de Guadalajara.
We're from Guadalajara.

Son muy inteligentes.
They're/All of you are very intelligent.

Son españolas.
They're/All of you are Spanish.

PRACTICE 2

Fill in the blanks with the correct form of **ser**.

1. Mi nombre _____ Marliz Camargo.

2. Yo _____ Ana Benavidez. _____ la secretaria de la universidad.

3. ¿Cuál _____ su número de teléfono, por favor?

4. Nosotros _____ abogados ¿y ustedes?

5. Vosotros _____ de Bolivia y ellas _____ de España.

6. Tú _____ profesora de inglés.

7. Él _____ soltero, y ella _____ casada.

8. Ellos _____ venezolanos.

9. ¿_____ usted casado o soltero?

10. Ustedes _____ muy inteligentes.

Culture note

As we saw earlier, Spanish has a formal and an informal way of addressing people. The pronouns **usted** and **ustedes** are used when addressing strangers or people older than you; **tú** and **vosotros/as** are used for family and friends. However, you'll find that in most of Latin America, people do not use **vosotros/as**. They simply use **usted/ustedes** for both formal and informal situations. This is one of the main differences between European (also called Castilian or Peninsular) Spanish and Latin American Spanish. In fact, if you're learning Spanish specifically for use in Latin America, you can ignore the **vosotros/as** forms in this course. This program focuses on Latin American Spanish, but the **vosotros/as** forms are used every now and then because you may encounter them in written language, in media from Spain, and so on.

ANSWERS
PRACTICE 1: 1. tú; **2.** yo; **3.** él or usted; **4.** yo; **5.** ella or usted; **6.** tú.

PRACTICE 2: 1. es; **2.** soy/Soy; **3.** es; **4.** somos; **5.** sois/son; **6.** eres; **7.** es/es; **8.** son; **9.** Es; **10.** son.

—————— Lesson 4 (conversations) ——————

CONVERSATION 1
The fourth lesson of each unit covers conversations in the form of two different dialogues. Catalina has been shopping all morning at the very famous department store Galerías 93. She is at the register and has just been offered an application for the store's card and rewards program, an offer she can't refuse.

Vendedora:	Para obtener la tarjeta de Galerías 93, necesito algunos datos personales. ¿Cuál es su nombre completo, por favor?
Catalina:	Mi nombre es María Catalina Esguerra Uribe.
Vendedora:	¿Cuál es su nacionalidad?
Catalina:	Soy argentina.
Vendedora:	¿Cuál es su número de teléfono?
Catalina:	Es el nueve, cinco, ocho, tres, cuatro, dos, uno.
Vendedora:	¿Cuál es su profesión?
Catalina:	Soy abogada.
Vendedora:	¿Es usted soltera o casada?
Catalina:	Soy soltera.
Vendedora:	Muy bien. Esta es su tarjeta provisional con su código personal, que es el tres, seis, tres, ocho.
Catalina:	¡Muchas gracias!
Vendedora:	¡No hay de qué! Mucha suerte en el próximo sorteo!

Saleswoman:	In order to apply for the Galerías 93 card, I need some personal information. What's your full name, please?
Catalina:	My name is María Catalina Esguerra Uribe.
Saleswoman:	What's your nationality?
Catalina:	I'm Argentinian.
Saleswoman:	What's your telephone number?
Catalina:	It's nine, five, eight, three, four, two, one.
Saleswoman:	What's your profession?
Catalina:	I'm a lawyer.
Saleswoman:	Are you single or married?
Catalina:	I'm single.
Saleswoman:	All right. This is your temporary card with your personal code, which is three, six, three, eight.
Catalina:	Thank you!
Saleswoman:	You're welcome! Good luck in the next raffle!

NOTES

Did you know that people in Spanish-speaking countries have last names that come from both the father and the mother? It might seem confusing at first, but that's mostly because it's different. The basic rule is that a person born into a Spanish-speaking family is given a first name followed by two last names, the first being the father's family name and the second, the mother's family name.

So, let's say that the woman in our conversation, María Catalina Esguerra Uribe, got married to Pablo Ocampo Hoyos. If they had a son, he could be called Pablito Ocampo Esguerra.

NUTS & BOLTS 1
COUNTRIES AND NATIONALITIES
Here's a list of a few nationalities and countries.

País (*country*)	Nacionalidad (*nationality*)
Argentina	argentino/a
Bolivia	boliviano/a
Brasil	brasilero/a
Canadá	canadiense
Chile	chileno/a
Colombia	colombiano/a
Ecuador	ecuatoriano/a
España	español/a
Estados Unidos	estadounidense
Inglaterra	inglés/inglesa
México	mexicano/a
Perú	peruano/a

País (*country*)	Nacionalidad (*nationality*)
Uruguay	uruguayo/a
Venezuela	venezolano/a

PRACTICE 1
Complete the following dialogue with words and/or phrases you've learned in this unit:

Pedro: Buenos 1 _____. Mi 2 _____ es Pedro Sánchez.
Ramón: Mucho 3 _____.
Pedro: Necesito unos 4 _____. ¿Cuál es su 5 _____?
Ramón: Es el tres, seis, nueve, nueve, dos, uno, tres.
Pedro: ¿Cuál es su 6 _____?
Ramón: 7 _____ abogado.
Pedro: ¿Es usted 8 _____ o casado?

CONVERSATION 2
After a few months, Catalina wins a state-of-the-art capuccino machine at Galerías 93. Mr. Scholl, the store manager, meets with her to give her the prize.

Señor Scholl: Buenas tardes, señora Esguerra. Soy Marcos Scholl, gerente de ventas de Galerías 93.
Catalina: ¡Mucho gusto! Es un placer.
Señor Scholl: El placer es mío. ¿Cómo está usted?
Catalina: ¡Pues, muy contenta, claro!
Señor Scholl: Su premio es la cafetera para capuccino. Necesito su código personal y su tarjeta de Galerías 93.
Catalina: Aquí tiene.
Señor Scholl: ¡Ah, usted es argentina! ¿De dónde es exactamente?
Catalina: Soy de Buenos Aires. ¿Es usted español?

Señor Scholl: No, soy alemán. Soy de Colonia . . . Bueno, eso es todo. Por favor firme aquí.

Catalina: Muchas gracias. Hasta luego, Sr. Scholl.

Señor Scholl: ¡Felicitaciones! Disfrute la nueva cafetera. Adiós, Sra. Esguerra.

Mr. Scholl: *Good afternoon, Ms. Esguerra. I'm Marcos Scholl, sales manager of Galerías 93.*

Catalina: *It's a pleasure meeting you!*

Mr. Scholl: *The pleasure is mine. How are you?*

Catalina: *Well, I'm very happy, of course!*

Mr. Scholl: *Your prize is the capuccino machine. I need your personal code and the Galerías 93 card.*

Catalina: *Here you are.*

Mr. Scholl: *Oh, so you're Argentinian! Where are you from, exactly?*

Catalina: *I'm from Buenos Aires. Are you Spanish?*

Mr. Scholl: *No, I'm German. I'm from Cologne . . . Well, that's all. Please sign here.*

Catalina: *Thank you very much. Good-bye, Mr. Scholl.*

Mr. Scholl: *Congratulations! Enjoy your new cappuccino maker. Good-bye, Ms. Esguerra.*

NOTES

So, if Spanish has a formal form and an informal form, how do you go about using them? Well, the general rule is that when you first meet someone, you should use the formal form. However, many times when the person you have just met is close to you in age or younger than you, you'll see that the informal form is used rather quickly and you'll be on a first name basis almost from the beginning.

There are circumstances in which, due to the nature of the situation, you'll be almost obliged to use the formal form regardless of age. The distinction is also useful when you, for whatever reason, want to place a distance between yourself and your audience. To be on the safe side, don't use the **tú** form when you first meet someone. This is particularly important in many parts of Latin America. If the person is older or has a higher rank than you, it could be interpreted as being disrespectful.

NUTS & BOLTS 2
GREETINGS
In this unit we've seen some expressions used to greet people and say good-bye. Now let's take a closer look at some more expressions. Here are some formal expressions.

¿Cómo está usted?	*How are you?*
Muy bien, gracias.	*Very well, thank you.*
Encantado (de conocerle).	*Nice to meet you.*
Mucho gusto (en conocerle).	*Very pleased to meet you.*
Igualmente.	*Likewise.*

Here are some informal expressions.

¿Cómo estás?	*How are you?*
¿Qué tal?	*What's going on? How's it going?*
¿Qué hay?	*What's up?*
¿Qué pasa?	*What's up?*
¡Hola!	*Hello!*
Hasta mañana.	*See you tomorrow.*
Nos vemos.	*See you.*

PRACTICE 2
Decide whether the following sentences are formal or informal:

1. ¡Hola! ¿Cómo estás?   4. Mucho gusto. ¿Cómo está?
2. ¿Eres venezolano?   5. ¿Qué tal?
3. ¿Es usted soltero o casado? 6. Usted es ecuatoriana.

Tip!

When listening to the recorded conversations, you might not understand all of what's said at first. Don't get frustrated! It's normal not to understand every word of a language you're starting to learn. Focus on the few words you do understand and try to use your imagination to figure out the rest. Listen to the conversations two or three times, but don't play them over and over in an attempt to finally get it right. You'll only get frustrated! Be patient with yourself. Learning another language takes time. For great tips on how to get the most out of the conversations in this book, take a look at the *Language learning tips* section.

ANSWERS
PRACTICE 1: 1: días; **2.** nombre; **3.** gusto; **4.** datos personales; **5.** número de teléfono; **6.** profesión; **7.** Soy; **8.** soltero.

PRACTICE 2: 1. informal; **2.** informal; **3.** formal; **4.** formal; **5.** informal; **6.** formal.

UNIT 1 ESSENTIALS
At the end of each unit, you'll find a list of essential phrases. The grammar and vocabulary used should be familiar to you.

¿Cómo está? Bien, gracias, ¿y usted?
How are you? Fine, thanks, and you?

¿Cómo estás? Bien, gracias, ¿y tú?
How are you? Fine, thanks, and you?

¿Cuál es su nombre?
What's your name?

¿Cuál es su nacionalidad?
What's your nationality?

¿Cuál es su número de teléfono?
What's your phone number?

¿Cuál es su profesión?
What's your profession?

(Yo) soy francés.
I'm French.

(Tú) eres abogada.
You're a lawyer.

(Él/Ella) es argrentino/a.
He/She is Argentinian.

(Usted) es boliviano.
You're Bolivian.

(Nosotros/as) somos artistas.
We're artists.

(Vosotros/as) sois profesionales.
You're professionals.

(Ellos/as) son colombianos/as.
They're Colombian.

(Ustedes) son mexicanos/as.
You're Mexican.

Unit 2
Talking about family

In this unit, you'll learn how to talk about your family and to describe where you live. You'll also continue to expand your knowledge of Spanish grammar by learning plurals, another form of *to be*, the verb *to have*, and more.

———————————— Lesson 5 (words) ————————————

WORD LIST 1

Here's a list of words that refer to family members. All of these nouns have their natural gender.

madre	*mother*
padre	*father*
niño/a	*boy/girl*
hijo/a	*son/daughter*
hermano/a	*brother/sister*
abuelo/a	*grandfather/grandmother*
tío/a	*uncle/aunt*
primo/a	*cousin*
sobrino/a	*nephew/niece*
esposo/a	*husband/wife*
nieto/a	*grandson/granddaughter*
suegro/a	*father-in-law/mother-in-law*
nuera	*daughter-in-law*
yerno	*son-in-law*
cuñado/a	*brother-in-law/sister-in-law*

NUTS & BOLTS 1
INDEFINITE ARTICLES AND PLURALS

Like English, Spanish has indefinite articles that translate as *a* or *an*. But in Spanish, they have to match the gender and number of the noun they precede. Singular indefinite articles are translated as *a/an*, while plurals are translated as *some*.

	masculine	feminine
singular	**un**	**una**
plural	**unos**	**unas**

un hombre (*a man*)	**unos niños** (*some boys, some children*)
una mujer (*a woman*)	**unas niñas** (*some girls*)

Notice that the plural masculine form **unos** is used as long as at least one of the members of the group is male. The feminine plural form **unas** is used exclusively for groups with only female members.

Now, let's take a look at how the plural is formed in Spanish. It's very simple; to pluralize a word ending in a vowel, add **-s** to the end.

un hombre (*a man*)	**unos hombres** (*some men*)
una abuela (*a grandmother*)	**unas abuelas** (*some grandmothers*)

To pluralize a word ending in a consonant other than **-z**, add **-es** to the end.

un señor (*a gentleman*)	unos señores (*some gentlemen*)
una mujer (*a woman*)	unas mujeres (*some women*)

Words ending in a -z are pluralized by dropping the -z and adding -ces.

un lápiz (*a pencil*)	unos lapices (*some pencils*)
una luz (*a light*)	unas luces (*some lights*)

Note that the plural of **padre** (*father*) means *parents*. Similarly, other masculine plural nouns referring to family members can take on a more general sense and do not necessarily refer to males only. This depends on context, of course.

hijos	*children (sons and daughters)*
abuelos	*grandparents*
hermanos	*brothers and sisters, siblings*
primos	*cousins*
nietos	*grandchildren*

PRACTICE 1
Make the following nouns plural, insert the correct indefinite article before each one, and translate your answers.

1. tarjeta
2. hermano
3. señor

4. abogado
5. hija
6. premio

7. nombre   9. madre

8. cafetera   10. padre

WORD LIST 2

Here are some words that can be used when talking about where we live. **El** and **la** are definite articles, meaning *the*. You'll learn about them in a moment.

la casa	*house*
el edificio	*building*
el apartamento	*apartment*
la sala	*living room*
el comedor	*dining room*
la cocina	*kitchen*
el baño	*bathroom*
la habitación	*bedroom*
el jardín	*garden*
el balcón	*balcony*
el escritorio	*desk, study*
la puerta	*door*
la ventana	*window*
la silla	*seat, chair*
la mesa	*table*

NUTS & BOLTS 2

DEFINITE ARTICLES

The definite article in Spanish corresponds to *the* in English. There are four forms that agree in gender and number with the nouns they modify.

	masculine	feminine
singular	**el**	**la**
plural	**los**	**las**

You saw **el** and **la** in the word list above. They're convenient ways to tell you whether a noun is masculine or feminine. As we saw in Unit 1, determining the gender of a noun is not very difficult. Most nouns ending in **-o** are masculine, and most ending in **-a** are feminine. Nouns ending in **-ión** and **-ad** are feminine, while nouns ending in **-e** are generally masculine. Sometimes, however, there will be nouns that can be either masculine or feminine. In such cases, the article will change depending on who or what you are talking about.

el estudiante (*the male student*)	**la estudiante** (*the female student*)
el bebé (*the baby boy*)	**la bebé** (*the baby girl*)

PRACTICE 2
Replace the indefinite article with the definite article, and then translate your answers.

1. unas habitaciones

2. un abuelo

3. unos padres

4. una cocina

5. una prima

6. unas hermanas

7. un niño

8. un jardín

Culture note

Spanish speakers around the world use slightly different words for the same things. Here are a few differences.

In Spain, for example, you will hear people talking about their **piso** when referring to **un apartamento** (*apartment*). They'll also refer to their parents as **madre** (*mother*) and **padre** (*father*). Spaniards usually talk about their young children as **el crío** (*kid, m.*) or **la cría** (*kid, f.*).

In Latin America, people will use the words **cuarto** and **dormitorio** to refer to **una habitación** (*bedroom*). There is also the word **estudio,** which is used instead of **escritorio,** in the sense of *study* or *office*. And you will hear Latin Americans use the words **mamá** (*mom*) and **papá** (*dad*), or even **mami** and **papi,** when talking about their parents. In some parts of Latin America, you'll hear the word **párvulo** in reference to young children.

The words **habitación** and **cuarto** are literally translated as *room*. However, in many countries they are used to mean specifically a *bedroom*. Spanish has two other words that literally mean *bedroom*: **alcoba** and **dormitorio**. But **habitación** is also commonly used to refer to rooms in a hotel.

ANSWERS

PRACTICE 1: 1. unas tarjetas (*some cards*); **2.** unos hermanos (*some brothers*); **3.** unos señores (*some gentlemen*); **4.** unos abogados (*some lawyers*); **5.** unas hijas (*some daughters*); **6.** unos premios (*some prizes*); **7.** unos nombres (*some names*); **8.** unas cafeteras (*some coffeemakers*); **9.** unas madres (*some mothers*); **10.** unos padres (*some fathers/parents*).

PRACTICE 2: 1. las habitaciones (*the bedrooms*); **2.** el abuelo (*the grandfather*); **3.** los padres (*the fathers/parents*); **4.** la cocina (*the kitchen*); **5.** la prima (*the female cousin*); **6.** las hermanas (*the sisters*); **7.** el niño (*the boy*); **8.** el jardín (*the garden*).

PHRASE LIST 1

Here are some phrases that can be used to talk about family and friends. You'll see them again in the conversations in this unit.

como ya sabes	*as you already know*
el mayor	*the oldest (male)*
la menor	*the youngest (female)*
diferencia de edades	*difference in ages*
el centro de atracción	*center of attraction*
es natural	*it's natural*
y encima . . .	*and on top of that . . .*
situación familiar	*family situation*
tienes que . . .	*you have to . . .*
en un mismo apartamento	*in the same apartment*

NUTS & BOLTS 1

Estar *(TO BE)*

In Spanish, the verb *to be* has two forms: **ser** and **estar.** In Unit 1, we learned a bit about **ser.** Now let's take a look at **estar.** We'll discuss the differences between the two verbs in the next lesson of this unit. Here's the full conjugation of **estar.** Note where the accents are.

yo estoy	*I am*
tú estás *(infml.)*	*you are*
él está	*he is*
ella está	*she is*
usted está *(fml.)*	*you are*

nosotros/as estamos	we are
vosotros/as estáis *(infml.)*	*(all of) you are*
ellos/ellas/ustedes están	*they/(all of) you are*

PRACTICE 1

Fill in the blanks with the correct form of the verb **estar.**

1. Yo _____ en el apartamento.

2. Vosotros _____ felices.

3. Ellos _____ en la casa.

4. ¿Cómo _____ usted?

5. ¿Cómo _____ vosotros?

6. Yo _____ bien, ¿y tú?

PHRASE LIST 2

Here are some common expressions using **estar.**

¿Cómo estás?	*How are you?*
Estoy bien, gracias.	*I'm fine, thanks.*
Estoy cansado.	*I'm tired. (male)*
Estoy cansada.	*I'm tired. (female)*
Estoy triste.	*I'm sad.*
Estás feliz.	*You're happy.*
Está mal.	*He/She is not doing well.*
¿Donde está la universidad?	*Where's the university?*
Está en la Avenida Palacios.	*It's on Avenida Palacios.*
El horno está caliente.	*The oven is hot.*
El agua está fría.	*The water is cold.*

Notice that you say **el agua** instead of **la agua**. That's because **agua** begins with a stressed vowel. If a feminine word begins with a stressed **a-** or **ha-**, use **el** instead of **la.** In the plural, though, use the regular **las.**

el agua/las aguas	*the water/the waters*
el hacha/las hachas	*the axe/the axes*

NUTS & BOLTS 2
THE NUMBERS 20–100

Let's take a look at numbers from 20 to 100 in Spanish.

20 veinte	30 treinta
21 veintiuno	31 treinta y uno
22 veintidós	32 treinta y dos
23 veintitrés	40 cuarenta
24 veinticuatro	50 cincuenta
25 veinticinco	60 sesenta
26 veintiséis	70 setenta
27 veintisiete	80 ochenta
28 veintiocho	90 noventa
29 veintinueve	100 cien

Notice that once you go above thirty, the numbers are formed with the tens followed by **y** (*and*) and then the number.

45	**cuarenta y cinco**	*(lit., forty and five)*
77	**setenta y siete**	*(lit., seventy and seven)*
82	**ochenta y dos**	*(lit., eighty and two)*

PRACTICE 2
Match the numbers in column A with those in column B.

A	B
1. 77 - 11 - 31	a. sesenta y siete, diez, veintiuno
2. 45 - 35 - 25	b. cien, ochenta y uno, veinte
3. 90 - 100 - 15	c. setenta y siete, once, treinta y uno
4. 67 - 10 - 21	d. cuarenta y cinco, treinta y cinco, veinticinco
5. 100 - 81 - 20	e. cuarenta y cinco, sesenta y cinco, diecinueve
6. 45 - 65 - 19	f. noventa, cien, quince

Culture note
You'll hear the word **hombre** (*man*) used conversationally when two men are addressing each other. This is very similar to the conversational English use of *man*. Today, women are also beginning to use the word **mujer** (*woman*) in the same way. Also, many times, a Spanish speaker will refer to his wife as **mi mujer,** which literally means **my woman.** It is, however, not meant in a disrespectful way;

ANSWERS
PRACTICE 1: 1. estoy; **2.** estáis; **3.** están; **4.** está; **5.** estáis; **6.** estoy.

PRACTICE 2: 1. c; **2.** d; **3.** f; **4.** a; **5.** b; **6.** e.

——————— Lesson 7 (sentences) ———————

SENTENCE LIST 1

¿Cuántos años tienen?	*How old are they?*
¿Cómo se llaman?	*What are their names?*
No me siento muy bien.	*I don't feel very well.*
Ella está un poco celosa.	*She's a bit jealous.*
Eso no es todo.	*That's not all.*
Hay cuatro alcobas.	*There are four rooms.*
Hay una cocina.	*There's a kitchen.*
Tengo dos hijos.	*I have two sons.*
No hay otra solución.	*There's no other solution.*
No me digas.	*Really? (lit., Don't tell me.)*

NUTS & BOLTS 1
USING SER AND ESTAR

So, how are **ser** and **estar** used? The major difference, in a nutshell, is that **ser** expresses permanent, or at least long-lasting, qualities, while **estar** expresses qualities that are likely to change, as well as location, even of something that's not likely to move. Let's start with **ser,** which is generally used in the following ways.

1. TO EXPRESS ORIGIN OR NATIONALITY
Soy de Argentina.

I'm from Argentina.

Eres francesa.
You're French.

2. To identify people and things
¿Cuál es su nombre?
What's your name?

Mi nombre es Marta.
My name is Marta.

¿Cuál es su número de teléfono?
What's your phone number?

Es el tres dos cero-tres cuatro cinco seis.
It's 320-3456.

3. To express occupation
Ella es profesora de matemáticas.
She's a professor of mathematics.

Ellos son ingenieros.
They're engineers.

4. To express permanent or inherent characteristics
El hielo es frío.
Ice is cold.

Las rosas son hermosas.
Roses are beautiful.

PRACTICE 1
Chose the correct form of **ser.**

1. Su número de fax (son, es, eres) tres cinco seis-tres cuatro nueve cero.

2. Juan y Pedro (sois, son, es) arquitectos.

3. María y yo (son, sois, somos) estudiantes.

4. Tú (soy, eres, es) una mujer celosa.

5. Vosotros (sois, son, eres) uruguayos./Ustedes (sois, son, eres) uruguayos.

6. Él (son, eres,es) brasilero.

7. Ella (eres, es, soy) doctora.

8. Yo (son, somos, soy) de los Estados Unidos. ¿Y tú?

SENTENCE LIST 2

In Unit 1, you learned the most common greetings. Here are a few more informal ways to greet someone and a few sentences that can be used to make small talk.

¿Qué tal?	*What's up?*
¿Qué pasa?	*How's it going?*
¿Qué hay?	*What's up? What's going on?*
¿Cómo va todo?	*How's everything?*
Así, así.	*So-so.*
Pues, nada.	*Not much.*
Pues, aquí estamos.	*Here we are.*
Y la familia, ¿cómo está?	*How's your family doing?*
Y su esposa/o, ¿cómo va?	*How's your wife/husband?*
¿Y sus hijos?	*What about your children?*
¿Que tal andan todos?	*How's everyone?*
Pues bien.	*Fine.*
¿Cómo te trata la vida?	*How's life treating you?*

NUTS & BOLTS 2

USING ESTAR

The verb **estar** is used in the following circumstances:

1. TO SHOW LOCATION

Mi hermana está en el apartamento.

My sister is in the apartment.

Londres está en Inglaterra.

London is in England.

2. TO EXPRESS WHAT IS TEMPORARY
El café está frío.

The coffee is cold (right now).

3. TO EXPRESS FEELINGS AND EMOTIONS
¡Estoy feliz!

I am happy (right now)!

As you can see, one of the main differences between **ser** and **estar** is the fact that **ser** expresses a permanent characteristic and **estar** a temporary condition or location. So, depending on the speaker's intention, in some cases either **ser** or **estar** can be used. Notice the differences.

Ella es bonita.

She's pretty (by nature).

Ella está bonita.

She looks pretty (right now).

Es borracho.

He's a drunk (as a characteristic).

Está borracho.

He's drunk (right now).

Es triste.

He's gloomy (by nature).

Está triste.

He's feeling down.

¿Cómo eres?

What are you like? (Describe yourself.)

¿Cómo estás?
How are you? (How's your current state?)

PRACTICE 2
Choose the verb that best completes the sentence.

1. Buenos Aires (es, está) en Argentina.
2. Juan, Pedro, y Miguel (están, son) profesores.
3. ¡Hola! ¿Cómo (estás, eres)?
4. Tú y María (sois, estáis) portuguesas.
5. Yo (estoy, soy) en mi casa.
6. Mi tía y mi hermana (están, son) en el apartamento.
7. Yo (estoy, soy) un estudiante.
8. ¡Hola! ¿Cómo (estáis, sois)?

Tip!
In trying to learn how to use **ser** and **estar**, don't get too hung up on the rules. Try to remember the basic differences and then experiment, and pay attention to how Spanish speakers use them. One way of exploring this difference is to type fragments like "**el presidente / la doctora / María es**" and "**el presidente / la doctora / María está**" into a search engine. See if you can decipher the results and identify the different nuances. You'll see that, with time, it will all start making more sense. Remember, be patient with yourself, and most of all, have fun learning the language.

ANSWERS
PRACTICE 1: 1. es; 2. son; 3. somos; 4. eres; 5. sois/son; 6.es; 7. es; 8. soy.

PRACTICE 2: 1. está; 2. son; 3. estás; 4. sois; 5. estoy; 6. están; 7. soy; 8. estáis.

CONVERSATION 1

Farina is on her third date with Jorge. She's telling him a little bit more about her personal life and her family.

Farina: Como ya sabes, estoy divorciada de mi segundo esposo y tengo dos hijos.

Jorge: ¿Cuántos años tienen?

Farina: Bueno, el mayor tiene venticinco años y la menor tiene ocho años.

Jorge: Es una diferencia de edades muy grande, ¿no? ¿Cómo se llaman?

Farina: Carlos es de mi primer matrimonio y Carolina del segundo. Carlos está casado y tiene una bebita de dieciséis meses.

Jorge: ¡Así que eres abuela!

Farina: Sí, soy abuela y me siento muy bien. ¡Estoy feliz!

Jorge: ¡Y tu hija ya es tía!

Farina: Sí, pero ella está un poco celosa de mi nieta.

Jorge: Es natural. La bebé es en este momento el centro de atracción de la familia.

Farina: *As you already know, I'm divorced from my second husband and I have two children.*

Jorge: *How old are they?*

Farina: *Well, the older one is twenty-five and the younger one is eight.*

Jorge: *That's a big age difference, don't you think? What are their names?*

Farina: *Carlos is from my first marriage and Carolina from the second. Carlos is married and has a sixteen-month-old baby.*

Jorge: *So, you're a grandmother!*

Farina: *Yes, I'm a grandmother and I'm okay with it. (lit., I feel good). I'm happy!*

Jorge:	*And your daughter is already an aunt!*
Farina:	*Yes, but she's a bit jealous of my granddaughter.*
Jorge:	*It's natural. Right now the baby is the center of attention of the whole family.*

NOTES

In Unit 1, you learned how to ask for someone's name like this: **¿Cuál es su nombre?** That's one possibility, but Spanish speakers generally use the verb **llamarse** (*to be called*) instead.

¿Cómo se llaman?

What are their names?

¿Cómo se llama?

What is your name?

Me llamo María.

My name is Maria.

In the next unit, we will learn how to conjugate regular verbs like this one.

NUTS & BOLTS 1

TENER *(TO HAVE)*

You might have noticed a new verb in the dialogue: **tener** (*to have*). It's an irregular verb, but a very common and important one, so let's look at its forms.

yo tengo	*I have*
tú tienes *(infml.)*	*you have*
él tiene	*he has*
ella tiene	*she has*
usted tiene *(fml.)*	*you have*

nosotros/as tenemos	*we have*
vosotros/as tenéis *(infml.)*	*(all of) you have*
ellos/ellas/ustedes tienen	*they/(all of) you have*

The verb **tener** has a few very common uses, such as telling a person's age.

¿Cuántos años tiene Pedro?
How old is Pedro? (lit., How many years does Pedro have?)

Pedro tiene veintitrés años.
Pedro is twenty-three years old.

It's also used to show possession, just like in English.

Tengo un apartamento en México y una casa en Paraguay.
I have an apartment in Mexico and a house in Paraguay.

In Spanish, the verb **tener** is also used to describe certain physical, mental, and emotional states. In most of the cases where Spanish uses **tener,** English uses *to be.*

tener frío	*to be cold*
tener calor	*to be warm*
tener sed	*to be thirsty*
tener hambre	*to be hungry*
tener sueño	*to be sleepy*
tener cansancio	*to be tired*

tener prisa	to be in a hurry
tener miedo	to be scared
tener razón	to be right

¿Tienes hambre?
Are you hungry?

Tengo sueño ahora.
I'm sleepy now.

Tenemos frío en enero.
We're cold in January.

PRACTICE 1
Fill in the blanks with the correct form of **tener.**

1. Nosotros _____ hambre y sed.

2. Ella _____ veintisiete años y él _____ cuarenta.

3. Vosotros _____ una casa grande./Ustedes _____ una casa grande.

4. Tú _____ sueño.

5. ¿Cuántos hijos _____ tú?

6. ¿Cuántos nietos _____ Sara?

7. Yo _____ tres primos.

8. Ella _____ siete sobrinos.

CONVERSATION 2
A day after his date, Jorge meets up with his friend Fabio and tells him about the woman he's been dating.

Fabio: ¡Está divorciada!

Jorge: ¿Tiene hijos?

Fabio: Sí, dos. ¡Y encima es abuela!

Jorge: ¡No me digas!

Fabio: Pero eso no es todo. Ella vive con sus hijos, su nuera, y su nieta en un mismo apartamento.

Jorge: ¿Es un apartamento grande o pequeño?

Fabio: Hay cuatro alcobas y una sala-comedor. Hay también una cocina y un balcón.

Jorge: No está mal.

Fabio: ¿No está mal? ¡Los dos ex esposos viven en el edificio también!

Jorge: Bueno, tienes razón. El problema es gordo.

Fabio: Farina es una mujer muy atractiva y divertida pero su situación familiar es difícil.

Fabio: *She's divorced!*

Jorge: *Does she have children?*

Fabio: *Yes, two. And, on top of that, she's a grandmother!*

Jorge: *No kidding!*

Fabio: *But that's not all. She lives with her children, her daughter-in-law, and her granddaughter in the same apartment.*

Jorge: *Is it a big or a small apartment?*

Fabio: *There are four bedrooms and a living room–dining room. There's also a kitchen and a balcony.*

Jorge: *Not bad.*

Fabio: *Not bad? Her two ex-husbands are living in the building too!*

Jorge: *Well, you're right. That's a major problem.*

Fabio: *Farina is a very attractive and fun woman, but her family situation is very difficult.*

NUTS & BOLTS 2

HAY *(THERE IS/THERE ARE)*

The word **hay** is used to mean both *there is* and *there are*.

Hay una persona en la clase.
There's one person in the classroom.

En la casa hay tres habitaciones y un estudio.
There are three bedrooms and a study in the house.

¿Cuántas personas hay en su familia?
How many people are there in your family?

PRACTICE 2

Translate the following sentences, writing out the numbers in Spanish.

1. *There are seventy men and twenty women in the room.*

2. *The house has fifteen bathrooms.*

3. *I'm hungry.*

4. *The coffee is hot.*

5. *She's sleepy.*

6. *You (fml. sg.) are right.*

7. *We're hot.*

8. *They're scared.*

Culture note

In Unit 1, we briefly mentioned **La Real Academia de la Lengua Española,** which is based in Madrid, Spain. The Academy was founded in 1713 by Juan Manuel Fernández Pacheco, Marquis of Villena and Duke of Escalona. It's affiliated with national academies in twenty-one Spanish-speaking countries. Because it's the institution responsible for regulating the Spanish language and reflecting the evolution of the language, it's a major publisher of grammars and dictionaries. The academy has its own website and an online dictionary that you might want to visit.

ANSWERS

PRACTICE 1: 1. tenemos; **2.** tiene, tiene; **3.** tenéis/tienen; **4.** tienes; **5.** tienes; **6.** tiene; **7.** tengo; **8.** tiene.

PRACTICE 2: 1. Hay setenta hombres y veinte mujeres en la habitación. **2.** La casa tiene quince baños. **3.** Tengo hambre. **4.** El café está caliente. **5.** Ella tiene sueño. **6.** Usted tiene razón. **7.** Tenemos calor. **8.** Tienen miedo.

UNIT 2 ESSENTIALS
un/una

a, an

unos/unas

some

el/la/los/las

the

Eres colombiano.

You're Colombian.

Su nombre es Angela.

Her name is Angela.

Somos estudiantes.

We're students.

El hielo es frío.

Ice is cold.

Estoy en el comedor.
I'm in the dining room.

Bogotá está en Colombia.
Bogotá is in Colombia.

El café está caliente.
The coffee is hot.

Están felices.
They're happy/You're happy.

Estáis felices.
You're happy. (infml. Spain)

Ella es bonita.
She's pretty.

Ella está bonita.
She looks pretty.

Tengo veinte años.
I'm twenty years old.

Tiene dos casas.
He/She has two houses.

En el apartamento hay dos dormitorios.
There are two bedrooms in the apartment.

En el apartamento hay un baño.
There's one bathroom in the apartment.

Unit 3
Everyday life

In this unit you'll learn some more numbers, as well as the days of the week and months of the year. You'll also learn how to ask questions in Spanish, how to describe things, and how to talk about your likes and dislikes.

———————————— Lesson 9 (words) ————————————

WORD LIST 1
Let's learn the days of the week in Spanish and some other useful vocabulary.

la semana	*week*
el día	*day*
lunes	*Monday*
martes	*Tuesday*
miércoles	*Wednesday*
jueves	*Thursday*
viernes	*Friday*
sábado	*Saturday*
domingo	*Sunday*
el fin de semana	*weekend*
semanal	*weekly*
diario	*daily*
la mañana	*morning*
la tarde	*afternoon*
la noche	*evening, night*

Notice that in Spanish, the days of the week are not written with a capital letter.

NUTS & BOLTS 1

NUMBERS ABOVE 100

You already know the numbers 0 to 100. So, let's keep on counting.

cien	100
ciento uno/una	101
ciento dos	102
doscientos/as	200
trescientos/as	300
cuatrocientos/as	400
quinientos/as	500
seiscientos/as	600
setecientos/as	700
ochocientos/as	800
novecientos/as	900
mil	1,000
mil novecientos noventa y ocho	1,998
diez mil	10,000
veinte mil	20,000
un millón	1,000,000

The hundreds not only have a masculine and a feminine form, but they are also plural.

doscientos hombres	200 men
cuatrocientas mujeres	400 women
quienientos treinta y tres niños	533 boys (children)
seiscientas quince niñas	615 girls

Usually the word **cien** is used before a noun, and the word **ciento** before any number except **mil** (*thousand*).

cien días	100 days
cien personas	100 people
ciento tres dólares	103 dollars
ciento setenta y siete años	177 years
cien mil pesos	100,000 pesos

Finally, the word **millón** (*million*) and others formed by using it are followed by the preposition **de** (*of*).

un millón de casas	1,000,000 houses
cuatro millones de personas	4,000,000 people

PRACTICE 1
Translate the following phrases. Write out the numbers in Spanish.

1. *365 days*

2. *52 weeks*

3. *10,000 people*

4. *1,565,000 houses*

5. *100 children*   7. *145 prizes*

6. *555 women*   8. *278 rooms*

WORD LIST 2

Here are the months of the year and other useful vocabulary.

el año	*year*
el mes	*month*
enero	*January*
febrero	*February*
marzo	*March*
abril	*April*
mayo	*May*
junio	*June*
julio	*July*
agosto	*August*
septiembre	*September*
octubre	*October*
noviembre	*November*
diciembre	*December*
la década	*decade*
el siglo	*century*
la estación	*season*
la primavera	*spring*
el verano	*summer*
el otoño	*fall*
el invierno	*winter*

Like the days of the week, the months and seasons are not capitalized in Spanish.

NUTS & BOLTS 2

TELLING TIME

The verb **ser** comes in very handy when telling time. You can ask for the time using any of the following expressions.

¿Qué hora es?
What time is it?

¿Qué horas son?
What time is it?

¿Qué hora tiene?
What time do you have?

Usually, you answer by using the verb **ser + la(s)**, because the noun **hora** is feminine. Notice that with most hours you use **son las . . .** , but with one o'clock you use **es la . . .**

Son las doce (en punto).
12:00/It's twelve o'clock (sharp).

Es la una.
1:00/It's one o'clock.

Son las dos.
2:00/It's two o'clock.

Son las seis en punto.
6:00/It's six o'clock sharp.

Use **y** (*and*) to add minutes past the hour. Notice that you can use **cuarto** (*quarter*) or **quince** (*fifteen*) for a quarter of an hour and **media** (*half*) or **treinta** (*thirty*) for a half an hour.

Es la una y diez.
1:10/It's ten after one.

Son las cuatro y veinte.
4:20/It's twenty after four.

Es la una y quince.
1:15/It's one fifteen.

Son las tres y cuarto.
3:15/It's a quarter after three.

Son las nueve y treinta.
9:30/It's nine thirty.

Son las once y media.
11:30/It's eleven thirty.

Son las siete y cuarenta y cinco.
7:45/It's seven forty-five.

When telling time past the half hour, you subtract the minutes from the hour and use **menos** (*less*), like this:

Es la una menos cinco.
12:55/It's five to one.

Es la una menos cuarto.
12:45/It's a quarter to one.

Son las cuatro menos veinte.
3:40/It's twenty to four.

Son las ocho menos cuarto.
7:45/It's a quarter to eight.

You learned a few words for divisions of the day in your word list. Here they are again, with a few more expressions that will come in handy in telling the time.

la mañana	*morning*
el mediodía	*noon*
la tarde	*afternoon*
la noche	*evening, night*
la media noche	*midnight*
la madrugada	*late night, early morning (from midnight till daybreak)*

Because we normally don't use military time, you can specify the time of day when telling time with phrases like the following.

Es la una y diez de la madrugada.

1:10/It's ten after one in the morning.

Son las cuatro menos veinte de la mañana.

3:40/It's twenty to four in the morning.

Son las nueve y treinta de la noche.

9:30/It's nine thirty at night.

Es la una y diez de la tarde.

1:10/It's ten after one in the afternoon

Notice that when the preposition **de** is followed by the masculine article **el,** it forms the contraction **del.**

Son las doce del mediodía.

It's twelve noon.

PRACTICE 2
What time is it? Write out your answers in complete words in Spanish.

1. *7:15 P.M.*

2. *3:20 P.M.*

3. *1:45 A.M.*

4. *8:00 A.M.*

5. *2:30 P.M.*

6. *12:55 P.M.*

7. *6:45 A.M.*

8. *1:35 P.M.*

9. *9:10 A.M.*

Tip!

Take a closer look at how numbers are written in Spanish and in English. Those little commas and periods we all love (especially when dealing with large amounts of money) signal something totally different:

5.000 cinco mil
5,000 *five thousand*

19,95 diecinueve coma noventa y cinco
19.95 *nineteen point ninety-five*

10.540,80 diezmil quinientos cuarenta coma ochenta
10,540.80 *ten thousand, five hundred forty point eighty*

ANSWERS

PRACTICE 1: 1. trescientos sesenta y cinco días **2.** cincuenta y dos semanas **3.** diez mil personas **4.** un millón quinientos sesenta y cinco mil casas. **5.** cien niños **6.** quinientas cincuenta y cinco mujeres **7.** ciento cuarenta y cinco premios **8.** doscientas setenta y ocho habitaciones

PRACTICE 2: 1. Son las siete y cuarto (y quince) de la noche.
2. Son las tres y veinte de la tarde. **3.** Es la una y cuarenta y
cinco de la madrugada./Son las dos menos cuarto de la
madrugada. **4.** Son las ocho de la mañana. **5.** Son las dos y
treinta (y media) de la tarde. **6.** Son las doce y cincuenta y cinco
del medio día./Es la una menos cinco. **7.** Son las seis y cuarenta
y cinco de la mañana./Son las siete menos cuarto de la mañana.
8. Es la una y treinta y cinco de la tarde./Son las dos menos
veinticinco de la tarde. **9.** Son las nueve y diez de la mañana.

———— Lesson 10 (phrases) ————

PHRASE LIST 1

You've already seen a number of different ways to greet someone.
How about saying good-bye? Here are a few phrases to help you
out:

Adiós.	*Good-bye.*
Hasta luego.	*Until later.*
Hasta pronto.	*See you soon. (lit., Until soon).*
Hasta mañana.	*Until tomorrow.*
Hasta más tarde.	*Until later.*
Hasta entonces.	*Till then.*
Chao.	*Bye.*
Nos vemos.	*See you. (lit., We see each other.)*
Que estés bien. *(infml.)*	*Take care.(lit., May you be well.)*
Que esté bien. *(fml.)*	*May you be well.*

NUTS & BOLTS 1
ADJECTIVE AGREEMENT

Remember that adjectives are words that you use to describe
nouns. So *big, intelligent, interesting,* and *horrible* are adjectives in
English. Don't forget that nouns in Spanish have gender (masculine or feminine) and number (singular or plural), and adjectives
must agree with the nouns that they describe or modify.

un hombre panameño	*a Panamanian man*
una mujer panameña	*a Panamanian woman*
unos hombres panameños	*a few Panamanian men*
unas mujeres panameñas	*a few Panamanian women*

As you can see from the above examples, adjectives usually come after the nouns they modify. The typical adjective endings are **-o** for masculine singular, **-a** for feminine singular, **-os** for masculine plural, and **-as** for feminine plural. If an adjective ends in **-e,** (**grande**, *big*), then it has the same form in the singular for both genders (**grande**) and adds **-s** for both genders in the plural (**grandes**). There are a few irregularities that we'll get to, but that's the basic picture.

Here are some adjectives you can use to describe people and things. Notice that just the singular forms are given. You can make the plurals just by adding **-s** to the appropriate singular form.

alto(a)/bajo(a)	*tall/short*
gordo(a)/delgado(a)	*fat/thin*
largo(a)/corto(a)	*long/short*
ancho(a)/angosto(a)	*wide/narrow*
grande/pequeño(a)	*big/small*
rico(a)/pobre	*rich/poor*
costoso(a)/barato(a)	*expensive/cheap*
limpio(a)/sucio(a)	*clean/dirty*

libre/ocupado(a)	*free/busy*
bueno(a)/malo(a)	*good/bad*
agradable/desagradable	*pleasant/unpleasant*
temprano/tarde	*early/late*
divertido(a)/aburrido(a)	*fun/boring*
bonito(a)/feo(a)	*pretty/ugly*

Here are some examples using **ser**. Notice the way the adjectives all agree with the person or thing they modify.

Soy alto.
I'm tall.

Eres delgada.
You're thin.

El apartamento es pequeño.
The apartment is small.

Ella es rica.
She's rich.

Somos pobres.
We are poor.

Vosotros sois divertidos.
You are fun.

Ellos son agradables.
They are pleasant.

Son bajos.
They are short.

Let's see some more examples, this time with **tener.**

Tengo una casa grande.
I have a big house.

Tiene una abuela rica.
He/She has a rich grandmother.

Tenemos un día libre.
We have a free day.

Tienen un tío divertido.
They have a fun uncle.

PRACTICE 1
Connect each noun with the appropriate adjective by using a form of **ser.**

1. el día	a. larga
2. el libro	b. costosas
3. las cafeteras	c. divertida
4. la semana	d. aburrido
5. los apartamentos	e. corto
6. la comedia	f. pequeños

PHRASE LIST 2

por la mañana	in the morning
por la tarde	in the afternoon
por la noche	in the evening, at night
al mediodía	at noon
a la medianoche	at midnight
en la madrugada	in the early morning, at dawn

al amanecer	*at dawn*
al atardecer	*at dusk*
Se me hace tarde.	*I'm late.*
Es muy temprano.	*It's very early.*

NOTE

Do you remember that **de + el = del**? Well, the same thing happens with **a** (*to, at*) plus **el**: **a + el = al** (*to the, at the*) in the expressions **al amanecer** and **al atardecer**.

NUTS & BOLTS 2
MORE ON ADJECTIVE AGREEMENT

Let's get back to adjectives and adjective agreement, so you know how to describe things in Spanish. Again, as with nouns, adjectives ending in **-o** are masculine, and the feminine is formed by changing the **-o** to **-a**. To form the plural, just add **-s** to the singular form.

	masculine singular	feminine singular	masculine plural	feminine plural
pretty	**bonito**	**bonita**	**bonitos**	**bonitas**
ugly	**fco**	**fea**	**feos**	**feas**

Es un jardín muy bonito.

It's a very pretty garden.

Es una foto muy fea.

It's a very ugly photo.

Tienen unos jardines bonitos.

They have some pretty gardens.

Tienen unas fotos feas.

They have some ugly pictures.

As you know, there are some adjectives that end in -e, like **grande** (*big*), **pobre** (*poor*), **libre** (*free*), and so on. These adjectives only have one singular form for both masculine and feminine. There are other adjectives that end in a consonant, like **trabajador** (*hardworking*), **difícil** (*difficult*), and **fácil** (*easy*). Adjectives that end in -or have two singular forms (**trabajador, trabajadora**), but adjectives like **difícil** and **fácil** only have one. Both of these types of adjectives end in -es in the plural.

Ella es una niña inteligente.
She's an intelligent girl.

Él es un chico inteligente.
He's an intelligent kid.

Son inteligentes.
They're intelligent.

Tienen un hermano trabajador.
They have a hardworking brother.

Ella es trabajadora.
She's hardworking.

Tienen unos padres trabajadores.
They have hardworking parents.

Most adjectives of nationality end in a consonant, and the feminine is formed by adding -a to the end.

Yo soy española y él es alemán.
I'm Spanish and he's German.

Ella es alemana y ellos son franceses.
She's German and they're French.

Tú eres francesa y él es español.
You're French and he's Spanish.

PRACTICE 2

Form sentences using the words given. Make sure you use the correct form of the verb. Adjectives are given in the singular, masculine form, so you may have to change them.

1. yo—tener—treinta—películas—divertido

2. casas—ser—feo

3. tú—tener—dos apartamentos—grande

4. ella—ser—inglés

5. las niñas—ser—alto y bonito

6. yo—tener—un día—libre

7. vosotros—tener—unos tíos—rico

8. ustedes—tener—unos tíos—rico

Culture note

You've probably heard the term **realismo mágico** (*magical realism*), which refers to a Latin American literary movement. The term has been attributed to the Cuban writer Alejo Carpentier, who first applied it to Latin American fiction in 1949. The main characteristic of magical realism is the matter-of-fact incorporation of fantastic or dreamlike elements into otherwise realistic fiction. The Colombian writer Gabriel García Márquez is probably the movement's best known proponent. His most famous novel is **Cien años de soledad** (*One Hundred Years of Solitude*). Other magic realist writers include Guatemala's Miguel Ángel Asturias, Argentina's Julio Córtazar, Mexico's Carlos Fuentes, and Chile's Isabel Allende.

Reading short stories by these writers might be a good way for you to get an introduction to Latin American literature and, in doing so, learn some adjectives! If you'd like a nice overview of magical realism, try this link:

http://en.wikipedia.org/wiki/Magical_realism

Don't forget that there's a Spanish version of Wikipedia as well! See if you can figure out how to find the article on **realismo mágico**.

ANSWERS

PRACTICE 1: 1. El día es corto. **2.** El libro es aburrido. **3.** Las cafeteras son costosas. **4.** La semana es larga. **5.** Los apartamentos son pequeños. **6.** La comedia es divertida.

PRACTICE 2: 1. Yo tengo treinta películas divertidas. **2.** Las casas son feas. **3.** Tú tienes dos apartamentos grandes. **4.** Ella es inglesa. **5.** Las niñas son altas y bonitas. **6.** Yo tengo un día libre. **7.** Vosotros tenéis unos tíos ricos. **8.** Ustedes tienen unos tíos ricos.

— Lesson 11 (sentences) —

SENTENCE LIST 1

¿Cómo estás de tiempo?	*Do you have time?/How are you doing for time?*
¿Qué tal si nos encontramos para almorzar?	*How about if we meet for lunch?*
¿Qué te parece si nos reunimos al mediodía?	*How about if we meet at noon?*
¿Conoces el lugar?	*Do you know the place?*
¿Qué tal si vamos al cine?	*How about if we go to the movies?*
¿Tienes la cartelera de cine a la mano?	*Do you have the movie listings handy?*
Quedamos a las ocho, ¿no?	*We meet at eight, don't we?*
¿Por qué no escogemos una comedia?	*Why don't we choose a comedy?*

NUTS & BOLTS 1
QUESTION WORDS

Back in Lesson 3, when you learned the forms of **ser,** you saw an example of a yes/no question.

¿Es Marta de Madrid o de Barcelona?
Is Marta from Madrid or Barcelona?

We'll come back to yes/no questions in a moment. For now let's look at questions with question words like *who, what, where, when,* and so on. Here are a few question words in Spanish.

cómo	*how*
qué	*what*
quién	*who*
cuándo	*when*

You already know how to use **cómo** to greet people and to ask for a description of something or someone. It's also used when you don't understand what has been said. Notice that **cómo** comes at the beginning of the question and that the subject (if it's not dropped) and verb are reversed.

¿Cómo estás?
How are you?

¿Cómo es la película?
How's the movie?

¿Cómo se llama?
What is your name? (lit., How are you called?)

¿Cómo se llama la profesora?
What's the teacher's name?

¿Cómo?
What?/Pardon me?

The word **qué** is used to ask for an explanation or an identification. It's also used to ask when something is happening.

¿Qué es eso?
What is that?

¿Qué es la filosofía?
What is philosophy?

¿Qué hora es?
What time is it?

¿A qué hora es la película?
At what time is the movie?

Quién is used to request the identification of a person. In Spanish it has a plural form (**quienes**).

¿Quién es ella?
Who is she?

¿Quiénes son ustedes?
Who are you?

¿Quién es su padre?
Who's your father?

¿Quiénes son sus padres?
Who are your parents?

Finally, **cuándo** is used to ask when something is taking place.

¿Cuándo es la película?
When is the movie?

¿Cuándo tienes el día libre?
When do you have a free day?

¿Cuándo está ocupada?
When is she busy?

PRACTICE 1
Translate the following sentences.

1. *When do you have time? (infml. sg.)*
2. *How are you doing? (infml. pl.)*
3. *At what time is the movie?*
4. *Who are the children?*
5. *How's the coffee?*
6. *What time is it?*

SENTENCE LIST 2

El lunes trabajo horas extras.	*On Monday I work extra hours.*
Los martes tengo clases en la universidad.	*On Tuesdays I have classes at the university.*
Esa es una mejor idea.	*That's a better idea.*
No, al mediodía no me va bien.	*No, noontime is not good for me.*
Hablamos luego.	*We'll talk later.*
A mí tampoco me gustan.	*I don't like them either.*
Estoy muy ocupada.	*I'm very busy.*
¿Tienes la cartelera de cine a la mano?	*Do you have the movie listings handy?*

NUTS & BOLTS 2
MORE QUESTION WORDS
Here are some more useful question words.

dónde	*where*
cuánto	*how much*
cuál	*which*
por qué	*why*

Dónde is used with **estar** to ask for the location of something or someone. In order to ask for the origin of something/someone, the phrase **de dónde** (*from where*) is used along with the verb **ser.**

¿Dónde está el restaurante?
Where is the restaurant?

¿Dónde están las niñas?
Where are the girls?

¿De dónde eres?
Where are you from?

Cuánto has a feminine form, **cuánta,** and the plural forms **cuántos/as.**

¿Cuánto es el apartamento?
How much is the apartment?

¿Cuánto dinero tienes?
How much money do you have?

¿Cuánta leche quieres?
How much milk do you want?

¿Cuántos días hay en una semana?
How many days are there in a week?

¿Cuántas horas tiene un día?
How many hours does a day have?

Cuál also has a plural form (**cuáles**) and is used when asking about something that belongs to a group.

¿Cuál es su casa?
Which is your house?

¿Cuáles son sus libros?
Which are your books?

Finally, there is **por qué,** which means *why.*

¿Por qué es delgado?
Why is he thin?

¿Por qué está María en Costa Rica?
Why is María in Costa Rica?

¿Por qué tienes sueño?
Why are you sleepy?

PRACTICE 2
Write a question for each of the following answers:

1. El hotel tiene cuatrocientas cincuenta habitaciones.

2. La película es a las tres y media de la tarde.

3. Colombia está en Sudamérica.

4. Estoy cansado.

5. Tengo cinco hermanos.

Tip!
In Spanish, the context of a sentence is very important, because speakers tend to drop the subject pronouns and only use them when they want to show emphasis or when they're absolutely necessary for clarity. In most cases, the verb ending helps you determine who the subject of the sentence is. But this is not the case

with the third person singular and plural, because these verb endings are used with a few different subjects. Let's take a look at the following question.

¿Cuándo está libre?

This could be referring to **usted, él,** or **ella.**

And how about this one:

¿Cuándo están libres?

It could be referring to **ustedes, ellos,** or **ellas.**

When you need to use the pronoun for clarification, simply insert it after the verb.

¿Cuándo está usted libre?
When are you free?

¿Cuándo está ella libre?
When is she free?

¿Cuándo están ustedes libres?
When are you free?

¿Cuándo están ellos libres?
When are they free?

ANSWERS

PRACTICE 1: 1. ¿Cuándo tienes tiempo? **2.** ¿Cómo estáis? **3.** ¿A qué hora es la película? **4.** ¿Quiénes son los niños? **5.** ¿Cómo está el café? **6.** ¿Qué hora es?

PRACTICE 2: 1. ¿Cuántas habitaciones tiene el hotel? **2.** ¿A qué hora es la película? **3.** ¿Dónde está Colombia? **4.** ¿Cómo estás/está? **5.** ¿Cuántos hermanos tienes/tiene?

CONVERSATION 1

Clara and Margarita have been friends since high school. They haven't seen each other since graduation, and they're trying to set up a time to meet.

Clara: ¿Cómo estás de tiempo? Cualquier día después del trabajo me viene bien.

Margarita: Estoy muy ocupada. El lunes trabajo horas extras en la oficina. Los martes y jueves tengo clases en la universidad. Y los miércoles practico deporte. El único día que tengo libre es el viernes y generalmente se lo dedico a mi novio.

Clara: Sí, entiendo . . . Bueno, y ¿qué tal si nos encontramos para almorzar?

Margarita: Esa es una mejor idea. ¿Qué te parece si nos reunimos este martes al mediodía?

Clara: No, el martes al mediodía no me va bien. Mejor por la tarde y tomamos un café. ¿Conoces un sitio que se llama "Chocolate y Churros"?

Margarita: Sí, es un lugar muy agradable. Me gustan mucho las tortas que tienen pero son un poco costosas.

Clara: Ay, lo siento Margarita, ya son las dos y media y se me hace tarde. Hablamos luego.

Margarita: Bueno, que estés bien. Adiós.

Clara: Chao.

Clara: *Do you have time? Any day after work is fine with me.*

Margarita: *I'm very busy. On Monday I work extra hours in the office. On Tuesdays and Thursdays I have classes at school. And Wednesdays I play sports. The only day I have free is Friday, and I usually set that aside for my boyfriend (lit., dedicate it to him, to my boyfriend).*

Clara:	Yes, I understand . . . Well, and how about if we meet for lunch?
Margarita:	That's a better idea. How about if we meet this Tuesday at noon?
Clara:	No, Tuesday at noon is not good for me. It'd be better in the afternoon for a coffee. Do you know a place called "Chocolate y Churros"?
Margarita:	Yes, it's a very nice place. I like the cakes they have very much, but they're a bit expensive.
Clara:	Oh, sorry, Margarita, it's already two thirty and I'm running late. We'll talk later.
Margarita:	Okay . . . take care. Good-bye.
Clara:	Bye.

NOTES

Notice that the days of the week are masculine, so the masculine article is always used except after the verb **ser**.

Trabajo horas extras el lunes.

I work extra hours on Monday.

Hoy es martes.

Today is Tuesday.

Also notice that when talking about an activity that happens with a certain frequency on a certain day of the week, the plural is used.

Los miércoles hago deporte.

I play sports on Wednesdays.

Estudio los sábados.

I study on Saturdays.

There are plenty of examples of new verbs in this dialogue: **trabajo** (*I work*), **practico** (*I play, I practice*), **dedico** (*I dedicate*), and so on. You'll learn all about verb conjugation in the next unit.

NUTS & BOLTS 1
YES/NO QUESTIONS

Question words like the ones we saw in Lesson 11 are one way of making questions. Yes/no questions are another type of question, and they're very simple to form. All you need to do is put the verb at the beginning of the sentence.

¿Eres boliviana?
Are you Bolivian?

¿Tienes hermanos?
Do you have brothers and sisters?

Notice that subject pronouns are often left out; they are only used for emphasis or to clarify. If they are used, or if a subject noun is used, they come after the verb.

¿Es (usted) profesora?
Are you a teacher?

¿Tiene (ella) el libro?
Does she have the book?

¿Es Marta de Costa Rica?
Is Marta from Costa Rica?

¿Tienen los niños tiempo?
Do the children have time?

Or-questions are formed in similar way.

¿Eres soltero o casado?
Are you single or married?

¿Está Jorge en la casa o en la oficina?
Is Jorge at home or in the office?

In English, you can ask what's called a *tag question,* as in *He's a blast, isn't he?* or *They aren't much fun, are they?* In Spanish, the equivalents of tag questions can be formed with either ¿no? (*no?*) or ¿verdad? (*right?*) at the end of the question. Notice the difference in punctuation.

Eres soltera, ¿no?
You're single, aren't you?

Tienes dos hermanos, ¿verdad?
You have two brothers, don't you?

Él está en Londres y ella en Bogotá, ¿no?
He's in London and she's in Bogotá, right?

PRACTICE 1
Fill in the blank with the correct form of the verb in parentheses.

1. Ellos _____ una casa en Madrid, ¿verdad? (tener)

2. ¿_____ usted colombiana? (ser)

3. Tú _____ en la oficina, ¿verdad? (estar)

4. ¿Cuántas habitaciones _____ el apartamento? (tener)

5. Nosotros _____ solteros. (ser)

6. Vosotros _____ en Quito, ¿verdad? (estar)

7. ¿Por qué _____ usted sed? (tener)

8. ¡Nosotros _____ hambre! (tener)

CONVERSATION 2
Clara and Margarita had so much fun having coffee together and remembering the good old days that they have decided to get together over the weekend and go to the movies with their boyfriends. They're setting it all up over the phone.

Clara: Bueno, y ¿qué tal si vamos los cuatro al cine este fin de semana?

Margarita: Sí, sería divertido.

Clara: ¿Qué películas les gustan?

Margarita: A mí me gustan mucho las películas de suspenso, pero Rafael las detesta.

Clara: A mí tampoco me gustan. Prefiero las películas románticas o las comedias.

Margarita: Bueno, ¿por qué no escogemos una comedia? ¿Tienes la cartelera de cine a la mano?

Clara: Sí, aquí la tengo. A ver . . . Bueno, solamente hay dos películas: *Dos bobos en apuros* y *Chanchitos en el espacio*.

Margarita: No sé . . . pero *Chanchitos en el espacio* suena divertida. La otra película parece aburrida, ¿no crees?

Clara: Sí, tienes razón.

Margarita: ¿A qué hora la dan?

Clara: A las diez menos cuarto de la noche.

Margarita: Ya está . . . Quedamos a las ocho en el bar que está al otro lado del teatro, ¿no?

Clara: A las ocho es muy temprano. Mejor a las nueve. Hasta entonces.

Margarita: Hasta luego.

Clara: *Well, how about if the four of us go to the movies this weekend?*

Margarita: *Yes, that would be fun.*

Clara: *What movies do you like?*

Margarita: *I like suspense movies very much, but Rafael hates them.*

Clara: *I don't like them either. I prefer romantic or funny movies.*

Margarita: *Well, how about if we choose a comedy? Do you have the movie listings handy?*

Clara: *Yes, here they are. Let's see . . . There are only two movies:* Two Dummies in a Jam *and* Piglets in Space.

Margarita:	I don't know . . . but Piglets in Space *sounds like fun.*
	The other movie seems boring, don't you think?
Clara:	Yes, you're right.
Margarita:	What time is it playing?
Clara:	At a quarter to ten.
Margarita:	That's it. We meet at eight at the bar that's across from
	the theater, right?
Clara:	Eight is too early. Nine is better. See you then.
Margarita:	See you then.

NOTES

In Spanish, a simple **sí** or **no** is enough to answer short yes/no questions. However, because this way of answering is a bit brief, it is better to try to give a little more information by using other short phrases or repeating the verb used in the question.

¿Tienes la cartelera de cine a la mano?

Do you have the movie listings handy?

Sí, aquí la tengo.

Yes, here they are (lit., Yes, I have it here.)

¿Están tus padres en casa?

Are you parents home?

Sí, sí están.

Yes, they are.

NUTS & BOLTS 2
SAYING WHAT YOU LIKE TO DO

Here are some verbs that may come in handy when talking about things you usually do.

trabajar	*to work*
bailar	*to dance*

cantar	*to sing*
comer	*to eat*
beber	*to drink*
nadar	*to swim*
trotar	*to jog*
escribir	*to write*
dormir	*to sleep*

All of these verbs are in the infinitive, or basic, form, which corresponds to the *to* form in English. In the next unit, you'll learn how verbs are conjugated in Spanish—for example, how to say *I swim* or *she swims* instead of *to swim*. But before that, you can start using these infinitive forms with the very useful expression **me gusta** (*I like*).

Me gusta bailar.
I like to dance.

Me gusta nadar.
I like to swim.

Me gusta hablar español.
I like to speak Spanish.

Gusta is a form of the verb **gustar,** which literally means *to be pleasing.* In Spanish, when you say *I like X*, you say *X is pleasing to me.* If the thing you like is a verb, the form **gusta** is always used, as in the above examples. You also use **gusta** if you like a singular person or thing.

Me gusta el libro.
I like the book.

Me gusta el nuevo profesor.
I like the new teacher.

If you like more than one person or thing, you use **gustan.**

Me gustan los fines de semana.
I like weekends.

Me gustan los libros interesantes.
I like interesting books.

Me gustan los actores mexicanos.
I like Mexican actors.

To say that you don't like something, use **no me gusta** or **no me gustan** (*I don't like*).

No me gusta cantar.
I don't like to sing.

No me gusta trotar.
I don't like to jog.

No me gustan los lunes.
I don't like Mondays.

No me gustan las películas de horror.
I don't like horror films.

PRACTICE 2
Fill in the blanks with the correct form of **gustar.**

1. Me _____ los apartamentos grandes.

2. No me _____ los gatos.

3. Me _____ los niños.

4. No me _____ trabajar.

5. Me _____ los viernes.

6. No me _____ los libros largos.

7. Me _____ las comedias.

Discovery activity

You may be wondering by now about accent marks on some words, like **cómo**. We covered them in the *Spelling and pronunciation* section at the beginning of this program, but let's go over them once again now that you have more Spanish under your belt. Accent marks are used for two purposes: to show where the stress or emphasis falls on a word when it's pronounced, and to help differentiate between identically spelled words. We won't get into all the rules here, but here are some general rules for when and why accents are used.

If a word ends in a vowel, **-n**, or **-s**, stress normally falls on the second-to-last syllable.

libro, **hom**bre, Es**pa**ña, computa**do**ra, **gus**tan, **tie**nen, **car**tas, **tie**nes, **es**tas

If a word ends in a consonant other than **-n** or **-s**, it is normally stressed on the last syllable.

mu**jer**, espa**ñol**, cele**brar**, ciu**dad**, escu**char**

An accent mark is used to "overrride" this pattern.

fotogra**fí**a, **cár**cel, to**mó**, **só**tano, es**tás**

An accent mark is also used to distinguish between two words that are pronounced the same way but mean different things.

solo (*adjective: sole, only, alone*)   **sólo** (*adverb: merely, solely, only*)

que (*conjunction: that, that which*)   **qué** (*interrogative: what*)

si (*if*)   **sí** (*yes*)

el (*the, masc.*)   **él** (*he*)

As a discovery activity, and as a great way to test your comprehension, go to an online Spanish newspaper. You can find a huge list of them at *www.onlinenewspapers.com*. Choose a country that interests you, select a newspaper, and pick an article at random. Scan the article, looking for accent marks on words you're unfamiliar with. Try to pronounce them, and then try to pronounce other unfamiliar words without accent marks. Do you see how helpful accents marks are?

ANSWERS
PRACTICE 1: 1. tienen; **2.** Es; **3.** estás; **4.** tiene; **5.** somos; **6.** estáis; **7.** tiene; **8.** tenemos.

PRACTICE 2: 1. gustan; **2.** gustan; **3.** gustan; **4.** gusta; **5.** gustan; **6.** gustan; **7.** gustan.

UNIT 3 ESSENTIALS
¿Qué hora es?
What time is it?

¿Qué horas son?
What time is it?

Es la una en punto.
It's one o'clock.

Son las dos y diez.
It's ten after two.

Son las tres y media de la tarde.
It's three thirty in the afternoon.

Tengo un apartamento bonito.
I have a pretty apartment.

Tienen un gato gordo.
They have a fat cat.

¿A qué hora es la película?
At what time is the movie?

¿Quién es él?
Who is he?

¿Cuándo estás ocupado?
When are you busy?

¿Dónde está el teatro?
Where is the theater?

¿Cuántas semanas hay en un año?
How many weeks are there in a year?

¿Cuál es su hija?
Which one is your daughter?

¿Por qué estás cansada?
Why are you tired?

¿Cómo es la película?
How's the movie?

UNIT 4
Health and the human body

In this unit you'll learn a lot of new and useful vocabulary related to the human body and health. You'll also learn how to express possession with the equivalents of *my, mine, Juan's,* and so on. And very importantly, you'll learn how to conjugate verbs in the present tense.

─────────────── Lesson 13 (words) ───────────────

WORD LIST 1
Let's learn a few words pertaining to the head and face.

la cabeza	*head*
la cara	*face*
el pelo	*hair*
la frente	*forehead*
la oreja	*ear*
el ojo	*eye*
la nariz	*nose*
la mejilla	*cheek*
la boca	*mouth*
el labio	*lip*
la lengua	*tongue*
el diente	*tooth*
la muela	*molar*
la garganta	*throat*
la barbilla	*chin*
el cuello	*neck*

NUTS & BOLTS 1
Possessive adjectives (singular)

Let's look at some useful little words called possessive adjectives, which correspond to the English *my, your, his, her, our,* and *their.* Because these are adjectives in Spanish, they must agree in gender and number with the nouns they modify. Let's start with the possessive adjectives that correspond to the singular personal pronouns (**yo, tú, él, ella, usted**).

mi(s)	*my*
tu(s)	*your (infml.)*
su(s)	*his, her, your (fml.)*

The possessive adjectives **mi, tu,** and **su** are used with singular possessions (**mi libro, tu casa**), and **mis, tus,** and **sus** are used with plural possessions (**mis libros, tus casas**). The gender of the possession doesn't make any difference in these cases. Let's see some more examples.

Mi pelo es rojo.
My hair is red.

Mis ojos son grandes.
My eyes are big.

Tu cara es bonita.
Your face is pretty.

Tus dientes son blancos.
Your teeth are white.

Su nariz es larga.
His/Her/Your nose is long.

Sus piernas son gordas.
His/Her/Your legs are fat.

Notice that there is only one form for *his, her,* and *your (fml.)*—**su**. The context will tell you what, exactly, **su** means.

PRACTICE 1
Translate the following sentences:

1. *I like your eyes.*

2. *His nose is long.*

3. *My family is in Caracas.*

4. *Your (infml.) granddaughter is hungry.*

5. *Her hair is short.*

6. *My apartment is small.*

7. *Your (fml.) grandparents are tired.*

8. *My house is your (fml.) house.*

WORD LIST 2
Here are some more words related to the rest of the human body.

el cuerpo	*body*
el brazo	*arm*
la espalda	*back*
la columna vertebral	*backbone, spinal column*
el hombro	*shoulder*
el codo	*elbow*
la muñeca	*wrist*
la mano	*hand*
el dedo	*finger, toe*
el estómago	*stomach*
el pecho	*chest*

la pierna	*leg*
la rodilla	*knee*
el pie	*foot*
el corazón	*heart*
la cadera	*hip*

NUTS & BOLTS 2
POSSESSIVE ADJECTIVES (PLURAL)

Let's take a look at the possessive adjectives that correspond to the plural subject pronouns (**nosotros, vosotros, ellos, ellas, ustedes**).

nuestro/a(s)	*our*
vuestro/a(s)	*your (infml.)*
su(s)	*their, your (fml.)*

Notice that the first two plural forms change depending on both the gender and the number of the possession—for example, **nuestro libro** (*our book*), **nuestra casa** (*our house*), **nuestros libros** (*our books*), and **nuestras casas** (*our houses*). Here are some more examples. Again, don't forget that the **vuestro** forms are not very common in Latin America, where **su(s)** is used instead.

Nuestra casa es grande.
Our house is big.

Nuestro apartamento está en Quito.
Our apartment is in Quito.

Vuestros hijos son altos.
Your children are tall.

Sus hijos son altos.
Their/Your children are tall.

Vuestras manos son pequeñas.
Your hands are small.

Sus manos son pequeñas.
Their/Your hands are small.

Su familia es boliviana.
Their/Your family is Bolivian.

Sus abuelos son italianos.
Their/Your grandparents are Italian.

PRACTICE 2
Fill in the blank with the correct form of the possessive adjective. The English possessive is given in parentheses.

1. _____ primos son venezolanos. (*their*)

2. En _____ casa hay catorce habitaciones. (*our*)

3. _____ padres están divorciados. (*your, fml.*)

4. _____ familias son grandes. (*our*)

5. En _____ familia hay muchos niños. (*your, infml.*)

6. _____ apartamento está en Nueva York. (*our*)

7. _____ libros están en la oficina. (*your, fml.*)

8. _____ coche no es muy grande. (*our*)

Tip!
Although names of body parts are used in much the same manner in Spanish as in English, there is one significant difference—in Spanish, they are frequently preceded by a definite article (**el, la, los,** or **las**). In most cases, the possessive adjective is only used when it's not clear from the context to whose body something belongs. Here are a few examples:

ANSWERS

PRACTICE 1: 1. Me gustan tus ojos. **2.** Su nariz es larga. **3.** Mi familia está en Caracas. **4.** Tu nieta tiene hambre. **5.** Su pelo es corto. **6.** Mi apartamento es pequeño. **7.** Sus abuelos están cansados. **8.** Mi casa es su casa.

PRACTICE 2: 1. Sus; **2.** nuestra; **3.** Sus; **4.** Nuestras; **5.** vuestra; **6.** Nuestro; **7.** Sus; **8.** Nuestro.

—————————— Lesson 14 (phrases) ——————————

PHRASE LIST 1

Here are some phrases you can use when visiting the doctor or talking about your physical state. Notice the use of **tener.**

tener dolor de cabeza	*to have a headache*
tener dolor de garganta	*to have a sore throat*
tener fiebre	*to have a fever*
tener tos	*to have a cough*
tener mal de estómago	*to have an upset stomach*
tener mareo	*to be dizzy*
tener la tensión alta	*to have high blood pressure*
tener la tensión baja	*to have low blood pressure*
tener náusea	*to be nauseated, to have nausea*
hacer un exámen de sangre	*to take a blood test*

| tomar la tension | to take the blood pressure |
| tomar un medicamento | to take medication |

NUTS & BOLTS 1
POSSESSION WITH DE + PRONOUN

A definite article and the preposition **de** (*of*) can be used with a subject pronoun in place of the more ambiguous **su(s).**

su pierna	his/her/their/your leg
la pierna de él	his leg
la pierna de ella	her leg
la pierna de ellos	their leg
la pierna de ellas	their leg
la pierna de usted	your leg
la pierna de ustedes	your leg

su cuerpo	his/her/their/your body
el cuerpo de él	his body
el cuerpo de ella	her body
el cuerpo de ellos	their body
el cuerpo de ellas	their body
el cuerpo de usted	your body
el cuerpo de ustedes	your body

In the plural form, simply use the plural feminine or masculine article, depending on the gender of the noun.

| las piernas de él | *his legs* |
| los cuerpos de ustedes | *your bodies* |

PRACTICE 1

Can you say each of the sentences below in another way? Follow the example:
Ex. Son los padres de mis padres.
Son mis abuelos.

1. Es el hijo de mi hermano.

2. Son los hermanos de mi esposo.

3. Es la esposa de tu padre.

4. Son las hijas de nuestra hija.

5. Son los padres de Juan.

6. Son los hijos de nuestra tía.

PHRASE LIST 2

Just like English, Spanish has a few idioms using words for parts of the body.

estar en buenas manos	*to be in good hands*
pararse de cabeza	*to go crazy, to go out of one's mind*
dar la cara	*to face the circumstances*
tener cara dura	*to be shameless*
tener los pies en la tierra	*to have both feet on the ground*
perder la cabeza	*to lose one's head*
tener la cabeza fría	*to keep a cool head*
ojo por ojo	*an eye for an eye*

NUTS & BOLTS 2
More possession with de

The preposition **de** comes in very handy when talking about possession. While English uses apostrophe -s, Spanish uses a phrase with **de**. This is similar to another way of showing possession in English with *of*. Let's take a look at some examples.

el corazón de la señora Suárez
Mrs. Suarez's heart

los primos de María
María's cousins

el restaurante de Jorge
Jorge's restaurant

las ventanas de la casa
the windows of the house

la puerta de la oficina
the door of the office

Remember that when **de** is followed by the masculine article (**el**), it becomes **del**.

la casa del padre de Juan.
Juan's father's house

la cola del caballo
the horse's tail

When using **de** + the masculine pronoun **él**, there is no contraction.

La casa de él es grande.
His house is big.

Here's how you can ask questions about possession. Notice that **¿de quién?** means *whose*.

¿De quién es la casa?
Whose house is it?

¿De quién es el restaurante?
Whose restaurant is it?

¿De quién son los primos?
Whose cousins are they?

PRACTICE 2
Translate the following sentences:

1. *His parents are divorced.*
2. *Whose heart is it?*
3. *Roberto's mother has high blood pressure.*
4. *It's María's sister's uncle.*
5. *Their sister's husband has a headache.*

Tip!
Here are some useful phrases you can use to describe yourself and others.

tener la cara larga	*to have a long face*
tener la cara redonda	*to have a round face*
ser rubio/a	*to be blond*
ser moreno/a	*to be dark skinned*
ser blanco/a	*to be white*
tener los ojos negros/ azules/marrones/verdes	*to have black/blue/brown/green eyes*
tener el cabello largo/ corto	*to have long/short hair*
ser calvo/a	*to be bald*

ser alto/a	*to be tall*
ser bajo/a	*to be short*

Let's take a look at some examples.

Soy bajo y rubio. Tengo los ojos verdes.
I'm short and blond. I have green eyes.

Soy morena de ojos azules.
I'm dark skinned with blue eyes.

Ella tiene el cabello largo y es alta.
She has long hair and is tall.

ANSWERS

PRACTICE 1: **1.** Es mi sobrino. **2.** Son mis cuñados. **3.** Es tu madre. **4.** Son nuestras nietas. **5.** Son sus padres. **6.** Son nuestros primos.

PRACTICE 2: **1.** Sus padres están divorciados. **2.** ¿De quién es el corazón? **3.** La madre de Roberto tiene la tensión alta. **4.** Es el tío de la hermana de María. **5.** El esposo de su hermana tiene dolor de cabeza.

—————— Lesson 15 (sentences) ——————

SENTENCE LIST 1
Here are sentences that may come in handy at a doctor's office.

¿Cuál es el problema?	*What's the problem?*
Tengo dolor de garganta y tos.	*I have a sore throat and a cough.*
Me siento mareado.	*I feel dizzy.*
Tengo náusea y diarrea.	*I have nausea and diarrhea.*
¿Toma algún medicamento en este momento?	*Are you taking any medication right now?*

¿Sufre de alguna enfermedad?	*Do you suffer from any illnesses?*
¿Fuma usted?	*Do you smoke?*
¿Tiene la presión/tensión alta?	*Do you have high blood pressure?*
¿Lo han operado de algo?	*Have you had any operations?*
¿En dónde tiene dolor?	*Where do you have pain?*
¿Tiene problemas de corazón?	*Do you have heart problems?*
¿Tiene alergias?	*Do you have any allergies?*
Soy alérgico a la penicilina.	*I'm allergic to penicillin.*
¿Tiene hijos?	*Do you have children?*
¿Hace deporte con frecuencia?	*Do you play sports regularly?*

NUTS & BOLTS 1
POSSESSIVE PRONOUNS

Another way to talk about the things we own is by using possessive pronouns, which are equivalent to the English *mine, yours, his, hers, ours,* and *theirs.* They usually take the place of a noun and are normally used with a definite article.

el mío/la mía, los míos/las mías	*mine*
el tuyo/la tuya, los tuyos/las tuyas	*yours (infml.)*
el suyo/la suya, los suyos/las suyas	*his, hers, yours (fml.)*
el nuestro/la nuestra, los nuestros/las nuestras	*ours*
el vuestro/la vuestra, los vuestros/las vuestras	*yours (infml.)*

el suyo/la suya, los suyos/ las suyas	*theirs, yours (fml.)*

Notice that all of the possessive pronouns agree in both gender and number with the nouns they stand in for. Let's look at some examples to see how this works.

Mi cara es redonda y la tuya es larga.
My face is round and yours is long.

Tu cabello es rubio y el nuestro es negro.
Your hair is blond and ours is black.

Vuestros hijos están en Brasil y los suyos en Costa Rica.
Your children are in Brazil and hers/his/theirs/yours (are) in Costa Rica.

In the first example, **la tuya** is standing in for **la cara.** In the second, **el nuestro** is standing in for **el cabello.** In the third, **los suyos** is standing in for **los hijos.**

As we saw in Lesson 14, the use of the possessive adjective **su** can be clarified by using the preposition **de** and the corresponding pronoun. The same thing can be done with possessive pronouns, but in this case, only a definite article is used before the **de** phrase. Let's first take a look at the feminine.

Mi casa es grande y la suya es pequena.
My house is big and his/hers/theirs/yours is small.

Mi casa es grande y la de él es pequeña.
My house is big and his is small.

Mi casa es grande y la de ella es pequeña.
My house is big and hers is small.

Mi casa es grande y la de ellos es pequeña.
My house is big and theirs is small.

Mi casa es grande y la de ellas es pequeña.
My house is big and theirs is small.

Mi casa es grande y la de usted es pequeña.
My house is big and yours is small.

Mi casa es grande y la de ustedes es pequeña.
My house is big and yours is small.

Now, let's take a look at the masculine.

Mi cabello es largo y el suyo es corto.
My hair is long and his/hers/theirs/yours is short.

Mi cabello es largo y el de él es corto.
My hair is long and his is short.

Mi cabello es largo y el de ella es corto.
My hair is long and hers is short.

Mi cabello es largo y el de ellos es corto.
My hair is long and theirs is short.

Mi cabello es largo y el de ellas es corto.
My hair is long and theirs is short.

Mi cabello es largo y el de usted es corto.
My hair is long and yours is short.

Mi cabello es largo y el de ustedes es corto.
My hair is long and yours is short.

Let's take a few examples with the plural feminine and masculine.

Nuestras manos son pequeñas y las de él son grandes.
Our hands are small and his are big.

Tus padres están en Londres y los de ellos en Guadalajara.
Your parents are in London and theirs are in Guadalajara.

When the possessive pronoun comes after the verb **ser,** the article is left out.

La casa grande es mía.
The big house is mine.

La habitación treinta y dos es tuya/suya.
Room 32 is yours.

PRACTICE 1
Join the two sentences by using a possessive pronoun. Follow the example:

Ex. El padre de Juan está en La Paz. El padre de Margarita está en Francia.

El padre de Juan está en La Paz y el suyo está en Francia.

1. Nuestra profesora es delgada. La profesora tuya y la de Luis es gorda.

2. Las manos de Angela son bonitas. Mis manos son feas.

3. La madre de Pedro tiene sesenta y siete años. La madre de Enrique y Sara tiene ochenta y ocho.

4. Mi hermano es abogado. Tu hermano es astronauta.

5. La habitación de María es grande. La habitación de Claudia es pequeña.

SENTENCE LIST 2

Tengo un cosquilleo muy desagradable.	*I have a very unpleasant tingling feeling.*
¿Se le hinchan los pies y las manos?	*Do your feet and hands swell?*
Sí, con mucha frecuencia.	*Yes, very frequently.*
¿Y, qué quiere decir eso?	*So, what does that mean?*
¿Es grave?	*Is it serious?*

¿Cuál es el tratamiento a seguir?	*What is the treatment to be followed?*
Tiene un brote en todo el cuerpo.	*She has a rash all over her body.*
¿Es él su pediatra de cabecera?	*Is he your regular pediatrician?*
Él tiene paciencia con los niños.	*He is patient with children.*
Le gusta mucho la homeopatía.	*He likes homeopathy very much.*

NUTS & BOLTS 2
CONJUGATION OF -AR VERBS

Now let's look at how to conjugate verbs in Spanish. A conjugation is the pattern of endings (or other changes) that a verb undergoes to agree with a subject, as in the English *I sing, you sing, she sings,* etc. In Spanish, there are slightly different conjugations for different types of verbs. Verbs are grouped according to three different infinitive endings: **-ar** verbs, **-er** verbs, and **-ir** verbs. Examples from each group are **hablar** (*to speak*), **comer** (*to eat*), and **vivir** (*to live*). There are both regular and irregular verbs—that is, those that follow a regular pattern of conjugation and those that don't. But don't panic. Most verbs are regular!

Let's start with a list of some common **-ar** verbs.

caminar	*to walk*
hablar	*to talk, to speak*
tocar	*to touch, to play an instrument*
escuchar	*to listen to*
saborear	*to taste*
estudiar	*to study*

To conjugate any verb, take off the infinitive ending, which, in these cases, is **-ar**. Then you're left with the verb stem, and you add certain endings to that stem depending on the subject. For example, with **caminar**:

yo camino	*I walk*
tú caminas	*you walk*
él/ella camina	*he/she walks*
usted camina	*you walk*
nosotros caminamos	*we walk*
vosotros camináis	*you walk*
ellos/ellas caminan	*they walk*
ustedes caminan	*you walk*

All of the **-ar** verbs from the list above are conjugated in exactly this way. Here are some examples:

Los fines de semana nosotros caminamos en el parque.
We walk in the park on weekends.

Yolanda toca la guitarra muy bien.
Yolanda plays the guitar very well.

Ellos hablan cuatro idiomas.
They speak four languages.

Yo escucho música todas las noches.
I listen to music every night.

Notice that in English, you *listen to* something, but in Spanish, you don't need a preposition; *escuchar* is perfectly fine on its own.

You'll see this sort of difference a lot when you compare two languages. Sometimes one language will use a preposition where the other won't, and sometimes the situation is reversed. As a general tip, be wary of translating prepositions literally; in fact, it's better not even to assume that you need one in another language just because your native language uses one. Prepositions are often used in very different ways from one language to another!

Let's look at those -ar endings once more.

-o	-amos
-as	-áis
-a	-an

PRACTICE 2
Fill in the blank with the appropriate form of the verb in parentheses.

1. Nosotros _____ por la mañana. (caminar)

2. Ustedes _____ el piano. (tocar)

3. Yo _____ música clásica los fines de semana. (escuchar)

4. Tú _____ el vino. (saborear)

5. Ellos _____ español. (hablar)

6. Él _____ por la mañana. (caminar)

7. Vosotras _____ por teléfono. (hablar)

8. Yo _____ la radio. (escuchar)

ANSWERS

PRACTICE 1: 1. Nuestra profesora es delgada y la vuestra es gorda. **2.** Las manos de Angela son bonitas y las mías son feas. **3.** La madre de Pedro tiene sesenta y siete años y la suya tiene ochenta y ocho. **4.** Mi hermano es abogado y el tuyo es astronauta. **5.** La habitación de María es grande y la suya es pequeña.

PRACTICE 2: 1. caminamos; **2.** tocan; **3.** escucho; **4.** saboreas; **5.** hablan; **6.** camina; **7.** habláis; **8.** escucho.

——————— Lesson 16 (conversations) ———————

CONVERSATION 1
Listen in while Gloria visits the doctor.

> **Médico:** Buenos días, Doña Solís, ¿cuál es el problema?
> **Gloria:** Tengo mucho dolor en las muñecas, sobre todo la derecha.
> **Médico:** ¿Tiene dolor en el cuello o la espalda?

Gloria: No, para nada. Pero por las noches tengo un cosquilleo muy desagradable en los dedos de mi mano derecha.

Médico: ¿Toma algún medicamento en este momento?

Gloria: Sí, estoy tomando una pastilla para bajar la tensión.

Médico: ¿Se le hinchan los pies o las manos, sobre todo por las tardes?

Gloria: Sí, con mucha frecuencia.

Médico: Bueno, son los clásicos síntomas del síndrome del túnel del carpio.

Gloria: ¿Y, qué quiere decir eso? ¿Es grave?

Médico: No, simplemente tiene bloqueados los nervios del carpio que son los que conectan la muñeca con el resto de la mano.

Gloria: ¿Y cuál es el tratamiento a seguir?

Médico: La acupuntura ayuda mucho. Así que vamos a comenzar con una sesión dos veces por semana por un mes.

Doctor: *Good morning, Mrs. Solís. What seems to be the problem?*

Gloria: *I have a lot of pain in my wrists, especially the right one.*

Doctor: *Do you have pain in your neck or your back?*

Gloria: *No, not at all. But at nighttime I have a very unpleasant tingling sensation in the fingers of my right hand.*

Doctor: *Are you taking any medication right now?*

Gloria: *Yes, I'm taking a pill to lower my blood pressure.*

Doctor: *Do your feet and hands swell, especially in the afternoons?*

Gloria: *Yes, very frequently.*

Doctor: *Well, those are the typical symptoms of carpal tunnel syndrome.*

Gloria: *What does that mean? Is it serious?*

Doctor: *No, it only means that the carpal nerves, which connect your wrist to the rest of the hand, are blocked.*

> Gloria: *What treatment is there?*
>
> Doctor: *Acupuncture helps a lot. So we're going to begin with one session twice a week for a month.*

NOTES

Two polite titles that you may hear are **Don** and **Doña,** although they're dying out. They are usually used before the first name of a person who deserves respect on the basis of his or her age or status in society. You will very often see them used to address the Spanish king and queen: **Don Juan Carlos y Doña Sofía.** In Latin America, they are commonly used by workers to address their employers, especially in rural areas.

Notice that the doctor asked: **¿Toma algún medicamento en este momento?** The English translation is: *Are you taking any medication right now?* In Spanish, the present tense (**toma,** for example) can be translated into English as the simple present (*you take*), the present continuous or progressive (*you are taking*), or even the present emphatic (*you do take*). It all depends on the context.

NUTS & BOLTS 1
CONJUGATION OF -ER VERBS AND VER *(TO SEE)*
Verbs with an **-er** infinitive ending are also very easy to conjugate. Here are some examples:

correr	to run
beber	to drink
comer	to eat
ver	to see
leer	to read

Let's take a closer look at the verb **correr.** First, remove the **-er** ending to get the stem, **corr-.** Then add the appropriate ending for each subject.

yo corro	*I run*
tú corres	*you run*
él/ella corre	*he/she runs*
usted corre	*you run*
nosotros corremos	*we run*
vosotros corréis	*you run*
ellos/ellas corren	*they run*
ustedes corren	*you run*

Here are those **-er** endings once again.

-o	**-emos**
-es	**-éis**
-e	**-en**

If you take a close look at the conjugation of **-ar** and **-er** verbs, you can see that they are almost identical except for one letter. Here are some more examples of **-er** verbs.

Ella bebe dos litros de agua a diario.
She drinks two liters of water a day.

Los niños comen dulces.
The children eat sweets.

Now, you may be a little bit puzzled when asked to conjugate the verb **ver.** Naturally so, because when you take the ending off, you're left with only one letter! Yes, that's actually the stem, and it's conjugated just like **correr,** with a small irregularity in the **yo** form.

yo veo	*I see*
tú ves	*you see*
él/ella ve	*he/she sees*
usted ve	*you see*
nosotros vemos	*we see*
vosotros veis	*you see*
ellos/ellas ven	*they see*
ustedes ven	*you see*

Vemos a nuestros amigos con frecuencia.
We see our friends often.

Sabina y Ana ven muchas películas.
Sabina and Ana see a lot of movies.

Take a look at that first example again. **Vemos a nuestros amigos . . .** Did you notice that little **a** in between the verb **vemos** and the phrase **nuestros amigos**? This is called the **a personal,** and it's used when a direct object is a person. We'll come back to that later on in the course.

PRACTICE 1
Choose the verb that best completes the sentence.

1. Nosotras (beben, bebemos, bebéis) mucha agua.

2. Ella (lees, leen, lee) un libro.

3. Tú (corro, corre, corres) por las tardes.

4. Vosotros (vemos, véis, ven) televisión.

5. Yo no (comes, coméis, como) carne.

6. Ustedes (bebéis, beben, bebés) vino tinto.

7. Yo (ve, ves, veo) a mi amigo.

8. ¿Qué (leo, lee, lees), Ana?

CONVERSATION 2

Isabel is at the pediatrician's office with her little daughter. She's talking to another mother in the waiting room.

Margarita:	Mi hija tiene tres años, ¿y la suya?
Isabel:	Tiene veintidós meses. Se llama Catherina, ¿y la suya?
Margarita:	Sofía. ¿Qué le pasa a Catherina?
Isabel:	Tiene una fiebre muy alta y un brote en todo el cuerpo. No tiene apetito y llora mucho.
Margarita:	Mi hija también tiene una fiebre muy alta.
Isabel:	¿Es este su pediatra de cabecera?
Margarita:	Sí, es muy bueno. Estoy muy contenta. Sobre todo porque le gusta mucho la homeopatía.
Isabel:	Qué bien. No me gusta darle medicinas a Catherina cuando no es absolutamente necesario.
Margarita:	Si, además es un médico que escucha a los padres y tiene mucha paciencia con los niños.
Isabel:	Bueno, ya estoy más tranquila.
Margarita:	No se preocupe. Catherina está en buenas manos.

Margarita:	*My daughter is three years old, and yours?*
Isabel:	*She's twenty-two months. Her name is Catherina. And yours?*

Margarita: *Sofía. What's wrong with Catherina?*
Isabel: *She has a very high fever and a rash all over her body.*
She has no appetite and cries a lot.
Margarita: *My daughter has a high fever, too.*
Isabel: *Is this your regular pediatrician?*
Margarita: *Yes, he's very good. I am very happy. Especially because*
he likes homeopathy very much.
Isabel: *That's good. I don't like to give Catherina medicine*
when it isn't absolutely necessary.
Margarita: *Yes, plus he's a doctor who listens to parents and has a*
lot of patience with the children.
Isabel: *Well, now I feel better.*
Margarita: *Don't worry. Catherina is in good hands.*

NOTES

Homeopathic medicine and other more natural approaches to treating illnesses are becoming the trend in Spanish-speaking countries. In most of Latin America, you'll find that people consider themselves much more in tune with nature and their bodies and prefer natural remedies and herbal teas to conventional Western medicine, which is considered by some to be very aggressive and hard on the body.

Some common herbs are **palo de aceite** (*oily stick*), which is used to treat intestinal problems, rheumatism, colic, and asthma; **cola de caballo** (*horse's tail*), which is used to treat wounds and infections of the gums; **uña de gato** (*cat's claw*), which is used to treat stomach and lung tumors; and **guayaba** (*guava*), which is a fruit whose parts are used to make an infusion to treat diarrhea.

You've probably also heard that in several South American countries, a tea made out of **mate de coca** (*coca leaf*) is a popular beverage. In fact, people living at very high altitudes either drink this tea or chew coca leaves to help fight altitude dizziness and sickness. The effects of this tea are similar to those of coffee. The tea is not considered a drug, and it is also used for medicinal and religious purposes.

NUTS & BOLTS 2
CONJUGATION OF -IR VERBS
The third group of verbs end in **-ir** in the infinitive.

percibir	*to perceive*
escribir	*to write*
vivir	*to live*
partir	*to leave*

Here's the **-ir** conjugation.

yo escribo	*I write*
tú escribes	*you write*
él/ella escribe	*he/she writes*
usted escribe	*you write*
nosotros escribimos	*we write*
vosotros escribís	*you write*
ellos/ellas escriben	*they write*
ustedes escriben	*you write*

Let's look at the **-ir** endings one more time.

-o	-imos
-es	-ís
-e	-en

If you take a closer look, you'll notice that the only difference between -er and -ir verbs is the ending used for **nosotros** and **vosotros**. Here are some example sentences with -ir verbs.

Nosotros escribimos muchas cartas.

We write a lot of letters.

Ellos viven en una ciudad grande, pero tú vives en una aldea pequeña.

They live in a big city, but you live in a little village.

Now you've learned how to conjugate all three types of Spanish verbs in the present tense. Don't forget that the Spanish present tense can be translated into English as the simple present (*she goes*), the present progressive or continuous (*she is going*), or the present emphatic (*she does go*). It can also be used to talk about something that will happen in the near future, as in the English *It's 3:00 now, and the train arrives in an hour.*

Here are some useful expressions of time that you can use with the simple present tense.

ahora	*now*
ahora mismo	*right now*
mañana	*tomorrow*
esta noche	*tonight*
siempre	*always*
con frecuencia	*frequently*
a veces	*sometimes*
casi nunca	*seldom, almost never*

nunca	never
todos los días	every day
todas las semanas	every week
una vez por semana	once a week
dos veces por semana	twice a week

PRACTICE 2
Translate the following sentences into Spanish.

1. *Right now she has a headache.*
2. *My parents leave tomorrow in the afternoon.*
3. *We live in a small apartment.*
4. *I always drink coffee in the morning.*
5. *She writes emails every day.*
6. *Sometimes we listen to jazz.*
7. *They never eat at night.*
8. *My wife leaves this evening.*

Discovery activity

Now that you've learned verbs in Spanish, you'll want to find plenty of creative ways to practice using them. The more you use them, the more automatic the verb conjugations will become for you. A simple way to lodge verb conjugations in your mind is repetition—listening to the audio, repeating aloud, reading the forms in the book, and writing them out. Check out the *Language learning tips* section for more suggestions. There's also a lot of information in the grammar summary on verbs, but for now it's probably best to stick with the present tense. To practice the present tense, make it a goal to learn three to five new and useful verbs every day, and write example sentences for them in your language journal. Tailor this exercise to your life and your routine, and look up any new vocabulary you need. Another activity that will help is to find a photo of people—in a magazine, in an old photo album, online—and write a few sentences describing what they're doing. Stick to regular verbs at first, because we'll cover the irregular ones in small groups as we move along.

ANSWERS

PRACTICE 1: 1. bebemos; **2.** lee; **3.** corres; **4.** veis; **5.** como; **6.** beben; **7.** veo; **8.** lees.

PRACTICE 2: 1. Ahora mismo ella tiene dolor de cabeza. **2.** Mis padres parten mañana por la tarde. **3.** Nosotros vivimos en un apartamento pequeño. **4.** Yo siempre bebo café por la mañana. **5.** Ella escribe emails todos los días. **6.** A veces nosotros escuchamos jazz. **7.** Ellos nunca comen por la noche. **8.** Mi esposa parte esta noche.

UNIT 4 ESSENTIALS

Mis ojos son grandes y los tuyos pequeños.
My eyes are big and yours are small.

Nuestra habitación es costosa y la vuestra es barata.
Our room is expensive and yours is cheap.

Sus padres son ecuatorianos.
His/Her/Your/Their parents are Ecuadorian.

Los suyos son hondureños.
His/Hers/Yours/Theirs are Honduran.

Vuestra hermana es soltera y la de él es casada.
Your sister is single and his is married.

¿De quién es el restaurante?
Whose restaurant is it?

Es el restaurante del hermano de Miguel.

It's Miguel's brother's restaurant.

Yo camino todos los días.

I walk every day.

Tú hablas por teléfono.

You talk on the phone./You're talking on the phone.

Él toca el piano.

He plays the piano./He's playing the piano.

Nosotros escuchamos jazz.

We listen to jazz./We're listening to jazz.

Vosotros coméis paella.

You eat paella./You're eating paella.

Ellos beben agua.

They drink water./They're drinking water.

Yo leo un libro.

I read a book./I'm reading a book.

Tú escribes un email.

You're writing an email.

Ella vive en París.

She lives in Paris.

Nosotros partimos por la mañana.

We leave in the morning.

UNIT 5
Using the telephone and making appointments

In this unit, you'll learn common vocabulary and phrases used when talking on the phone, including how to make an appointment with someone. You'll also learn a few key irregular verbs, as well as the Spanish equivalents of *this, that, these,* and *those.*

——————————— Lesson 17 (words) ———————————

WORD LIST 1

el contestador automático	*answering machine*
la llamada	*phone call*
la operadora	*operator*
la guía telefónica	*phone book*
las páginas amarillas	*yellow pages*
la cabina telefónica	*telephone booth*
el mensaje	*message*
el buzón de voz	*voice mail*
la centralita	*switchboard*
eliminar	*to eliminate*
borrar	*to erase*

NUTS & BOLTS 1
DEMONSTRATIVE ADJECTIVES

Demonstratives, or words like *this* and *that,* show or point to places, people, or things. When a demonstrative is used right before a noun, as in *this book,* it's called a demonstrative adjective. In Spanish, demonstrative adjectives must agree in gender and number with the nouns they point to. Also, Spanish distinguishes among three spatial relations, while English recognizes only two. Let's look at each one.

The first set of demonstratives is used to point to things that are relatively close to the speaker. They can be translated as *this* in the singular and *these* in the plural.

este libro	*this book (m. sg.)*
esta casa	*this house (f. sg.)*
estos profesores	*these teachers (m. pl.)*
estas computadoras	*these computers (f. pl.)*

The second set of demonstratives is used to point to things that are farther away from the speaker but perhaps closer to the listener. The translation is *that* or *those.*

ese niño	*that boy (m. sg.)*
esa mujer	*that woman (f. sg.)*
esos cuadernos	*those notebooks (m. sg.)*
esas llaves	*those keys (f. sg.)*

Finally, the third set is used to point to things that are relatively far away from both the speaker and the listener. The most appropriate English translation is *that (over) there* or *those (over) there.*

aquel edificio	*that building there (m. sg.)*
aquella oficina	*that office over there (f. sg.)*
aquellos coches	*those cars there (m. pl.)*
aquellas calles	*those streets over there (f. pl.)*

Let's see some more examples in sentences.

Este teléfono no funciona.
This phone doesn't work.

Esa línea está ocupada.
That line is busy.

Aquella cabina telefónica está libre.
That phone booth over there is free.

PRACTICE 1
Choose the correct demonstrative adjective to fill in the blank.

1. (Este, Esta, Estos, Estas) llamada es importante.
2. (Aquellos, Aquel, Aquella, Aquellas) oficinas están ocupadas.
3. (Esas, Esa, Ese, Esos) contestador no funciona.
4. (Esas, Esa, Ese, Esos) teléfonos son de la oficina de mi tío.
5. (Este, Esta, Estos, Estas) mensajes son para Julián.
6. (Aquellos, Aquel, Aquella, Aquellas) hombre es mi padre.

WORD LIST 2

el fax	*fax*
el móvil	*mobile phone*
el celular	*cell phone*
la internet	*internet*
la computadora	*computer*
el teclado	*keyboard*
la pantalla	*screen*
la impresora	*printer*
el ratón	*mouse*
los audífonos	*headphones*
la conexión	*connection*

NUTS & BOLTS 2
DEMONSTRATIVE PRONOUNS

Words like *this* and *that* not only function as adjectives in English, as in *this book* or *that house,* but can also be used as pronouns, as in *I like this (one) and you like that (one).* In Spanish, demonstrative pronouns have an accent mark that distinguishes them from demonstrative adjectives.

éste/ésta	*this (one)*
éstos/éstas	*these (ones)*
ése/ésa	*that (one)*
ésos/ésas	*those (ones)*
aquél/aquélla	*that (one) over there*
aquéllos/aquéllas	*those (ones) over there*

Let's take a look at some examples. Notice the difference between demonstrative adjectives, which are used right before nouns, and demonstrative pronouns, which stand on their own in place of nouns.

Este número de fax es el mío y éste es el tuyo.
This fax number is mine and this one is yours.

Esa pantalla es plana y ésa no.
That screen is flat and that one is not.

Aquella computadora es nueva y aquélla no.
That computer is new and that one is not.

There are three neuter demonstrative pronouns that are used to refer to abstract concepts or unspecified objects. They're also used when the speaker doesn't necessarily have a specific noun in mind, so the gender is unknown; the neuter form is used instead.

esto	*this (one, thing)*
eso	*that (one, thing)*
aquello	*that (one, thing) further away*

Here are some examples.

Esto es un desastre.
This is a disaster.

Eso es verdad.
That's true.

Aquello no me gusta.
I don't like that.

PRACTICE 2
Choose either the demonstrative adjective or the demonstrative pronoun to complete the sentence.

1. (Ese,Ése) teléfono está ocupado.

2. (Este, Éste) es mi número de celular.

3. (Estos, Éstos) meses son largos.

4. (Esta, Ésta) pantalla es oscura y (aquella, aquélla) es pequeña.

5. (Estas, Éstas) computadoras son costosas.

6. (Esta, Ésta) semana tengo dos reuniones.

7. (Esas, Ésas) son nuestras oficinas.

8. (Ese, Ése) teclado no me gusta.

Demonstrative adjectives can also be used with time expressions, just as they are in English.

esta mañana	*this morning*
esta tarde	*this afternoon*
esta noche	*tonight*
esta semana	*this week*
este día	*this day*
este mes	*this month*
este año	*this year*
este siglo	*this century*

Here are some examples.

Este mes tengo mucho trabajo.
I have a lot of work this month.

Esta tarde tenemos dos reuniones.
We have two meetings this afternoon.

ANSWERS
PRACTICE 1: 1. Esta; **2.** Aquellas; **3.** Ese; **4.** Esos; **5.** Estos; **6.** Aquel.

PRACTICE 2: 1. Ese; **2.** Éste; **3.** Estos; **4.** Esta, aquélla; **5.** Estas; **6.** Esta; **7.** Ésas; **8.** Ese.

─────────── Lesson 18 (phrases) ───────────

PHRASE LIST 1
Here are a few verb phrases you'll use when talking on the phone or sending e-mail. They're all regular verbs, except for **colgar** and **hacer,** which we'll come back to later.

llamar por teléfono	*to make a phone call*
contestar el teléfono	*to answer the phone*
colgar el teléfono	*to hang up the phone*

marcar un número de teléfono	to dial a phone number
dejar un mensaje después de oír la señal	to leave a message after the tone
enviar un mensaje	to send a message
borrar un mensaje	to erase a message
copiar un mensaje	to copy a message
recibir un fax	to receive a fax
hacer una llamada internacional	to make an international call
hacer una llamada nacional/ local	to make a domestic/local call
enviar un correo electrónico	to send an e-mail
contestar un correo electrónico	to reply to an e-mail
enviar un archivo	to send a file
bajar un archivo	to download a file

NOTE

Notice that in English, you need a preposition after *reply*, but in Spanish, you can use **contestar** on its own. This is very similar to what you saw with **escuchar** (*to listen to*).

NUTS & BOLTS 1
NEGATION

Making a negative statement in Spanish is very easy—simply place the word **no** (*not*) before the verb.

Tengo conexión de internet en mi casa.
I have an internet connection at home.

No tengo conexión de internet en mi casa.
I don't have an internet connection at home.

La línea está ocupada.
The line is busy.

La línea no está ocupada.
The line isn't busy.

Hay tono.
There's a dial tone.

No hay tono.
There's no dial tone.

Eres un arquitecto.
You are an architect.

No eres un arquitecto.
You're not an architect.

When the answer to a question is negative, the word **no** is used twice—once to mean *no,* and once to mean *not.*

¿Está la señora Ruiz en su oficina?
Is Mrs. Ruiz in her office?

No. Ella no está en su oficina.
No. She's not in her office.

¿Tienes tiempo para tomar un café?
Do you have time for a coffee?

No. No tengo tiempo.
No. I don't have time.

PRACTICE 1
Make the following statements negative.

1. Éste es mi número de teléfono.

2. Las secretarias hablan por teléfono.

3. Tus padres tienen una casa pequeña.

4. Yo escribo un correo electrónico.

5. Tenemos tu número de celular.

6. Leo un fax.

7. Estas oficinas son muy grandes.

8. La línea está ocupada.

PHRASE LIST 2

Here are some phrases you'll use when talking on the phone.

¿Dígame?	*Hello? (lit., Tell me?)*
¿Aló?	*Hello?*
Le paso.	*I'm putting you through.*
La línea está ocupada.	*The line is busy.*
Está comunicando.	*The line is ringing.*
No hay tono.	*There is no dial tone.*
No cuelgue, por favor.	*Do not hang up, please.*
Espere, por favor.	*Hold on, please.*
poner en espera	*to put on hold*

NUTS & BOLTS 2
INDEFINITE PRONOUNS

An indefinite pronoun is a pronoun that doesn't refer to anyone in particular. Here are some indefinite pronouns and other words that will come in handy in Spanish. Notice that they're all affirmative. We'll look at their negative counterparts in a moment.

algo	*something*
alguien	*somebody, someone*
algún (-o/-a/-os/-as)	*some, something*
siempre	*always*
también	*also, too*
o . . . o	*either . . . or*

Here's how they're used in a sentence.

Hay algo diferente en esta habitación.
There's something different in this room.

Alguien llama por teléfono.
Somebody's calling on the phone.

Algunos teléfonos no funcionan.
Some phones don't work.

Ella siempre escribe emails.
She always writes emails.

Nosotros también tocamos el piano.
We also play the piano.

Yo o corro o camino por las mañanas.
I either run or walk in the mornings.

Notice that **o . . . o** is used to introduce two different options, and each **o** is placed in front of one the options. In the example above, the two options are actions, so each **o** is placed before the verb.

Here are their negative counterparts. **Ni . . . ni** functions just like **o . . . o.**

nada	*nothing*
nadie	*nobody, no one*
ningún (-o/-a/-os/-as)	*none, not any*
nunca	*never*
tampoco	*neither, not either*
ni . . . ni	*neither . . . nor*

Negative words can be used alone, preceding the verb.

Jorge nunca come.
Jorge never eats.

Él tampoco canta.
He doesn't dance either.

Nadie habla italiano aquí.
No one here speaks Italian.

Double negation is perfectly correct in Spanish. Usually the word **no** immediately precedes the verb and another negative word follows the verb.

No funciona ni el teléfono ni el fax.
Neither the phone nor the fax works.

No hay conexión nunca.
There's never a connection.

No hay nadie en la oficina.
There's nobody in the office/There isn't anyone in the office.

PRACTICE 2
Translate the following sentences. When appropriate, use single (instead of double) negation.

1. *I always have a copy of my messages.*

2. *Nobody answers the phone.*

3. *They never erase their messages.*

4. *Someone receives a fax.*

5. *Someone also receives an email.*

6. *He doesn't have a phone or a fax in his office.*

Tip!

Later on in this unit, you'll be learning how to make polite requests. In doing so, the phrase **por favor** (*please*) comes in very handy. Another phrase that you'll often hear is **hágame el favor de** (*lit., do me the favor of*). You'll never be wrong to use **por favor**. However, you might be surprised not to hear the words when asking someone to do something that he or she is expected to do (as when ordering a meal from a server). As in English, your tone of voice can have as much to do with how your request is received as does its grammatical form.

ANSWERS

PRACTICE 1: 1. Éste no es mi número de teléfono. **2.** Las secretarias no hablan por teléfono. **3.** Tus padres no tienen una casa pequeña. **4.** Yo no escribo un correo electrónico. **5.** No tenemos tu número de celular. **6.** No leo un fax. **7.** Estas oficinas no son muy grandes. **8.** La línea no está ocupada.

PRACTICE 2: 1. Siempre tengo una copia de mis mensajes. **2.** Nadie contesta el teléfono. **3.** Nunca borran sus mensajes. **4.** Alguien recibe un fax. **5.** Alguien también recibe un correo electrónico. **6.** No tiene ni un teléfono ni un fax en su oficina.

―――――――――― Lesson 19 (sentences) ――――――――――

SENTENCE LIST 1

Quisiera hablar con . . .	*I'd like to talk to . . .*
Lo siento, tiene un número equivocado.	*Sorry, you have the wrong number.*
¿De parte de quién?	*Who's calling?*
¿Quién lo llama?	*Who's calling?*
¿Con quién hablo?	*Who am I talking to?*
Ahora no está.	*He/She isn't in right now.*
Está ocupada.	*She's busy.*
Por favor, llame más tarde.	*Please call later.*

Llame en cinco minutos.	*Call in five minutes.*
No está en su oficina.	*He/She is not in his/her office.*
Ya salió.	*He/She already left.*
¿Desea dejar un mensaje?	*Would you like to leave a message?*

NUTS & BOLTS 1

IRREGULAR VERBS HACER *(TO MAKE, TO DO)*, PONER *(TO PUT)*, TRAER *(TO BRING)*, AND CAER *(TO FALL)*

As you know, there are a few verbs in Spanish that are irregular. Most of the time, these verbs follow the pattern of endings you learned in Unit 4, but their stems change a bit when conjugated. For example, you already know the verb **tener,** which has a **g** before the ending for the first person singular (**yo tengo**), and the **e** in its stem changes to **ie** in several forms (**tienes, tiene, tienen**).

There are a few other verbs that add **g** in the first person singular: **hacer** (*to make, to do*), **poner** (*to put*), **traer** (*to bring*), and **caer** (*to fall*). For all other persons, they are conjugated just like regular **-er** verbs.

hacer (*to make, to do*)

yo hago	nosotros/as hacemos
tú haces	vosotros/as hacéis
él/ella/usted hace	ellos/ellas/ustedes hacen

poner (*to put*)

yo pongo	nosotros/as ponemos
tú pones	vosotros/as ponéis
él/ella/usted pone	ellos/ellas/ustedes ponen

The verb **traer** (*to bring*) also takes an **i** before the **g** in the **yo** form.

traer (*to bring*)

yo traigo	nosotros/as traemos
tú traes	vosotros/as traéis
él/ella/usted trae	ellos/ellas/ustedes traen

The verb **caer** (*to fall*) is conjugated just like **traer.**

caer (*to fall*)

yo caigo	nosotros/as caemos
tú caes	vosotros/as caéis
él/ella/usted cae	ellos/ellas/ustedes caen

PRACTICE 1
Complete the following sentences with the correct form of the verb.

1. Nosotros no _____ llamadas locales. (hacer)

2. Ustedes _____ los contratos. (traer)

3. Ella _____ a María en espera. (poner)

4. Yo _____ llamadas internacionales todos los días. (hacer)

5. Ellas no _____ en la oficina en este momento. (estar)

6. Usted _____ la línea equivocada. (tener)

7. Ella _____ buenas noticias. (traer)

8. Tú _____ ocupado todos los días. (estar)

9. Vosotros _____ la computadora en la oficina. (poner)

10. Yo _____ una reunión el martes. (tener)

SENTENCE LIST 2

¿Quiere esperar un momento?	*Do you want to wait a moment?*
No hay nadie disponible en este momento.	*There's no one available at the moment.*
Por favor, anote mi número de teléfono.	*Please write down my telephone number.*
Necesito hablar con el señor Sánchez lo antes posible.	*I need to speak to Mr. Sánchez as soon as possible.*
Que tenga un buen día.	*Have a nice day.*
Casi no reconozco tu voz.	*I almost don't recognize your voice.*
Tengo los contratos listos pero falta tu firma.	*I have the contracts ready, but your signature is missing.*
Salgo de viaje ese mismo día.	*I go on a trip that very same day.*
El martes por la mañana me viene bien.	*Tuesday morning suits me fine.*
Tengo una reunión muy temprano.	*I have a meeting very early.*
¿Cuál es su dirección de correo electrónico?	*What's your e-mail address?*
¿Su compañía tiene un sitio web?	*Does your company have a website?*
El informe está en un anexo al correo electrónico.	*The report is in an e-mail attachment.*

NUTS & BOLTS 2

IRREGULAR VERBS SALIR *(TO GO OUT)* AND DECIR *(TO SAY)*

Let's look at some more irregular verbs. The verbs **salir** (*to go out*) and **decir** (*to say*) are irregular **-ir** verbs that also have the **g** in the first person singular.

salir (*to go out*)

yo salgo	nosotros/as salimos
tú sales	vosotros/as salís
él/ella/usted sale	ellos/ellas/ustedes salen

Notice that **decir** (*to say*) also has a vowel change from **e** to **i** in its stem.

decir (*to say*)

yo digo	nosotros/as decimos
tú dices	vosotros/as decís
él/ella/usted dice	ellos/ellas/ustedes dicen

Yo salgo del trabajo a las tres de la tarde.
I leave work at 3:00 P.M.

Ella dice siempre la verdad.
She always tells the truth.

So far you've learned two verbs that have vowel changes in their stems: **tener** and **decir**. In tener, **e** become **ie,** and in **decir, e** becomes **i.** Notice that these changes do not happen in the **nosotros/as** and **vosotros/as** forms. You'll learn more about stem changing verbs later, but for now keep in mind that if there is a stem change, it doesn't affect the first and second person plural forms, **nosotros/as** and **vosotros/as.**

PRACTICE 2

Rewrite the following sentences using the subject pronoun given in parentheses.

1. Yo digo pocas palabras. (nosotros)

2. Tú sales de viaje el domingo. (yo)

3. Ustedes dicen la verdad. (ella)

4. Él sale de su oficina a las tres de la tarde. (tú)

5. Nostros salimos de nuestra casa a las nueve de la mañana. (vosotros)

6. Ellos no dicen nada. (yo)

Tip!

Don't get too worked up about learning irregular verbs. You'll see that the most frequently used verbs are the ones with the most irregularities—you'll hear them so often that you'll end up learning them very quickly. Also, the most irregular person in the conjugation of verbs is the first person singular, or **yo** form (*I*). So, even though a verb maybe called irregular, it may only mean that the first person singular is irregular and the rest of the conjugation follows a regular pattern, as you saw with some of the verbs in this lesson. If you're a stickler for memorizing irregular forms, though, here are some suggestions. Make flash cards for each new irregular verb, following the two-column format in which the irregular verbs are presented in this lesson. Keep them in your pocket, and when you have a few spare moments, take them out, glance over them, and repeat the forms aloud to yourself. You'll have them memorized pretty quickly. You can find more tips in the *Language learning tips* sections.

ANSWERS

PRACTICE 1: 1. hacemos; **2.** traen; **3.** pone; **4.** hago; **5.** están; **6.** tiene; **7.** trae; **8.** estás; **9.** ponéis; **10.** tengo.

PRACTICE 2: 1. Nosotros decimos pocas palabras. **2.** Yo salgo de viaje el domingo. **3.** Ella dice la verdad. **4.** Tú sales de tu oficina a las tres de la tarde. **5.** Vosotros salís de nuestra casa a las nueve de la mañana. **6.** Yo no digo nada.

CONVERSATION 1

Juan Fernández is calling Nova Limitada to speak with Miguel Sánchez. He dials the switchboard and gets the operator.

Operadora: Nova Limitada, buenos días, ¿con quién desea hablar?

Juan: Buenos días. Me llamo Juan Fernández y necesito hablar con el gerente de ventas, el señor Miguel Sánchez.

Operadora: Le comunico. Un momento por favor.

Operadora: La línea está ocupada. ¿Quiere esperar un momento?

Juan: No, no tengo tiempo. ¿Hay alguien más?

Operadora: No. Lo siento. En ese departamento no hay nadie disponible en este momento. Todos están en una reunión fuera de la ciudad.

Juan: Bueno, por favor anote mi número de teléfono. Necesito hablar con el señor Sánchez lo antes posible.

Operadora: ¿Quiere su buzón de voz?

Juan: Buena idea.

Operadora: Ya le conecto. Que tenga un buen día.

Juan: Muchas gracias. Igualmente.

Operator: *Nova Limitada, good morning; who would you like to speak to?*

Juan: *Good morning. My name is Juan Fernández, and I need to speak to the sales manager, Mr. Miguel Sánchez.*

Operator: *I'll put you through. One moment please.*

Operator: *The line is busy. Do you want to wait a moment?*

Juan: *No, I don't have time. Is there anybody else?*

Operator:	No. I'm sorry. There's no one available in that department at the moment. Everyone is at a meeting out of town.
Juan:	Well, please write down my phone number. I need to speak to Mr. Sánchez as soon as possible.
Operator:	Do you want his voice mail?
Juan:	Good idea.
Operator:	I'll put you through right now. Have a nice day.
Juan:	Thank you; same to you.

NOTES

As briefly mentioned in Lesson 16, when the direct object of a verb is a person, you must introduce it with the preposition **a**. This **a** has no real meaning, and when it's followed by the masculine article **el**, it forms the contraction **al**.

Invitamos al gerente de ventas.

We're inviting the sales manager.

Traigo a mis amigos.

I'm bringing my friends.

Veo a mis amigos todas las semanas.

I see my friends every week.

Quieren mucho a sus padres.

They love their parents very much.

The only exception is the verb **tener.** If **tener** has a person as a direct object, the preposition **a** is not used.

Tiene muchos amigos.

She/He has a lot of friends.

Tengo un hermano y una hermana.

I have a brother and a sister.

NUTS & BOLTS 1

IR *(TO GO)*

The verb **ir** *(to go)* is used in many situations, and it is also an irregular verb.

yo voy	nosotros/as vamos
tú vas	vosotros/as vais
él/ella/usted va	ellos/ellas/ustedes van

Notice that we generally use the preposition **a** *(to)* with the verb **ir**. And remember that **a** + the masculine article **el** forms the contraction **al**.

Esta tarde voy a mi oficina.
This afternoon I'm going to my office.

Nosotros vamos al cine los fines de semana.
We go to the movies on weekends.

PRACTICE 1

Match the phrases in column A with the appropriate responses in colmn B.

A	B
1. ¿Quién lo llama?	a. No, gracias, llamo más tarde.
2. ¿Cuál es su número?	b. Le paso.
3. ¿Desea dejar un mensaje?	c. Lo siento. Ella ya salió.
4. ¿Es el tres, ocho, nueve , uno, dos?	d. Sí, gracias, necesito hablar con el Señor Almirante.

A	B
5. Quisiera hablar con el señor Martínez, por favor.	e. Es el siete, tres, cero, nueve, dos, dos.
6. Qusiera hablar con la señora Marcos.	f. No. Tiene el número equivocado.
7. Cienfuentes abogados, ¿dígame?	g. Soy Manuel Marcos, de Industrias Talia.

CONVERSATION 2
Later that afternoon, Miguel returns Juan's call.

Secretaria: Trías y Trías abogados, buenas tardes.

Miguel: Buenas tardes. Soy Miguel Sánchez. Necesito hablar con el señor Fernández.

Secretaria: Le paso.

Juan: ¿Dígame?

Miguel: ¿Con quién hablo?

Juan: ¡Hola Miguel; soy yo, Juan!

Miguel: Hola Juan. Casi no reconozco tu voz. ¿Cómo van las cosas?

Juan: Pues más o menos. Necesito reunirme contigo urgentemente. Tengo los contratos listos, pero falta tu firma.

Miguel: ¿Qué te parece si nos vemos el miércoles a eso de las nueve?

Juan: Salgo de viaje ese mismo día. Y el lunes . . . ¿tienes tiempo?

Miguel: Pero, hombre si es día festivo. Pero, el martes por la mañana me viene bien.

Juan: Listo. Voy primero a los juzgados y luego a tu oficina.

Miguel: Tengo una reunión muy temprano . . . Si vienes después de las diez, mejor.

Juan: Perfecto. Entonces, nos vemos el martes.
Miguel: Hasta luego.

Secretary: *Trías and Trías lawyers, good afternoon.*
Miguel: *Good afternoon. I'm Miguel Sánchez. I need to speak to Mr. Fernández.*
Secretary: *I'll put you through.*

Juan: *Hello?*
Miguel: *Who am I speaking to?*
Juan: *Hi, Miguel; it's me, Juan!*
Miguel: *Hi, Juan. I almost don't recognize your voice. How are things?*
Juan: *Well, so-so. I need to meet with you urgently. I have the contracts ready, but your signature is missing.*
Miguel: *How about getting together on Wednesday at about nine?*
Juan: *I leave on a trip that same day. What about Monday . . . Do you have time?*
Miguel: *Come on now, that's a holiday! But Tuesday morning is fine with me.*
Juan: *Good. I'll go to court first and then to your office.*
Miguel: *I have a meeting very early. If you come after ten, that's better.*
Juan: *Perfect. So, see you Tuesday.*
Miguel: *Till later.*

NOTES

Don't confuse **sí** with **si**. When **sí** is spelled with an accent mark, it means *yes*; when it is spelled without the accent mark, it means *if*.

Notice that Miguel said: **Pero hombre, si es día festivo.** The words **hombre** and **si** are used as flavoring words, giving emphasis to what Miguel is saying. The sentence could be translated in a number of ways to capture the same sentiment, for example: *Come on now, that's a holiday!*

NUTS & BOLTS 2

QUERER (TO WANT, TO LOVE)

When making polite requests you will very often use the verb **querer** (*to want*). This is an irregular verb, conjugated as follows.

querer (*to want*)

yo quiero	nosotros/as queremos
tú quieres	vosotros/as queréis
él/ella/usted quiere	ellos/ellas/ustedes quieren

Querer can be used right before another verb in the infinitive, just as *to want to* is in English.

Quiero una habitación grande, por favor.
I want a big room, please

Quiero hablar con Patricia.
I want to speak to Patricia.

Quiero escribir un correo electrónico.
I want to write an e-mail.

A much nicer and more polite way of making requests is by using the form **quisiera** (*would like*).

Quisiera una cerveza, por favor.
I would like a beer, please.

Quisiera hablar con Patricia.
I'd like to speak to Patricia.

Quisiera hacer una llamada internacional.
I'd like to make an international call.

Note that this verb is often used to mean *to love*. So, a common way of saying *I love you* is to say **Te quiero.** Spanish does have the verb **amar,** which means *to love,* but it is not used as often, and it is usually used strictly in a romantic way. Don't forget to use the preposition **a** if the direct object of **querer** is a person.

Gloria quiere mucho a su papá.
Gloria loves her daddy very much.

Queremos a nuestros amigos.
We love our friends.

Anther verb that can be used to make a polite request is **gustar** (*to like*). Again, you would use the form **me gustaría** (*I would like*).

Me gustaría un café.
I would like a cup of coffee.

Me gustaría llamar por teléfono.
I'd like to make a phone call.

PRACTICE 2
Translate the following sentences.

1. *I would like to speak to the manager, please.*
2. *We want a new computer.*
3. *I'd like to go to my brother's office.*
4. *He wants your telephone number.*
5. *I'd like to leave a message.*

Culture note
Every country in the Spanish-speaking world celebrates different national, religious, and local **fiestas** or **días festivos** (*holidays*) depending on heritage and tradition. For economic reasons, in some countries the government has decided to move the celebration of

religious holidays to the following Monday in order to avoid the very long **puentes** (*long weekends, lit., bridges*) that would result in a holiday being on a Tuesday or Thursday, for example.

You might want to check out the internet for information on holidays like **el día de los Reyes Magos** (*Three Kings Day*), **el día de los Muertos** (*All Souls Day*), **la Noche Buena** (*Christmas Eve*), **La Pascua** (*Easter*), or **el carnaval** (*carnival*) to learn more about Spanish and Latin American holidays and traditions.

ANSWERS
PRACTICE 1: 1. g; **2.**e; **3.** a; **4.** f; **5.** b; **6.** c; **7.** d

PRACTICE 2: 1. Me gustaría/Quisiera hablar con el gerente, por favor. **2.** Queremos una computadora nueva. **3.** Me gustaría/Quisiera ir a la oficina de mi hermano. **4.** Él quiere tu número de teléfono. **5.** Me gustaría/Quisiera dejar un mensaje.

UNIT 5 ESSENTIALS
Este teléfono no funciona y éste tampoco.
This phone doesn't work, and this one either.

Esa pantalla es plana y ésa no.
That screen is flat and that one isn't.

Aquella computadora es nueva.
That computer over there is new.

Nuestra compañía no tiene un sitio web.
Our company doesn't have a website.

Hay algo diferente en la oficina hoy.
Today there is something different in the office.

Alguien llama por teléfono.
Someone is calling on the phone.

No funciona ni el teléfono ni el fax.
Neither the phone nor the fax works.

Nosotros hacemos llamadas locales.
We make local calls.

Ustedes traen los contratos.
You bring the contracts.

Ella pone a María en espera.
She puts María on hold.

Tú sales de viaje el domingo.
You go on a trip on Sunday.

Ustedes dicen la verdad.
You tell the truth.

Esta tarde voy a mi oficina.
This afternoon I go to my office.

Quiero hablar con Patricia.
I want to speak to Patricia.

Quisiera hacer una llamada internacional.
I would like to make an international call.

Me gustaría un café.
I'd like a cup of coffee.

Nos gustaría enviar un correo electrónico.
We'd like to send an e-mail.

UNIT 6
Getting around town

In this unit, you'll learn how to ask for and give directions. You'll learn a lot of important vocabulary that will help you talk about running errands and getting around cities and towns. Because you'll often hear command forms when you ask someone for directions, this unit will cover commands, as well as a lot of practical irregular verbs. You'll also learn about those very useful little words, prepositions.

———————— Lesson 21 (words) ————————

WORD LIST 1

norte	*north*
sur	*south*
este/oriente	*east*
oeste/occidente	*west*
izquierda	*left*
derecha	*right*
la carretera/la autopista/ la autovía	*highway, freeway*
la salida	*exit*
el peaje	*toll*
el carril/la vía	*lane*
de sentido unico	*one-way*
el mapa	*map*
el cruce	*intersection*
las afueras	*outskirts*
el pueblo	*town*
el subterráneo/el metro	*subway/metro*

el edificio	*building*
el edificio de apartamentos	*apartment building*

NUTS & BOLTS 1

SABER AND CONOCER *(TO KNOW)*

In Spanish, there are two different verbs that can be translated as *to know*: **saber** and **conocer.** They have different meanings and are not interchangeable. Let's start with **saber.**

saber (*to know*)

yo sé	nosotros/as sabemos
tú sabes	vosotros/as sabéis
él/ella/usted sabe	ellos/ellas/ustedes saben

Saber means *to know* as in to know a fact, to know something thoroughly, or to know how to do something. It can be followed by a noun like **su nombre** (*her name*) or **la respuesta** (*the answer*), by **que** . . . (*that* . . .), **donde** . . . (*where* . . .), and **cuando** . . . (*when* . . .) to introduce facts, or by another verb in the infinitive, in which case it's translated as *to know how to.*

Saben mi nombre.
They know my name.

No sé la respuesta.
I don't know the answer.

Yo sé hablar francés.
I know how to speak French.

Ella sabe mucho sobre geografía.
She knows a lot about geography.

Nosotros sabemos que tienes un secreto.
We know that you have a secret.

Tú sabes donde está la salida.
You know where the exit is.

Ustedes no saben cuando parte el tren.
You don't know when the train leaves.

Now let's look at **conocer.**

conocer (*to know*)

yo conozco	nosotros/as conocemos
tú conoces	vosotros/as conocéis
él/ella/usted conoce	ellos/ellas/ustedes conocen

Conocer means *to know* as in to know a person or to be familiar with something—a city, a book, a film, a restaurant, and so on. If the direct object of **conocer** is a person, don't forget to use the preposition **a.**

Conocemos a tus padres.
We know your parents.

Pedro conoce un restaurante italiano estupendo.
Pedro knows an excellent Italian restaurant.

Marta no conoce Nueva York.
Marta doesn't know New York / Marta isn't familiar with New York.

Yo conozco a mucha gente famosa.
I know many famous people.

Sometimes **conocer** can even be used to mean *to meet*, especially in the past tense, which you'll learn a bit later. But for now, learn the following expression.

Gusto en conocerle.
Pleased to meet you.

PRACTICE 1

Complete the phrases with the correct form of either **saber** or **conocer**:

1. Nosotros no _____ la ciudad de Moscú.

2. Yo _____ bailar salsa.

3. ¿Vosotros _____ historia antigua?

4. Ella no _____ hablar alemán.

5. ¿(Tú) _____ a mi hermana Luisa?

6. Mi familia no _____ a mi esposo.

7. Ella no _____ esquiar.

8. Yo no _____ este restaurante.

WORD LIST 2

la avenida	*avenue*
la calle	*street*
la cuadra/la manzana	*block*
la esquina	*corner*
la biblioteca	*library*
el restaurante	*restaurant*
la tienda	*store*
el parque	*park*
el banco	*bank*
la iglesia	*church*
el templo	*temple*
la mezquita	*mosque*
la acera / el andén	*sidewalk*
la panadería	*bakery*
la carnicería	*butcher shop*
la cafetería	*café/coffee shop*

la farmacia	*drugstore/pharmacy*
el supermercado	*supermarket*
la tienda de ropa	*clothing store*
la tienda por departamentos	*department store*
derecho	*straight*
el semáforo	*traffic light*
doblar	*to turn*
dar la vuelta	*to turn around*
ir a pie/caminar	*to walk*
seguir	*to follow*
el peatón	*pedestrian*

NUTS & BOLTS 2
PODER (CAN), DEBER (MUST), AND TENER QUE (TO HAVE TO)
The verb **poder** means *can, to be able to*, or *to have permission to.*

poder (*can*)

yo puedo	nosotros/as podemos
tú puedes	vosotros/as podéis
él/ella/usted puede	ellos/ellas/ustedes pueden

Just like **querer** (*to want to*), it's followed by another verb in the infinitive.

¿Puedes esquiar?
Can you ski?

Yo puedo hablar chino.
I'm able to speak Chinese/I can speak Chinese.

¿Podemos usar su teléfono?
May we use your phone?

Aquí no podemos fumar.
We cannot smoke here.

Ella no puede trabajar con música.
She can't work while listening to music.

The verb **deber** means *must* or *to have to*. **Deber** is a regular -er verb.

deber (*must*)

yo debo	nosotros/as debemos
tú debes	vosotros/as debéis
él/ella/usted debe	ellos/ellas/ustedes deben

Debo estudiar español.
I have to study Spanish.

Debemos entregar este informe hoy.
We have to submit this report today.

Spanish also uses the expression **tener que** + a verb in the infinitive, which is a bit stronger than using **deber**.

Tienen que comprar una nueva computadora.
They have to buy a new computer.

Tenéis que hacer las reservaciones de hotel esta tarde.
You have to make the hotel reservations this afternoon.

PRACTICE 2
Fill in the blanks with the correct form of the verb in parentheses.

1. _____ ir a la oficina esta tarde. (yo/tener)

2. ¿_____ hacer una llamada internacional? (nosotros/poder)

3. _____ partir a las siete y media. (nosotros/deber)

4. _____ hacer las reservaciones por internet. (ustedes/poder)

5. _____ doblar a la izquierda. (usted/tener que)

6. _____ hablar con nuestro jefe. (nosotros/tener que)

7. ¿_____ salir temprano de la oficina hoy? (ustedes/poder)

8. _____ traer su pasaporte. (él/deber)

9. _____ hablar por teléfono en este momento. (ella/no poder)

10. _____ partir por la mañana. (usted/tener que)

Tip!

Here are a few expressions you'll often hear using **saber** and **conocer**.

no saber ni jota de algo
to not have a clue about something

¿Quién sabe?
Who knows?

¡Yo qué sé!
How do I know!?/How should I know!?

conocer palmo a palmo
to know like the back (lit., palm) of one's hand

No sé.
I don't know.

conocer de vista
to know by sight

dar a conocer
to make known

Conozco la ciudad de Nueva York palmo a plamo.
I know New York like the back of my hand.

Ella no sabe ni jota de algebra.
She has no clue about algebra.

Concemos a tu esposo de vista.
We know your husband by sight.

ANSWERS
PRACTICE 1: 1. conocemos; 2. sé; 3. sabéis; 4. sabe;
5. Conoces; 6. conoce; 7. sabe; 8. conozco.

PRACTICE 2: 1. Tengo que; 2. Podemos; 3. Debemos;
4. Pueden; 5. tiene que; 6. Tenemos que; 7. Pueden; 8. Debe;
9. No puede; 10. Tiene que.

—————————— Lesson 22 (phrases) ——————————

PHRASE LIST 1
Here are some phrases you can use when traveling by car.

¡Pare!/¡Alto!	*Stop!*
el embotellamiento	*traffic jam*
apagar las luces	*to turn off the lights*
pagar el peaje	*to pay the toll*
abrocharse el cinturón de seguridad	*to buckle up*
poner el pie en el freno	*to hit the brakes*
exceder el límite de velocidad	*to exceed the speed limit*
saltarse el semáforo	*to go through a light*
ir en dirección opuesta	*to go in the opposite direction*
reducir la velocidad	*to slow down*
pagar una multa	*to pay a fine*

NUTS & BOLTS 1

VER *(TO SEE)*, VENIR *(TO COME)*, **AND** DAR *(TO GIVE)*

In this section, we'll take a look at two more irregular verbs, **venir** *(to come)* and **dar** *(to give)*. But first let's start with a review of **ver**.

ver *(to see)*

yo veo	nosotros/as vemos
tú ves	vosotros/as véis
él/ella/usted ve	ellos/ellas/ustedes ven

Ver means *to see*, but it is also used to mean *to watch*—for example, to watch TV, a play, a sports event, or a movie. You will also often hear Spanish speakers using the expression **a ver**, which literally means *let's see*.

A ella le gusta ver películas de horror.
She likes to watch horror movies.

Nosotros vemos televisión todas las noches.
We watch TV every evening.

A ver, la calle Alcalá está a dos cuadras de aquí.
Let's see, Alcalá Street is two blocks from here.

Veis/Ven un partido de tenis.
You are watching a tennis match.

The verb **venir** *(to come)* is an irregular verb.

venir *(to come)*

yo vengo	nosotros/as venimos
tú vienes	vosotros/as venís
él/ella/usted viene	ellos/ellas/ustedes vienen

Notice that it's often used with the preposition **de**—take a look.

Ellos vienen de Brasil.
They come from Brazil.

Nosotros venimos de trabajar.
We're coming from work.

¿Vienes del supermercado?
Are you coming from the supermarket?

The verb **dar** (*to give*) is also an irregular verb.

dar (*to give*)

yo doy	nosotros/as damos
tú das	vosotros/as dáis
él/ella/usted da	ellos/ellas/ustedes dan

Dar is used in a variety of common expressions.

dar (las) gracias	*to give thanks*
dar a luz	*to give birth*
dar con algo	*to find something*
dar de narices	*to fall flat on one's face (lit., nose)*
dar la hora	*to tell time*
dar la mano	*to shake hands*

Ella no quiere dar a luz en el hospital.
She doesn't want to give birth in the hospital.

El reloj da la hora exacta.
The clock shows/gives the exact time.

No me gusta dar la mano a personas extrañas.
I don't like to shake hands with strangers.

PRACTICE 1

Fill in the blanks with the correct form of the verbs in parentheses.

1. ¿Disculpe, me _____ la hora? (poder/dar)
2. Mis abuelos _____ en el tren de las once. (venir)
3. Yo _____ una comedia esta noche. (querer/ver)
4. En su país las personas no _____ la mano. (dar)
5. No me _____ televisión. (gustar/ver)
6. Los padres _____ regalos a sus hijos en Navidad. (dar)
7. Yo _____ de la universidad. (venir)
8. Ellos _____ un partido de fútbol. (ver)

PHRASE LIST 2

The following phrases will help you get around town and ask for directions.

cruzar la calle	to cross the street
caminar dos cuadras/manzanas	to walk two blocks
al lado de	next to
enfrente de	in front of
a mano izquierda	on the left-hand side
a mano derecha	on the right-hand side
en la esquina	at the corner
a la vuelta de la esquina	around the corner
por el andén	on the sidewalk
por el callejón	through the alley

NUTS & BOLTS 2
THE PRESENT PROGRESSIVE

We've seen a lot of verbs in the simple present tense. But Spanish, like English, also has a present progressive tense, which expresses actions happening at the very moment you are speaking. The formation is similar to English: use the verb **estar** (*to be*) followed by the present participle, which is like the *-ing* form of the verb in English. The present participle is formed as follows.

For **-ar** verbs, take off the **-ar** and add **-ando** to the stem.

For **-er** and **-ir** verbs, take off the **-er** or **-ir** and add **-iendo** to the stem.

Estoy caminando por el callejón.
I'm walking through the alley.

Estás hablando por teléfono.
You're talking on the phone.

Está comiendo churros.
He/She is eating churros.

¿Usted está viendo televisión?
Are you watching TV?

Estamos dando las gracias.
We're giving thanks.

Estáis conociendo la ciudad.
You're getting to know the city.

No están escribiendo cartas.
They/You aren't writing letters.

There are, of course, a few irregular verbs that you will learn as we go along, and those irregularities may include the present participle. Here are the present participles of the irregular verbs we have seen so far.

---

traer—trayendo	to bring—bringing
decir—diciendo	to say—saying
ir—yendo	to go—going
venir—viniendo	to come—coming
poder—pudiendo	to be able to—being able to

Unlike English, Spanish does not use this tense to express a future action. It is only used to talk about an action that is happening at the moment of speech. Here are a few time expressions you're likely to use with this tense.

ahora	now
ahora mismo	right now
en este momento	at this moment

PRACTICE 2
Change the verbs in the following sentences from the simple present to the present progressive.

1. Cantamos en el coro de la iglesia.

2. Él envía un fax.

3. Ustedes dicen pocas palabras.

4. Visito la ciudad de Nueva York.

5. Ellos salen de la oficina.

6. Vosotros habláis con vuestro jefe.

7. ¿Lees el periódico?

8. Él toma café.

Culture note

Muletillas or frases de relleno (*filler words*) are used when the speaker doesn't know what to say next or is looking for a word. These phrases are the equivalents of the English filler words *well, um, you know, err,* and so on. Spanish speakers prefer to use words like **este, pues, a ver, por así decir, es decir, vamos,** or **bueno.** There is some regional variation in the use of Spanish filler phrases. People from Argentina, for example, are known around the world for using the word **che** at the beginning of their sentences, and Spaniards tend to use **vamos** fairly often. In many regions, the word **mira** or **mire** (*look*) is used to start a sentence.

Mire, el teatro queda a dos cuadras.
Look, the theater is two blocks away.

A ver, cruce la calle y doble a la derecha.
Let's see, cross the street and turn right.

Pues, es muy fácil.
Well, it's very easy.

ANSWERS

PRACTICE 1: 1. puede dar; **2.** vienen; **3.** quiero ver; **4.** dan; **5.** gusta ver; **6.** dan; **7.** vengo; **8.** ven.

PRACTICE 2: 1. Estamos cantando en el coro de la iglesia. **2.** Él está enviando un fax. **3.** Ustedes están diciendo pocas palabras. **4.** Estoy visitando la ciudad de Nueva York. **5.** Ellos están saliendo de la oficina. **6.** Vosotros estáis hablando con vuestro jefe. **7.** ¿Estás leyendo el periódico? **8.** Él está tomando café.

Lesson 23 (sentences)

SENTENCE LIST 1

Siga derecho hasta . . .	*Go straight till . . .*
Le agradezco mucho su ayuda.	*Thanks a lot for (lit, I thank you for) your help.*

¿Sabe cómo llegar a . . . ?	Do you know how to get to . . . ?
Aquí en el mapa está muy claro.	Here on the map, it is very clear.
Buen viaje.	Have a good trip.
Siga por el carril de la derecha.	Stay in the right lane.
A más o menos dos kilómetros hay un peaje.	At more or less two kilometers, there is a toll.
Tome la rampa en dirección . . .	Take the ramp towards . . .

NUTS & BOLTS 1
COMMON PREPOSITIONS OF LOCATION

Prepositions are those little words we use to connect other words in order to show spatial, temporal, or other kinds of relationships. Examples of prepositions are *on, in,* and *at*. In Spanish, prepositions function almost the same way as in English, but their precise usage often has to be memorized. Let's first take a look at prepositions that show spatial relationships.

en	*in, on*
entre	*between*
delante de	*in front of*
enfrente de	*in front of*
detrás de	*behind*
debajo de	*underneath*
encima de	*on top of*
sobre	*above*
contra	*against*

cerca de	close to
lejos de	far away from
dentro de	inside of
fuera de	outside of

When showing spatial relationships, either **estar** or **hay** (*there is/are*) is typically used. Take a look at how the above prepositions are used in a sentence.

Madrid está en España.
Madrid is in Spain.

Antonio está sentado entre Marta y Alejandra.
Antonio is seated between Marta and Alejandra.

El teatro está delante de mi oficina.
The theater is in front of my office.

Hay un edificio alto enfrente de nuestra casa.
There's a tall building in front of our house.

La tienda está detrás del museo.
The shop is behind the museum.

Hay un gato debajo de la mesa.
There's a cat underneath the table.

La computadora está encima del escritorio.
The computer is on top of the desk.

Hay dos lámparas sobre la cama.
There are two lamps above the bed.

El armario está contra la pared.
The closet is against the wall.

La universidad está cerca de aquí.
The university is close to here.

Su oficina está lejos de su casa.
His office is far away from his house.

Los huevos están dentro de la nevera.
The eggs are inside the refrigerator.

El museo está fuera de la ciudad.
The museum is outside of the city.

PRACTICE 1

Replace each of the underlined prepositions with one that means the opposite. For example, if you see **debajo de** (*underneath*), change it to **encima de** (*on top of*).

1. Delante del armario hay una puerta.

2. Los turistas están dentro del museo.

3. Mi familia vive lejos de mi casa.

4. Enfrente de su casa hay un bar.

5. El niño está debajo de la cama.

6. Cerca de mi casa está la universidad.

7. Los archivos están detrás de esos libros.

8. Los documentos están dentro del sobre.

SENTENCE LIST 2

El teatro está a mano izquierda.	*The theater is on the left-hand side.*
Seguid derecho por está calle.	*Go straight down this street.*
¿Me puede decir cómo llegar a . . . ?	*Can you tell me how to get to . . . ?*
La entrada para visitantes está en la parte de atrás.	*The visitors' entrance is in back.*

Queremos tomarnos un café para coger fuerzas.	*We want to have a cup of coffee to wake us up a bit (lit., to get some strength).*
En la esquina de la plaza hay un café.	*On the corner of the plaza there's a coffee place.*
Vamos, es muy fácil.	*Let's see—it's very easy.*
Ahí queda el teatro de la ópera.	*That's where the opera theater is located.*

NUTS & BOLTS 2
COMMON PREPOSITIONS OF TIME

Now let's look at some prepositions and phrasal prepositions of time.

antes de	*before*
después de	*after*
desde	*since, from*
durante	*during*
hasta	*until, till*

Antes de salir, leo el periódico.
Before leaving, I read the newspaper.

Después del trabajo, hacemos deporte.
After work, we play sports.

Desde esta mañana estoy trabajando en este proyecto.
I've been working (lit., I am working) on this project since this morning.

Están de vacaciones desde enero hasta abril.
They are on vacation from January till April.

Generalmente tomo una siesta durante el día.
I usually take a nap during the day.

¡Hasta mañana!
See you tomorrow!/Until tomorrow!

Here are other common prepositions, some of which you already know.

a	to, at
con	with
de	of
hacia	toward
sin	without
sobre	about/on top of

The preposition **a** has several uses. First, it's a common preposition of motion.

Vamos a Caracas.
We're going to Caracas.

Ellos viajan a Chile todos los veranos.
They travel to Chile every summer.

In the last unit, you learned about the preposition **a** when it introduces a direct object that is a person. **A** is also used to introduce an indirect object, like the English *to*.

Ella da su comida a los pobres.
She gives her food to the poor.

Enviamos muchos mensajes a nuestros amigos.
We send many messages to our friends.

A is also used after certain verbs, such as **aprender** and **comenzar**.

Tengo que aprender a escribir a máquina.
I need to learn how to type.

Tengo que comenzar a estudiar con más frecuencia.
I need to start studying more often.

Some verbs are followed by **de** before an infinitive. Here are a few examples of common expressions using **de** + an infinitive.

acabar de hacer algo	*to have just done something*
tratar de hacer algo	*to try to do something*
cesar de hacer algo	*to stop doing something*

Juan acaba de salir de la oficina.
Juan just left the office.

Ella trata de aprender a esquiar.
She tries to learn how to ski.

Mi hija no cesa de llorar.
My daughter doesn't stop crying.

Finally, here are examples of how to use **hacia, sin,** and **sobre:**

Ellos van hacia Madrid.
They are going towards Madrid.

Me gusta el café sin azúcar.
I like coffee without sugar.

El libro es sobre turismo en España.
The book is about tourism in Spain.

PRACTICE 2
Choose the preposition that best completes the sentence:

1. No queremos ir de viaje _____ nuestros hijos. (sobre, sin, a)

2. El mapa es _____ Carlos. (de, hacia, a)

3. _____ hoy hago dieta. (hasta, antes de, desde)

4. _____ partir, quiero ir a la catedral otra vez. (después de, antes de, durante)

5. _____ la mañana bebo mucho café. (durante, sin, a)

6. Aprender _____ hablar otro idioma no es fácil. (de, a, con)

7. Tenemos que comenzar _____ preparar la presentación. (a, con, de)

8. El mensaje es _____ algo personal. (de, sobre, a)

Tip!

When you're learning another language, it's not always easy to meet native speakers. But it's important to give yourself the chance to hear native speakers, even if you can't interact with them. Listening to the radio provides one opportunity to do that. Here are a few links that will help you find different radio stations in Spanish. The phrase that you should look for is **escucha en vivo** (*listen direct/live*):

www.radiocentro.com.mx/ (Mexico)

www.continental.com.ar/ (Argentina)

www.caracol.com.co/ (Colombia)

www.rtve.es/rne/envivo.htm (Spain)

Newspapers are also a great way to practice Spanish. A single site that will direct you to a huge number of newspapers from around the world, including, of course, Spanish-speaking countries, is *www.onlinenewspapers.com/*. Just select the country that you're interested in.

Of course, you won't be able to follow everything that you read or hear at this point, but a good strategy is to look for stories that you're already familiar with, perhaps from English-language media. Alternatively, focus on a very small piece of real Spanish, maybe a paragraph or a very short audio clip, and read or listen along with a dictionary as many times as it takes to really become familiar with it. Just be patient, and be adventurous. You'll be surprised at how easy it is to practice your new language online!

ANSWERS
PRACTICE 1: 1. Detrás del armario hay una puerta. **2.** Los turistas están fuera del museo. **3.** Mi familia vive cerca de mi casa. **4.** Detrás de su casa hay un bar. **5.** El niño está encima de la cama. **6.** Lejos de mi casa está la universidad. **7.** Los archivos están enfrente de esos libros. **8.** Los documentos están fuera del sobre.

PRACTICE 2: 1. sin; **2.** de; **3.** desde; **4.** antes de; **5.** durante; **6.** a; **7.** a; **8.** sobre

--------- Lesson 24 (conversations) ---------

CONVERSATION 1
Alfonso and Luisa are on their honeymoon in Madrid. Today they're going to visit the palace of **El Escorial,** in the foothills of the **Sierra de Guadarrama** to the northwest of Madrid. Alfonso is asking the hotel receptionist for driving directions.

Recepcionista: Este . . . ¿Sabe cómo llegar a la Gran Vía?
Alfonso: Sí, claro que sí. Hasta ahí, no me pierdo.
Recepcionista: Bien. Pues siga derecho por la Gran Vía, luego tome la avenida de la Victoria. Siga derecho hasta la salida número seis.

Alfonso:	Aquí tengo un mapa. A ver . . . sí, aquí está: salida seis, autovía del Noreste, ¿verdad?
Recepcionista:	Exactamente. Siga por ahí hasta la salida dieciocho. Siga por el carril de la derecha y tome la rampa en dirección las Rosas/el Escorial.
Alfonso:	Pues, es muy fácil. Aquí en el mapa está muy claro.
Recepcionista:	A más o menos dos kilómetros hay un peaje.
Alfonso:	¿Cuánto hay que pagar?
Recepcionista:	Mire . . . No sé. Pero no es mucho. Cuando pase el peaje, doble a la izquierda. El Escorial no está muy lejos de ahí.
Alfonso:	Bueno, le agradezco mucho su ayuda.
Recepcionista:	De nada. Buen viaje.
Alfonso:	Gracias.

Hotel clerk:	Well . . . Do you know how to get to the Gran Vía?
Alfonso:	Yes, of course. Up until there I won't get lost.
Hotel clerk:	Good. Then, go straight along the Gran Vía, then take the Avenida de la Victoria. Go straight until exit number 6.
Alfonso:	I have a map here. Let's see . . . yes, here it is: Exit 6, Northeast highway, is that right?
Hotel clerk:	Exactly. Go down through there until exit 18. Take the right lane up the ramp towards "las Rosas/el Escorial."
Alfonso:	Well, it's very easy. Here on the map, it is very clear.
Hotel clerk:	At about two kilometers, there's a toll.
Alfonso:	How much is it?
Hotel clerk:	Hmm, I don't know. But it's not much. Once you pass the toll, make a left turn. The Escorial is not far from there.
Alfonso:	Well, thank you very much for your help.
Hotel clerk:	Not at all. Have a good trip.
Alfonso:	Thank you.

NOTES

The Royal Monastery of San Lorenzo del Escorial was built between 1563 and 1584 for Felipe II and is traditionally believed to have been built in honor of St. Lawrence. Its severe and non-ornamental style became one of the most influential in Spain. The palace is a monastery, a museum, a library, and the burial place of Spanish sovereigns. The complex is a UNESCO world heritage site.

There are many myths about the **Sierra de Guadarrama,** the mountains to the northwest of Madrid. One such myth, known as **La Sima de los Pastores** (*the Shepherd's Chasm*), tells of a hidden treasure buried in one of the mountains. It is believed that a certain Rafael Corraliza, who was in charge of the financial affairs of the monastery, decided one day to run off to Portugal with the treasure. He took a route that he thought would be less guarded towards the town of **Robledondo.** It was already dark, and when he reached the area known as **Sima de los Pastores,** he was swallowed by the earth, treasure and all. It is said that St. Lawrence had something to do with this, and with time, the abyss was covered with rocks and leaves to prevent something similar from ever happening again.

NUTS & BOLTS 1
THE IMPERATIVE

Let's look at the imperative, or command form, which you would use, for instance, when giving directions.

Because there are different ways of expressing *you* in Spanish, there are different command forms, informal and formal, corresponding to **tú, usted, vosotros,** and **ustedes.** For the **tú** (infml.) command forms, just take the final **-s** off the present **tú** form of a regular verb. For example, from **tú hablas** (*you speak*), the imperative is **¡habla!** (*speak!*) In the same way, **comer** (*to eat*) becomes **¡come!** (*eat!*) and **escribir** (*to write*) becomes **¡escribe!** (*write!*) There are, of course, some irregular verbs. Here are a few:

salir (*to leave, to go out*)	¡sal! (*leave! go out!*)
decir (*to say, to tell*)	¡di! (*say! tell!*)
venir (*to come*)	¡ven! (*come!*)
hacer (*to do, to make*)	¡haz! (*do! make!*)
tener (*to have*)	¡ten! (*have!*)
poner (*to put*)	¡pon! (*put!*)
ver (*to see*)	¡ve! (*see!*)
ir (*to go*)	¡ve! (*go!*)

The command with **vosotros** (also informal) is even easier. Just take the infinitive form of the verb, drop the final **-r**, and add a **-d**! This works for all verbs. So **hablar** becomes ¡**hablad!**, **comer** becomes ¡**comed!**, **escribir** becomes ¡**escribid!**, **decir** becomes ¡**decid!**, **poner** becomes ¡**poned!**, and so on.

Let's now take a look at how to make formal commands with **usted** and **ustedes**. Take the present form of the first person singular (**yo**) of the verb, drop the final **-o**, and add **-e** or **-en** for **-ar** verbs, and add **-a** or **-an** for **-er** and **-ir** verbs.

trabajar	*to work*
¡(usted) trabaje!	*work! (sg.)*
¡(ustedes) trabajen!	*work! (pl.)*
comer	*to eat*
¡(usted) coma!	*eat! (sg.)*

¡(ustedes) coman!	eat! (pl.)
escribir	to write
¡(usted) escriba!	write! (sg.)
¡(ustedes) escriban!	write! (pl.)

As usual, there are a few irregular verbs.

saber (to know)	sepa, sepan (know!)
ser (to be)	sea, sean (be!)
ir (to go)	vaya, vayan (go!)
dar (to give)	dé, den (give!)
estar (to be)	esté, estén (be!)

PRACTICE 1
Rephrase each sentence as a command.

1. Tienes que llamar a mi secretaria.

2. Tenéis que partir a las seis de la mañana.

3. Tienen que hacer las reservaciones por internet.

4. Tienes que caminar dos cuadras y doblar a la derecha.

5. Tiene que enviar el informe hoy por la tarde.

6. Tenéis que decir la verdad.

7. Tienes que contestar el mensaje.

8. Tenéis que seguir derecho por esta calle.

9. Tiene que llamar a Marta a las diez en punto.

10. Tienen que regresar temprano.

CONVERSATION 2

Alfonso and Luisa are now at **la Puerta del Sol** in Madrid. They are lost, and Luisa is asking a woman on the street for directions to **el Palacio Real**.

Luisa: Disculpe, ¿nos puede decir cómo llegar al Palacio Real?

Señora: Vamos, es muy fácil. Está a unas pocas cuadras de aquí. Seguid derecho por esta calle que se llama calle del Arenal hasta llegar a la plaza.

Luisa: Ahí queda el teatro de la ópera, ¿no?

Señora: Sí, el teatro está a mano izquierda. Tenéis que seguir por ahí e inmediatamente doblar a mano derecha y continuar por una calle muy pequeña . . . no recuerdo el nombre.

Luisa: No importa. Podemos preguntar a alguien.

Señora: Desde allí se puede ver la Plaza de Oriente. El palacio está en frente. Y la entrada para visitantes está en la parte de atrás.

Luisa: Muchas gracias.

Señora: Si queréis tomar un café para coger fuerzas, hay una cafetería que está muy bien en la esquina de la plaza a mano izquierda.

Luisa: Con este frío, creo que un chocolate con churros es mejor idea.

Señora: ¡Vamos, en este lugar los churros son deliciosos!

Luisa: *Excuse me, could you please tell us how to get to the Royal Palace?*

Woman: *Come on, it's very easy. It's a few blocks away from here. Go straight down this street, which is called Calle del Arenal, until you reach the square.*

Luisa:	The opera theater is there, isn't it?
Woman:	Yes, the theater is on the left-hand side. You have to go through there and immediately turn right and go along a very short street . . . I don't remember its name.
Luisa:	It doesn't matter. We can ask someone.
Woman:	From there, you can see the Plaza de Oriente. The palace is in front. And the visitors' entrance is in back.
Luisa:	Many thanks.
Woman:	If you'd like to have a coffee to pick yourself up (lit., regain strength) to go on, there's a café on the corner on the left-hand side that is pretty good.
Luisa:	It's so cold, I think a chocolate with churros is a better idea.
Woman:	Well, at this place, the churros are delicious!

NOTES

La Puerta del Sol (*the Gateway of the Sun*) is Madrid's center square, one of the busiest points and one of the city's most popular meeting places. The square marks the site of the original eastern entrance to the city through a gatehouse in a castle. These have long since disappeared, and in their place there has been a succession of churches. In the late nineteenth century, the area was turned into a square, becoming the center of café society. Shaped like a half-moon, the square features a red brick building with a clock tower, which is the focus of the city's New Year's Eve celebration. Crowds fill the square on that day, and at midnight, people swallow a single grape with each toll of the bell. According to tradition, this is supposed to bring good luck through out the year.

The **Palacio Real** (*Royal Palace*) is no longer used as a residence for the royal family, who live instead in **El Palacio de la Zarzuela,** a more modest palace outside Madrid. The Royal Palace, lavish and built to impress, is used for state occasions. Construction lasted twenty-six years, and its decor reflects the exuberant tastes of two Bourbon kings: Charles III and Charles IV.

NUTS & BOLTS 2

PARA AND POR *(FOR)*

You've probably already seen the prepositions **para** and **por** in the dialogues. Both of them are usually translated into English as *for*, but they have different uses.

Para indicates a purpose (*in order to*), an intention (*intended for*), a limit in time (*by/until a certain time*), a length of time (*for*), or a destination (*towards*). Note that when used to show an intention, **para** is followed by a verb in the infinitive. Here are a few examples.

Esta carta es para Julián.
This letter is for Julián.

Este nuevo programa es para hacer diseños gráficos.
This new program is for making graphic designs.

Necesitamos el informe para mañana a las nueve en punto.
We need the report by tomorrow morning at nine o'clock.

Queremos una habitación para diez noches.
We want a room for ten nights.

Voy para Cuernavaca.
I'm going to Cuernavaca.

On the other hand, **por** is used to indicate cause or reason (*because of, due to*), or to indicate exchange (*in place of, in exchange for*). It can also mean *through*.

El viaje está cancelado por la tormenta.
The trip is canceled because of the storm.

Necesito cambiar unos dólares por pesos.
I need to exchange some dollars for pesos.

El hombre salió por esa puerta.
The man left through that door.

Pasamos por Miami de camino a Chile.
We went through Miami on our way Chile.

PRACTICE 2
Take a look at the following sentences and decide what preposition you would use in Spanish.

1. Puedes cambiar el suéter _____ otro en una talla más grande.
(*You can exchange the sweater for another one in a bigger size.*)

2. Tenemos que terminar el proyecto _____ la próxima semana.
(*We have to finish the project by next week.*)

3. El regalo es _____ su hermana. (*The present is for her daughter.*)

4. Ella está mirando _____ la ventana. (*She is looking through the window.*)

5. Ella está ahorrando _____ comprar una casa. (*She is saving in order to buy a house.*)

6. Ellos están partiendo _____ Londres. (*They are leaving for London.*)

7. _____ su retraso, no podemos empezar la conferencia. (*Because of his delay, we cannot begin the conference.*)

8. Queremos alquilar el apartamento _____ tres años. (*We want to rent the apartment for three years.*)

Tip!

Learning **por** and **para** is, again, a question of practice and being very patient with yourself. Just remember that it is not a big deal if you get these prepositions wrong. Most people will appreciate your effort and won't mind the mistakes you make.

To help you a bit, here are some colloquial expressions that you will often hear using **por**. Try to familiarize yourself with them, and experiment with using them from time to time.

¡Por Dios!	For God's sake!
¡Por fin!	At last!
por lo visto	apparently
por eso	for this reason
por lo tanto	therefore
por desgracia	unfortunately
por una parte	on the one hand
por otra parte	on the other hand
por supuesto	of course
por casualidad	by chance

Por lo visto el vuelo está retrasado.
Apparently, the flight is delayed.

Nos encontramos con María por casualidad.
We bumped into María by chance.

Por desgracia no podemos viajar mañana.
Unfortunately, we can't travel tomorrow.

ANSWERS
PRACTICE 1: 1. ¡Llama a mi secretaria! **2.** ¡Partid a las seis de la mañana! **3.** ¡Hagan las reservaciones por internet! **4.** ¡Camina dos cuadras y dobla a la derecha! **5.** ¡Envíe el informe hoy por la tarde! **6.** ¡Decid la verdad! **7.** ¡Contesta el mensaje! **8.** ¡Seguid derecho por esta calle! **9.** Llame a Marta a las diez en punto. **10.** Regresen temprano.

PRACTICE 2: 1. por; **2.** para; **3.** para; **4.** por; **5.** para; **6.** para; **7.** por; **8.** por.

UNIT 6 ESSENTIALS
Sabemos hablar italiano.
We know how to speak Italian.

Conozco Buenos Aires.
I know Buenos Aires.

¿Podemos usar tu teléfono?
Can we use your phone?

Debemos entregar este informe hoy.
We have to hand in this report today.

Él tiene que viajar a Madrid.
He has to travel to Madrid.

Vemos un partido de fútbol.
We watch a football game.

Ellos vienen de Guatemala.
They come from Guatemala.

Ese reloj da la hora exacta.
That clock tells the exact time.

Estoy hablando por teléfono.
I am talking on the phone.

Estamos comprando un regalo para Inés.
We are buying a present for Inés.

¡Haz tus deberes!
Do your homework!

¡Ven a casa después del trabajo!
Come home after work!

¡Hablad con vuestro jefe antes de partir!
Speak to your boss before leaving!

Esta tarjeta es para Manuela por su cumpleaños.
This card is for Manuela for her birthday.

Por la tormenta tomamos un tren más tarde para Berlín.
Because of the storm, we took a later train to Berlin.

UNIT 7
Shopping

In this unit, you'll learn vocabulary related to clothing and colors, as well as some useful shopping expressions. You'll also learn how to make comparisons and how to talk about future plans.

——————— Lesson 25 (words) ———————

WORD LIST 1

el cinturón	*belt*
la chaqueta	*jacket*
los pantalones	*pants*
el traje	*suit*
la camisa	*shirt*
la corbata	*tie*
los calcetines	*socks*
los vaqueros	*jeans*
la camiseta	*T-shirt*
la gabardina	*raincoat*
el saco/la chaqueta	*jacket*
el jersey/el suéter	*sweater*
los zapatos	*shoes*

NUTS & BOLTS 1
STEM-CHANGING VERBS

In previous units, you learned the conjugations of a few irregular verbs. Now we'll take a closer look at verbs that undergo stem changes when conjugated in the simple present tense. The first group includes verbs in which the -o of the infinitive changes to -ue, as in **almorzar** (*to have lunch*). Notice that this change happens in all the forms except **nosotros** and **vosotros**.

yo almuerzo	nosotros/as almorzamos
tú almuerzas	vosotros/as almorzáis
él/ella/usted almuerza	ellos/ellas/ustedes almuerzan

Here are a few more common **o to ue** verbs.

costar	*to cost*
dormir	*to sleep*
encontrar	*to find, to meet*
morir	*to die*
mostrar	*to show*
volver	*to return*
volar	*to fly*
oler	*to smell*
recordar	*to remember*
soñar	*to dream*
mover	*to move*
poder	*can, to be able*

Notice that **h-** is added to **oler** (*to smell*) in the forms where the vowel changes.

yo huelo	nosotros/as olemos
tú hueles	vosotros/as oléis
él/ella/usted huele	ellos/ellas/ustedes huelen

A second common stem change is -e to -ie, as in **pensar** (*to think*). Again, the **nosotros** and **vosotros** forms are not affected.

yo pienso	nosotros/as pensamos
tú piensas	vosotros/as pensáis
él/ella/usted piensa	ellos/ellas/ustedes piensan

Here are some other **e** to **ie** verbs.

mentir	to lie, to tell lies
entender	to understand
sentir	to feel
cerrar	to close
comenzar	to begin
despertarse	to wake up
sentarse	to sit down

¿Cuánto cuesta esa camisa?
How much does that shirt cost?

Ellos sueñan con tener mucho dinero.
They dream about having a lot of money.

La clase comienza en veinte minutos.
The class begins in twenty minutes.

No entiendo lo que estás diciendo.
I don't understand what you are saying.

PRACTICE 1
Complete the following sentences with one of the following verbs:

pensar/dormir/sentir/costar/comenzar/cerrar/encontrar/entender/mostrar/volar

1. Yo _____ dolor en la espalda.

2. Yo no _____. ¿Puede hablar más despacio por favor?

3. Las tiendas abren a las nueve y media de la mañana y _____ a las ocho de la noche.

4. Ella _____ las camisetas de algodón al cliente.

5. ¿Cuánto _____ esa blusa roja?

6. Tú no _____ una corbata que combine con la camisa.

7. Mi bebita _____ once horas todas las noches.

8. Nosotros siempre _____ con la misma aerolínea.

9. La película _____ a las cinco.

10. Tú _____ demasiado en tus problemas.

WORD LIST 2

la falda	*skirt*
el vestido	*dress*
el abrigo	*overcoat*
la blusa	*blouse*

el bolso	*handbag*
el traje de baño/el bañador	*bathing suit*
la bata	*robe*
las sandalias	*sandals*
la bufanda	*scarf*
los guantes	*gloves*
las medias	*stockings*

NUTS & BOLTS 2
MORE STEM-CHANGING VERBS

There is another group of verbs with stems that change from -e to -i. **Pedir** (*to ask for*) is one example.

pedir (*to ask for*)

yo pido	nosotros/as pedimos
tú pides	vosotros/as pedís
él/ella/usted pide	ellos/ellas/ustedes piden

Here are some other common -e to -i verbs.

conseguir	*to find, to get, to obtain*
medir	*to measure*
reír	*to laugh*
repetir	*to repeat*
servir	*to serve*
impedir	*to prevent*
sonreír	*to smile*

Take a look at **sonreír** (*to smile*), which is just like **reír** (*to laugh*). Notice where the accent goes.

sonreír (*to smile*)

yo sonrío	nosotros/as sonreímos
tú sonríes	vosotros/as sonreís
él/ella/usted sonríe	ellos/ellas/ustedes sonríen

Finally, some verbs ending in **-cer** or **-cir** have the irregularity of adding a **-z** before the ending in the first person singular. Take **agradecer** (*to be thankful*) as an example.

agradecer (*to be thankful*)

yo agradezco	nosotros/as agradecemos
tú agradeces	vosotros/as agradecéis
él/ella/usted agradece	ellos/ellas/ustedes agradecen

Other common examples include the following.

ofrecer	*to offer*
producir	*to produce*
conducir	*to drive*
traducir	*to translate*

Verbs ending in **-ger** and **-gir** change the **-g** to **-j** in the first person singular. One example is **escoger** (*to choose*).

escoger (*to choose*)

yo escojo	nosotros/as escogemos
tú escoges	vosotros/as escogéis
él/ella/usted escoge	ellos/ellas/ustedes escogen

Here are some other examples.

elegir	*to choose*
exigir	*to demand*
proteger	*to protect*
dirigir	*to direct*

Él no consigue trabajo.
He doesn't find work.

Tú sonríes poco.
You don't smile a lot. (lit., You smile little.)

Yo conduzco un auto verde.
I drive a green car.

Yo exijo una explicación.
I demand an explanation.

PRACTICE 2
Conjugate the verb in parentheses.

1. La maestra _____ las oraciones varias veces. (repetir)
2. Yo _____ un auto viejo. (conducir)

3. El presidente _____ la reunión. (dirigir)

4. Ella siempre _____ películas extranjeras. (escoger)

5. Tú _____ demasiado dae tus empleados. (exigir)

6. Ellos _____ la mesa. (medir)

7. La estación de televisión _____ siete series cada año. (producir)

8. Ellos _____ una película de cine. (escoger)

Tip!

There will be times when you're speaking to a native Spanish speaker when you will simply not understand what he or she has just said. The best thing you can do in such circumstances is to let the person know that you are having a bit of trouble. Here are a few phrases that can help you.

Disculpe, ¿puede repetir lo que acaba de decir, por favor?
Sorry, could you please repeat what you just said?

No entiendo.
I don't understand.

¿Qué significa . . . ?
What does . . . mean?

Disculpe, ¿cómo dijo?
Sorry, what did you say?

ANSWERS

PRACTICE 1: **1.** siento; **2.** entiendo; **3.** cierran; **4.** muestra; **5.** cuesta; **6.** encuentras; **7.** duerme; **8.** volamos; **9.** comienza; **10.** piensas

PRACTICE 2: **1.** repite; **2.** conduzco; **3.** dirige; **4.** escoge; **5.** exiges; **6.** miden; **7.** produce; **8.** escogen

PHRASE LIST 1

ir de compras	*to go shopping*
llevar una prenda puesta	*to wear something*
ir de escaparates	*to go window-shopping*
buscar gangas	*to look for bargains*
comprar en rebaja	*to buy on sale*
comprar en el mercado de pulgas/comprar en el mercadillo	*to buy at the flea market*
probarse algo	*to try something on*
hacer a la medida	*to custom sew*
lavar en seco	*to dry-clean*
lavar a mano	*to hand wash*

NUTS & BOLTS 1
COMPARATIVES

In English, you can compare things with the formula *more/-er* or *less* + adjective/adverb/noun + *than*. In Spanish, the *more* comparative formula is **más** + adjective/adverb/noun + **que.**

Mi hermana es más alta que mi madre.
My sister is taller than my mother.

Tú caminas más rápido que yo.
You walk faster than I (do).

Juan tiene más camisas que su hermano.
Juan has more shirts than his brother.

But just like in English, there are a few exceptions. The following adjectives have a different form for the comparative.

bueno/a—mejor	*good—better*
malo/a—peor	*bad—worse*
grande—mayor	*big—bigger/older*
pequeño/a—menor	*small—smaller/younger*

Esta camisa me queda mejor que la azul.
This shirt fits me better than the blue one.

Esta corbata se ve peor que la otra.
This tie looks worse than the other.

Ella es mayor que nuestra hija.
She is older than our daughter.

Mi hermana es dos años menor que yo.
My sister is two years younger than I (am).

When you want to show inferiority, you will use **menos** + adjective/adverb/noun + **que.**

Yo soy menos tímida que mi amiga Rocío.
I am less shy than my friend Rocío.

Nosotros vamos al cine menos frecuentemente que vosotros.
We go to the movies less often than you (do).

Pedro tiene menos dinero que su esposa.
Pedro has less money than his wife.

PRACTICE 1
Fill in the blank with the words in parentheses.

1. Yo trabajo _____ tú. (*fewer hours than*)

2. Vosotros viajáis _____ nosotros. (*more frequently than*)

3. Esa película es _____ la de las once y media. (*longer than*)

4. Este bolso es _____ el negro. (*more expensive than*)

5. Tú lees _____ yo. (*fewer books than*)

6. Ellos tienen _____ sus padres. (*more problems than*)

7. Esta chaqueta es _____ la otra. (*more elegant than*)

8. Carlos es _____ su esposa. (*ten years older than*)

PHRASE LIST 2

¿Qué desea?	*What would you like?*
¿De qué color?	*What color?*
¿Cuánto vale?	*How much is it?*
¿Algo más?	*Anything else?*
No, gracias; eso es todo.	*No, thanks; that's all.*
Me queda mal.	*It doesn't fit me.*
Te quedan bien.	*They fit you well.*
¡Qué elegante!	*How elegant!*
Me lo llevo.	*I'll take it.*
Es muy costoso.	*It's very expensive.*

NUTS & BOLTS 2
EQUAL COMPARISONS AND SUPERLATIVES
There will be times when you want to compare two people or things that are equal. In this case, you will use the form **tan** + adjective/adverb + **como.**

Madrid es tan interesante como Nueva York.
Madrid is as interesting as New York.

La vida en Madrid es tan rápida como en Nueva York.
Life in Madrid is as fast as in New York.

To compare two phrases, you need to use **tanto,** which will agree in gender and number with the noun it precedes.

Carmen tiene tanta paciencia como tú.

Carmen has as much patience as you (do).

Ella tiene tanto dinero como su padre.

She has as much money as her father (does).

Ella tiene tantos gastos como ustedes.

She has as many expenses as you (do).

Ella tiene tantas sandalias como yo.

She has as many sandals as I (do).

When you use expressions like *the biggest, the worst, the most exciting,* and *the least difficult,* you are using superlatives. Forming superlatives in Spanish is very easy: simply add the corresponding definite article (**el, la, los, las**) to the patterns you've already learned, and use the preposition **de** when you want to express *in/of.*

Este vestido es el más costoso (de todos).

This dress is the most expensive (of all) .

La falda roja es la más fea.

The red skirt is the ugliest.

Marta es la menos extrovertida de la familia.

Marta is the least extroverted in the family.

Ellos son los menos puntuales de todos mis amigos.

They are the least punctual of all my friends.

Mis hermanas son las más altas de la clase.

My sisters are the tallest in the class.

Ese edificio es el más alto.

That building is the highest.

PRACTICE 2

Fill in the blanks with the Spanish equivalents of the words in parentheses.

1. Mi oficina es _____ la tuya. (*as big as*)
2. Estos tiquetes son _____. (*the least expensive*)
3. Nuestra habitación es _____ las tres. (*the smallest of*)
4. Es _____ película del año. (*the worst*)
5. Ella lleva el vestido _____. (*the prettiest*)
6. Los zapatos cafés son _____. (*the most comfortable*)
7. Me gusta el chocolate _____ a ti. (*as much as*)
8. Él tiene _____ trabajo del mundo. (*the best*)

Tip!

A good way to improve your Spanish vocabulary is to read short passages from newspapers or magazines, many of which you can, of course, find online. Before you begin to read an article, it is important that you focus on the title of the article and look at any pictures that are attached to it. Skim quickly over the entire text, looking for information that will help you get the gist of the content. In this way, you can familiarize yourself with the topic and begin to anticipate the information that you'll read. Read the text only a couple of times, and don't focus on each individual word. It's more important that you get the overall picture. Trying to understand and learn each little word will only cause you to give up and feel frustrated. For now, focus on the big picture, and then move on to something else. Soon enough, you'll be able to worry about all the little details! To find some practice material, go to your favorite search engine and type in **revistas en español** (*magazines in Spanish*) or **periódicos en español** (*newspapers in Spanish*).

ANSWERS

PRACTICE 1: 1. menos horas que; **2.** más frecuentemente que; **3.** más larga que; **4.** más costoso que; **5.** menos libros que; **6.** más problemas que; **7.** más elegante que; **8.** diez años mayor que.

PRACTICE 2: 1. tan grande como; **2.** los menos costosos; **3.** la más pequeña de; **4.** la peor; **5.** más bonito; **6.** los más cómodos; **7.** tanto como; **8.** el mejor.

Lesson 27 (sentences)

SENTENCE LIST 1

¿Qué número calza?	*What shoe size do you wear?*
Calzo el número treinta y siete.	*I wear shoe size 37.*
¿Qué talla lleva usted?	*What size do you wear?*
No estoy seguro.	*I'm not sure.*
Mi talla es cuarenta.	*I wear size 40.*
¿Le gustaría probarse este suéter?	*Would you like to try this sweater on?*
¿Ya lo atendieron?	*Has someone helped you?*
Gracias, sólo estoy mirando.	*Thanks, I'm just looking.*
¿Dónde está el probador?	*Where is the dressing room?*
Estoy buscando un vestido de noche informal.	*I'm looking for a casual evening dress.*

NUTS & BOLTS 1

DIRECT OBJECT PRONOUNS

A direct object is a noun (or pronoun) that shows you what the verb is acting on. For example, in the sentence *Manuel is buying a sweater,* the direct object is the noun *sweater*—it's the answer to the question *what is Manuel buying?* A direct object can also be a person, as in *Manuel sees the salesperson,* in answer to the question *who does Manuel see?*

Direct object pronouns are the pronouns used to replace direct object nouns, such as *sweater* or *salesperson* in our examples above. In English, there are some different pronouns used as direct objects: *me* instead of *I*, *her* instead of *she*, *him* instead of *he*, etc. Spanish is no different. Here are all of the direct object pronouns in Spanish.

me	*me*	nos	*us*
te	*you (infml.)*	os	*all of you (infml.)*
lo	*him, it, you (fml.)*	los	*them, you*
la	*her, it, you (fml.)*	las	*them, you*

Don't forget that nouns in Spanish can be feminine or masculine, even if they're inanimate. So, **lo** can mean *he* or *it* for a masculine noun, and **la** can mean *she* or *it* for a feminine noun. The same is true of **los** and **las**, in the plural. The direct object pronouns that correspond to **usted** are **lo** and **la**, and the ones that correspond to **ustedes** are **los** and **las**. The difference depends on whether you are talking to a man or a woman.

Yo amo a María.
I love María.

Yo la amo.
I love her.

Manuela llama a Pedro.
Manuela calls Pedro.

Manuela lo llama.
Manuela calls him. ·

Ellos visitan a María y Clara.
They visit María and Clara.

Ellos las visitan.

They visit them.

Now let's look at how direct object pronouns are used. In Spanish, as you saw in the examples above, they come right before the verb.

Carlos no te conoce.

Carlos doesn't know you.

Los oigo pero no los veo.

I hear them, but I don't see them.

Nosotros no la olvidamos.

We don't forget her.

However, if the main verb appears in the infinitive form (ending in **-ar**, **-er**, or **-ir**), the direct object pronoun can come either before the verbal phrase or after the infinitive, in which case the pronoun is attached to it.

Carlos te quiere conocer.

Carlos wants to meet you.

Carlos quiere conocerte.

Carlos wants to meet you.

Los puedo oír pero no los puedo ver.

I can hear them, but I can't see them.

Puedo oírlos pero no puedo verlos.

I can hear them, but I can't see them.

Nosotros no queremos olvidarla.

We don't want to forget her.

Nosotros no la queremos olvidar.

We don't want to forget her.

A similar thing happens with the present participial (**-ando**, **-endo**) form. Notice the use of the accent mark, which ensures that the stress remains on the same syllable as it would if there were no participial ending.

Te estoy ayudando.
I am helping you.

Estoy ayudándote.
I am helping you.

PRACTICE 1

Replace the direct object noun with a pronoun.

1. La señorita atiende al cliente.

2. Ella está comprando unos zapatos.

3. Mis hijas van a hacer una fiesta el viernes.

4. Yo voy a traer unas flores.

5. Vais a escribir una carta.

6. Estoy enviando un mensaje a Roberto.

7. Manuel conoce a tu familia.

8. Mis amigos llaman a María todos los días.

SENTENCE LIST 2

¿Puedo probarme esta falda?	*Can I try this skirt on?*
¿Me puede hacer un descuento?	*Can you give me a discount?*
¿Está rebajado?	*Is it reduced/on sale?*
¿Cómo le quedan?	*How do they fit?*
Me quedan un poco cortos.	*They are a bit short.*
Ese color es el último grito de la moda.	*That color is very trendy right now.*

¿Cuánto cuesta la cartera negra de cuero?	*How much is the black leather handbag?*
¿Dónde se encuentran chaquetas para caballero?	*Where can I find men's jackets?*
La chaqueta no combina bien con los pantalones.	*The jacket doesn't go well with the pants.*

NUTS & BOLTS 2

THE FUTURE WITH IR A *(GOING TO)*

Now let's take a look at how we can talk about things we are planning on doing tomorrow or in the near future. In Spanish, there is a very simple formula: **ir** (*to go*) + **a** (*to*) + verb in the infinitive. This is the equivalent of *going to* in English.

Yo voy a comprar un traje.
I am going to buy a suit.

Tú vas a ir de compras por la tarde.
You are going to go shopping in the afternoon.

Ella va a estrenar su chaqueta el martes.
She is going to wear her jacket for the first time on Tuesday.

Usted va a viajar a España.
You are going to travel to Spain.

Nosotros vamos a mirar escaparates.
We are going to go window-shopping.

Vosotros vais a buscar zapatos.
You are going to look for shoes.

Ellos van a probarse los vestidos.
They are going to try the dresses on.

Ustedes van a descansar.
You are going to rest.

Here are some useful time expressions that you can use to show a time in the future.

hoy	today
hoy por la tarde	today in the afternoon
hoy por la noche	today in the evening
mañana	tomorrow
mañana por la mañana	tomorrow morning
mañana por la tarde	tomorrow afternoon
mañana por la noche	tomorrow evening
más tarde	later
esta tarde	this afternoon
esta noche	this evening
la semana que viene	next week
el mes que viene	next month
el año que viene	next year

PRACTICE 2
Answer the following questions using the information in parentheses.

1. ¿Cuándo van a ir a Los Ángeles? (ellos—en diciembre)

2. ¿Qué vas a comprar? (yo—unos pantalones y unos zapatos)

3. ¿A dónde vais de vacaciones? (nosotros—Costa Rica)

4. ¿Cuántas personas va a invitar a la fiesta? (ella—45 personas)

5. ¿Qué película van a ver? (nosotros—una película de Almodóvar)

6. ¿A qué hora vas a salir de la oficina? (yo—a las 3:30 P.M.)

7. ¿Cuántas camisas tengo que comprar? (tú—tres)

8. ¿Cuándo van a hacer la presentación? (ellas—el martes por la tarde)

Tip!

You're probably going to need a few more adjectives to describe the way clothes and shoes fit. Here is a very useful list.

ajustado/a	*tight*
suelto/a	*loose/flowing*
escotado/a	*low-cut*
ancho/a	*baggy/wide*
enterizo/a	*one-piece*
de dos piezas	*two-piece*
cómodo/a	*comfortable*
incómodo/a	*uncomfortable*
suave	*soft*
duro	*hard*

Los vestidos sueltos y escotados son perfectos para noches de verano.
Loose and low-cut dresses are perfect for summer nights.

Estos zapatos no son tan suaves como los negros.
These shoes are not as soft as the black ones.

Los trajes de baño enterizos son más cómodos que los de dos piezas.
One-piece bathing suits are more comfortable than two-piece ones.

Estos pantalones están muy ajustados.
These pants are very tight.

ANSWERS

PRACTICE 1: 1. La señorita lo atiende. **2.** Ella los está comprando/Ella está comprándolos. **3.** Mis hijas la van a hacer el viernes. **4.** Yo las voy a traer/Yo voy a traerlas. **5.** Vais a escribirla/La vais a escribir. **6.** Estoy enviándolo a Roberto/Lo estoy enviando a Roberto. **7.** Manuel la conoce. **8.** Mis amigos la llaman todos los días.

PRACTICE 2: 1. Ellos van a ir en diciembre. **2.** Voy a comprar unos pantalones y unos zapatos. **3.** Vamos a ir a Costa Rica. **4.** Ella va a invitar a cuarenta y cinco personas. **5.** Vamos a ver una película de Almodóvar. **6.** Voy a salir a las tres y media de la tarde. **7.** Tienes que comprar tres camisas. **8.** Ellas van a hacer la presentación el martes por la tarde.

--------------------- Lesson 28 (conversations) ---------------------

CONVERSATION 1

Juan is at a men's shop trying on some clothes, because he is going on vacation with his girlfriend next week and he needs a few things.

Vendedora:	**¿Qué tal le quedan los pantalones, señor?**
Juan:	**Estos vaqueros azul claro son muy anchos y estos negros son demasiado ajustados. ¿Tiene una talla intermedia?**
Vendedora:	**Espere un momento. Voy a buscar a ver qué encuentro. Y las camisetas, ¿qué tal?**
Juan:	**La anaranjada parece ser de un material más ligero que la verde, ¿no es verdad?**
Vendedora:	**Sí, la anaranjada es cien por ciento de algodón. El color es el último grito de la moda y le queda mejor que la verde. Claro, es también más costosa.**
Juan:	**¿Tiene más en mi talla?**
Vendedora:	**Sí, creo que sí. ¿Tiene algún color en mente?**

Juan:	Me gustaría llevar dos blancas, una azul oscura y otra en amarillo o rojo.
Vendedora:	Si gusta esperar un momento, voy a buscar los vaqueros y otras camisetas. Ya regreso.
Juan:	Mientras espero voy a mirar por ahí a ver qué más encuentro.
Vendedora:	Muy bien. Hay pantalones cortos y bañadores en descuento allá enfrente.

Saleswoman:	*Do the pants fit, sir?*
Juan:	*These light blue jeans are too loose, and these black ones are too tight. Do you have something in between?*
Saleswoman:	*Wait a moment. I'll take a look and see what I can find. What about the T-shirts?*
Juan:	*The orange one seems to be made of a lighter material than the green one, right?*
Saleswoman:	*Yes, the orange one is one hundred percent cotton. The color is very trendy nowadays, and it suits you better than the green one. Of course, it's more expensive.*
Juan:	*Do you have more in my size?*
Saleswoman:	*Yes, I think so. Do you have a color in mind?*
Juan:	*I'd like to take two white ones, a dark blue one, and another one in yellow or red.*
Saleswoman:	*If you'd like to wait a moment, I'll go get the jeans and the T-shirts. I'll be back soon.*
Juan:	*While I wait, I'll take a look over there to see what else I find.*
Saleswoman:	*Very well. There are shorts and bathing suits on sale over there in the front.*

NOTES

When it comes to clothes, you'll find that there are different words for the same item across the Spanish-speaking world. In Latin America, for example, *blue jeans* are **los jeans,** *sweater* is **un suéter,** and *jacket* is **una chaqueta, un saco,** or **una americana.** But in Spain, a pair of blue jeans is **un vaquero,** a sweater is **un suéter** or **un jersey,** and a jacket may be referred to as **un saco.**

And when it comes to talking about underwear, no one seems to agree: *women's underwear* can be **bragas, bombachas, calzoncitos,** or **pantis,** and *men's underwear* may be **calzones** or **calzoncillos.** *Stockings* are **medias** or **pantymedias,** and *socks* are **calcetines** or **medias.** *Slippers* are known as **zapatillas, pantuflas,** or **chinelas,** and a *robe* is a **bata, albornoz,** or **deshabillé.** So, what to do? When in Rome do, as the Romans, and simply use the words people use where you are!

NUTS & BOLTS 1
REFLEXIVE VERBS

Reflexive verbs are verbs in which the subject performs the action on him- or herself. Spanish reflexive verbs often correspond to English verbs that use reflexive pronouns, like *to wash oneself, to dress oneself,* and so on. But there are also many verbs that are reflexive in Spanish but are not reflexive in English. Spanish reflexive verbs are conjugated following the same rules as **-ar, -er, -ir,** or irregular verbs, but their infinitives always end in **-se.** When reflexive verbs are conjugated, they always take the following reflexive pronouns.

me (*myself*)	nos (*ourselves*)
te (*yourself*)	os (*yourselves*)
se (*himself, herself, itself, yourself*)	se (*themselves, yourselves*)

These pronouns come before the conjugated verb. Let's take a look at **levantarse,** which means *to get up.*

(yo) me levanto	*I get up*
(tú) te levantas	*you get up*
(él/ella/usted) se levanta	*he/she/it gets up*

(nosotros/as) nos levantamos	*we get up*
(vosotros/as) os levantáis	*you get up*
(ellos/ellas/ustedes) se levantan	*they/you get up*

When a reflexive verb is used with other verbs, like in the present continuous with **estar** or the immediate future with **ir,** the reflexive pronoun can be placed either before the verb phrase or after it. If it comes after, it's attached to the end of the main verb.

(Yo) me levanto a las seis todos los días.
I get up at six every day.

En este momento me estoy levantando.
Right now, I am getting up.

En este momento estoy levantándome.
Right now, I am getting up.

Mañana me voy a levantar tarde.
Tomorrow I'm going to get up late.

Mañana voy a levantarme tarde.
Tomorrow I'm going to get up late.

Here are some more common reflexive verbs in Spanish. Again, notice that some of them can be translated reflexively in English, but not all of them.

acostarse	*to go to bed*
llamarse	*to be called*
vestirse	*to get dressed, to dress oneself*

ponerse	to put something on
divertirse	to have fun
ducharse	to shower
bañarse	to bathe (oneself)
sentarse	to sit down, to seat oneself
sentirse	to feel
despedirse	to say good-bye

You've probably noticed that if you take off the -se ending of the reflexive infinitive, you're left with another, non-reflexive verb. Our first example, **levantarse**, is like this. **Levantarse** means *to get up, to rise,* or *to lift oneself from a seated or reclining position,* but **levantar** simply means *to lift* or *to raise (something else).* Similar pairs are **llamar** (*to call*) and **llamarse** (*to call oneself, to be called*), **vestir** (*to dress someone else*) and **vestirse** (*to get dressed, to dress oneself*), and so on. Here are some more examples of reflexive verbs.

Me siento muy feliz.
I feel very happy.

Ella se va a despedir de su familia esta tarde.
She's going to say good-bye to her family this afternoon.

Ellos se están vistiendo para la fiesta.
They are getting dressed for the party.

Also note that reflexives can have a reciprocal sense. In the plural form, the reflexive pronoun can sometimes mean *each other* or *one another,* as in these sentences.

Nos miramos.
We look at each other.

Ellos se están besando.
They are kissing each other.

Los perros se huelen.
The dogs smell one another.

PRACTICE 1
Combine the following words to form sentences, conjugating the verbs as necessary.

1. Yo/llamarse/Pedro Campos.

2. Ellos/ir a divertirse/en la fiesta de esta noche.

3. Él/ir a sentarse/a leer el periódico.

4. En este momento/estar probándose/el vestido.

5. ¿A qué hora/levantarse/usted todos los días?

6. Ellos/acostarse/muy tarde los fines de semana.

7. ¿Vosotros/estar mirando/en el espejo ahora?

8. Después de/trotar/ella/ir a bañarse.

CONVERSATION 2
Now listen in as Sara, Juan's girlfriend, does some shopping of her own.

Vendedora:	¿Ya la atendieron?
Sara:	Gracias. ¿Cuánto cuesta la cartera negra de cuero? No tiene una etiqueta con el precio.
Vendedora:	Vamos a ver . . . Tiene razón. Estos bolsos están rebajados y tienen un treinta por ciento de descuento.
Sara:	¡Es una ganga! Me lo llevo. También me gustaría probarme unos zapatos.
Vendedora:	¿Qué número calza?
Sara:	Treinta y siete.

Vendedora:	La talla treinta y siete está en esta sección. ¿Busca algún color en particular?
Sara:	Sí, quiero unos zapatos que vayan con el bolso negro.
Vendedora:	Aquí hay unos muy bonitos y con un tacón no muy alto. Son muy cómodos. ¿Le gustan?
Sara:	A ver . . . me los voy a probar. ¡Me quedan como anillo al dedo! ¡Me los llevo! ¿Están también rebajados?
Vendedora:	Soñar no cuesta nada, ¿verdad? Desafortunadamente, no.
Sara:	Bueno, no importa. Son bonitos y me quedan bien.

Saleswoman:	Is someone helping you?
Sara:	Thank you. How much is the black leather bag? It doesn't have a price tag.
Saleswoman:	Let's see . . . You're right. These handbags are on sale, and they are thirty percent off.
Sara:	That's a bargain! I'll take it. I'd also like to try on some shoes.
Saleswoman:	What size do you wear?
Sara:	Thirty-seven.
Saleswoman:	Size thirty-seven is in this section. Are you looking for any particular color?
Sara:	Yes, I'd like a pair of shoes that go with the black bag.
Saleswoman:	Here are some very pretty ones with a not-so-high heel. They are very comfortable. Do you like them?
Sara:	Let's see . . . I'm going to try them on. They fit me like a glove! I'll take them! Are they also on sale?
Saleswoman:	It doesn't hurt to ask! (lit., "To dream doesn't cost anything, right?") Unfortunately, no . . .
Sara:	Well, it doesn't matter. They're pretty and they fit me well.

NOTES

As you learn Spanish, you'll see that there's a saying for just about anything and everything. There are two sayings in the above dialogue. The first one, **Me queda como anillo al dedo,** is equivalent of the English saying *It fits me like a glove.* The second one, **Soñar no cuesta nada,** literally means *To dream doesn't cost anything,* but in this context, you can translate it as *It doesn't hurt to ask.*

NUTS & BOLTS 2
COLORS, PATTERNS, AND FABRICS
Here are the colors in Spanish.

amarillo	*yellow*
azul	*blue*
celeste	*sky blue*
azul marino	*navy blue*
rojo	*red*
verde	*green*
marrón/café	*brown*
negro	*black*
blanco	*white*
gris	*gray*
naranja/anaranjado	*orange*
morado	*purple*
rosa/rosado	*pink*
dorado	*gold*
plateado	*silver*

Remember that most colors have to agree in gender and number with the noun they modify. Exceptions are those ending in -e or in a consonant like, **verde, azul, marrón, café,** and **celeste,** which only have to agree in number.

Este vestido plateado no combina con esos zapatos rojos.
This silver dress doesn't match those red shoes.

Las camisas amarillas son más costosas que las azules.
The yellow shirts are more expensive than the blue ones.

Los zapatos cafés no me gustan.
I don't like the brown shoes.

Here are a few more adjectives you can use with colors to describe clothes.

a rayas	*striped*
a cuadros	*plaid*
estampado	*with a pattern, patterned*
de lunares	*polka-dot*
oscuro	*dark*
claro	*light*

And here are some types of fabric.

algodón	*cotton*
lana	*wool*
lino	*linen*

seda	silk
cuero	leather
plástico	plastic
gamuza	suede
poliéster	polyester

Me gusta la camisa de algodón de rayas azules y grises.
I like the blue and gray striped cotton shirt.

Quiero una chaqueta de gamuza café.
I want a brown suede jacket.

La falda roja a cuadros de lana es muy costosa.
The red plaid wool skirt is very expensive.

PRACTICE 2
Answer using complete sentences. ¿De qué color son estas cosas?

1. las naranjas
2. el océano
3. la luna
4. los limones

5. el sol
6. la sangre
7. el césped
8. el carbón

Culture note
Just like in English, there are many idiomatic expressions in Spanish using colors. Here are a few.

ponerse rojo como un tomate	*to be embarrassed (lit., to turn red like a tomato)*
ponerse colorado	*to be embarrassed (lit., to turn red)*
estar rojo de la ira	*to be very angry (lit., to be red with fury)*

contar un chiste verde	to tell an obscene joke (lit., to tell a green joke)
ver todo negro	to be a pessimist (lit., to see everything as black)
ver todo color de rosa	to be an optimist, to wear rose colored glasses (lit., to see everything pink)
ir de punta en blanco	to be dressed to the nines (lit., to go from the tip in white)
ser de sangre azul	to have blue blood (lit., to be of blue blood)
estar negro de la risa	to laugh very hard (lit., to turn black with laughter)

ANSWERS

PRACTICE 1: 1. Yo me llamo Pedro Campos. 2. Ellos van a divertirse/se van a divertir en la fiesta de esta noche. 3. Él se va a sentar/va a sentarse a leer el periódico. 4. En este momento me estoy probando/estoy probándome el vestido. 5. ¿A qué hora se levanta usted todos los días? 6. Ellos se acuestan muy tarde los fines de semana. 7. ¿Os estáis mirando en el espejo ahora? 8. Después de trotar, ella se va a bañar/va a bañarse.

PRACTICE 2: 1. Las naranjas son anaranjadas. 2. El océano es azul. 3. La luna es blanca. 4. Los limones son amarillos. 5. El sol es amarillo. 6. La sangre es roja. 7. El césped es verde. 8. El carbón es negro.

UNIT 7 ESSENTIALS

La clase comienza a las tres y media de la tarde.

The class starts at 3:30 P.M.

Yo siempre pienso en ti.

I always think about you.

Tú pides demasiado de una relación.

You ask too much out of a relationship.

Yo agradezco tu ayuda.
I am thankful for your help.

Yo escojo siempre el mismo color.
I always choose the same color.

Juan tiene más camisas cafés que su hermano.
Juan has more brown shirts than his brother.

Pedro tiene menos dinero que su esposa.
Pedro has less money than his wife.

Esta camisa me queda mejor que la azul.
This shirt fits me better than the blue one.

Ella tiene tantas sandalias como yo.
She has as many sandals as I do.

Carlos no te conoce.
Carlos doesn't know you.

Carlos quiere conocerte.
Carlos wants to meet you.

Carlos te quiere conocer.
Carlos wants to meet you.

Yo voy a comprar un traje.
I am going to buy a suit.

Ellas van a probarse los vestidos.
They are going to try the dresses on.

Ellos se están vistiendo para la fiesta.
They are getting dressed for the party.

UNIT 8
Let's eat!

In this unit, you'll learn how to order food at a restaurant and how to do some grocery shopping in Spanish. You will also learn how to talk about things that happened in the past.

———————————— Lesson 29 (words) ————————————

WORD LIST 1

el desayuno	*breakfast*
el almuerzo	*lunch*
la merienda	*snack time*
la cena	*dinner*
la comida	*food, dinner*
la cuchara	*spoon*
el tenedor	*fork*
el cuchillo	*knife*
el vaso	*glass*
la copa	*wineglass*
la taza	*cup*
el plato	*plate, dish*
la servilleta	*napkin*
la carta, el menú	*menu*
la cuenta	*bill, check*
la propina	*tip*

NUTS & BOLTS 1
INDIRECT OBJECT PRONOUNS
Take a look at this sentence: *I gave him the book.* You already know that *the book* is the thing given; it's the direct object. But there's a second type of object in that sentence, too. *Him* is an indirect ob-

ject pronoun. It could also be expressed as *to him,* as in *I gave the book to him.* Indirect object pronouns tell us to whom or for whom an action is done. Let's take a look at them in Spanish.

me	*(to/for) me*
te	*(to/for) you (infml. sg.)*
le	*(to/for) him, her, it, you (fml. sg.)*
nos	*(to/for) us*
os	*(to/for) you (infml. pl.)*
les	*(to/for) them, you (fml. pl.)*

Indirect object pronouns can be used to replace indirect object nouns.

¿Qué vas a ofrecer a tus invitados?
What are you going to offer your guests?

Les voy a ofrecer champaña.
I'm going to offer them champagne.

¿Qué le vas a regalar a Pablo?
What are you going to give Pablo?

Le voy a regalar una guitarra.
I'm going to give him a guitar.

Notice that since **le** and **les** can refer to several things, you can also use them along with a phrase like **a él, a ella, a Pablo, a usted, a ellos, a ellas,** or **a ustedes** to avoid misunderstanding.

No les voy a comprar nada a ellos.
I'm not going to buy anything for them.

Le dijimos la verdad a él.

We told him the truth.

In addition, you'll see that Spanish speakers often like to emphasize the indirect object pronoun by using **a mí, a ti, a nosotros/ as, a vosotros/as,** and so on, even when these expressions are not necessary for clarification.

Ellas nos dan la receta a nosotros.

They give us the recipe.

Tú me escribes una carta a mí.

You write a letter to me.

¿Qué nos vas a comprar a nosotros?

What are you going to buy for us?

Les voy a enviar unas tarjetas a mis primos.

I'm going to send some cards to my cousins.

Just like direct object pronouns, indirect object pronouns are placed before a single conjugated verb or verb phrase; or attached to the end of a verbal phrase.

Margarita le da el plato a Laura.

Margarita gives Laura the dish.

Margarita le está dando el plato a Laura.

Margarita is giving Laura the dish.

Margarita está dándole el plato a Laura.

Margarita is giving Laura the dish.

Margarita le va a dar el plato a Laura.

Margarita is going to give Laura the dish.

Margarita va a darle el plato a Laura.

Margarita is going to give Laura the dish.

With commands, the indirect object pronoun is attached to affirmative commands, but placed before negative ones.

Por favor, póngame tres kilos de limones.
Please give me three kilos of lemons.

No nos dé leche en polvo.
Do not give us powdered milk.

Tráigame una servilleta.
Bring me a napkin.

No me sirva el almuerzo frío.
Don't serve me a cold lunch.

PRACTICE 1
Fill in the blank with the appropriate indirect object pronoun.

1. Ella _____ sirve la comida a él.

2. Él _____ regala unas flores a ella.

3. Voy a escribir_____ una carta a ellas.

4. El mesero _____ trae la carta a nosotras.

5. Ella _____ trae un regalo a ustedes.

6. Tú _____ das los dos litros de leche a mí.

7. _____ vamos a enviar una invitación muy especial a vosotros.

8. Por favor, traiga_____ un cuchillo a nosotros.

WORD LIST 2
Here is some more useful vocabulary you can use to talk about food.

la comida	*food*
el pan	*bread*

la carne	*meat*
el pollo	*chicken*
el cerdo	*pork*
el vegetal	*vegetable*
el tomate	*tomato*
el frijol	*bean*
la mantequilla	*butter*
el jugo	*juice*
el arroz	*rice*
duro/a	*hard*
sobrecocido/a	*overcooked*
quemado/a	*burnt*
picante	*spicy*
podrido/a	*bad, rotten*
pasado/a	*spoiled*
agrio/a	*sour*
dulce	*sweet*
salado/a	*salty*
amargo/a	*bitter*
a la parrilla	*grilled*
frito/a	*fried*
ahumado/a	*smoked*

NUTS & BOLTS 2
ADVERBS

Adverbs are words that are used to describe a verb, an adjective, or another adverb, like the word *happily*. In English, a lot of adverbs are formed by adding -*ly* to the end of an adjective, as in *happy–happily*. Similarly, in Spanish, adverbs are formed by adding -**mente** to the feminine form of adjectives ending in -**a** and to the final -**e** or consonant of any other adjective. Here are a few adjective-adverb pairs.

feliz–felizmente	*happy–happily*
triste–tristemente	*sad–sadly*
lento–lentamente	*slow–slowly*
rápido–rápidamente/rápido	*quick–quickly*
nuevo–nuevamente	*new–once again*
frecuente–frecuentemente	*frequent–frequently*
normal–normalmente	*normal–normally*

When an adverb is describing a verb, telling you how something is done, it's placed after the verb, regardless of whether it is a single verb or a verb phrase.

Ella come lentamente.
She eats slowly.

Ellos trabajan rápidamente.
They work quickly.

Nosotros vamos a comer rápidamente.
We're going to eat quickly.

But an adverb can also come at the beginning of a sentence if it describes a characteristic of, or expresses an attitude toward, the whole sentence.

Normalmente trabajo ocho horas diarias.
I normally work eight hours a day.

Tristemente no podemos viajar el mes entrante.
Sadly, we won't be able to travel next month.

When an adverb describes an adjective or another adverb, it's placed in front of the word it is modifying.

Sus respuestas son completamente absurdas.
Your answers are completely absurd.

Yo duermo muy bien.
I sleep very well.

Tienes que trabajar más rápidamente.
You need to work more quickly.

When using two or more adverbs in a series, the suffix **-mente** is dropped from all except the very last one.

Ella trabaja rápida, diligente y eficientemente.
She works quickly, diligently, and efficiently.

La serpiente se mueve lenta y silenciosamente.
The snake moves slowly and quietly.

PRACTICE 2
Fill in the blank with the appropriate adverb.

1. Necesito el informe (inmediato).

2. Marcos hace su trabajo (rápido y eficiente).

3. (Frecuente) corremos por las mañanas en el parque.

4. Marta habla (lento y claro).

5. Ella no contesta el teléfono (rápido).

6. (Nuevo) tenemos un problema con la computadora.

7. El problema se va a resolver (fácil)

8. Vosotros (normal) vais al cine los sábados por la tarde.

Tip!

Watch out for those false cognates! False cognates are words that look the same or similar in English and in Spanish but actually have very different meanings. Here are three examples of adverbs that look the same but mean different things (immediately after each is the Spanish equivalent of the English word).

actualmente	*at the present time*
(efectivamente/realmente	*actually)*
en absoluto	*absolutely not*
(totalmente	*absolutely)*
sensiblemente	*perceptibly*
(sensatamente	*sensibly)*

Here are a few other words that are false cognates.

embarazada	*to be pregnant*
el delito	*crime*
contestar	*to answer*
atender	*to take care of*
asistir	*to be present*
éxito	*success*
suceso	*an event or happening*

ANSWERS

PRACTICE 1: 1.le; **2.** le; **3.** (escribir)les; **4.** nos; **5.** les; **6.** me; **7.** Os; **8.** (tráiga)nos

PRACTICE 2: **1.** inmediatamente; **2.** rápida y eficientemente; **3.** Frecuentemente; **4.** lenta y claramente; **5.** rápidamente; **6.** Nuevamente; **7.** fácilmente; **8.** normalmente

————————— Lesson 30 (phrases) —————————

PHRASE LIST 1

Me gustaría . . .	*I would like . . .*
Me puede traer . . .	*Could you bring me . . .*
Tengo ganas de . . .	*I feel like . . .*

No huele bien.	*It doesn't smell good.*
Huele mal.	*It smells bad.*
Sabe a vinagre.	*It tastes like vinegar.*
La leche está cortada.	*The milk is sour.*
¿Algo más?	*Anything else?*
No, nada más gracias.	*No, nothing else, thanks.*
Las papayas tienen buena pinta.	*The papayas look good.*
¿Cuánto es?	*How much is it?*

NUTS & BOLTS 1
MORE ON ADVERBS

There are, of course, a few adverbs that do not follow the pattern described in the previous lesson. Let's break them down into groups, starting with adverbs of quantity or degree.

bastante	*quite, enough*
poco	*a few, a little*
mucho	*a lot*
demasiado	*too (much)*
muy	*very*
tanto	*as much*
más	*more*
menos	*less*
mucho	*very*
nada	*nothing*
algo	*somewhat*

And here are adverbs of time that don't end in **-mente**.

ahora	*now*
ya	*already, now*
tarde	*late*
temprano	*early*
pronto	*soon*
por fin	*finally*

And finally, here are adverbs of manner that don't end in **-mente**.

bien	*well*
mal	*badly, poorly*
mejor	*better*
peor	*worse*

Ella siempre se sirve demasiada comida.
She always serves herself too much food.

La comida está muy condimentada.
The food is very spicy.

Tengo poco tiempo para almorzar.
I have little time for lunch.

Yo desayuno temprano.
I have an early breakfast.

PRACTICE 1

Give the adverb that means the opposite of each of the adverbs below.

1. mal

2. felizmente

3. poco

4. lentamente

5. temprano

6. algo

7. más

8. mejor

PHRASE LIST 2

la lata de atún	*can of tuna*
la tajada de jamón	*slice of ham*
la pieza de pollo	*piece of chicken*
la bolsa de papas	*sack of potatoes*
la botella de agua mineral	*bottle of mineral water*
el cartón de jugo	*carton of juice*
el racimo de uvas	*bunch of grapes*
el frasco de mermelada	*jar of jam*
el manojo de zanahorias	*handful of carrots*
el paquete de galletas	*package of cookies*
la rebanada de pan	*slice of bread*
un litro de leche	*a liter of milk*
dos kilos de naranjas	*two kilos of oranges*

NUTS & BOLTS 2

THE PRETERITE OF -AR VERBS AND ESTAR

Now that you're able to talk about things that are happening in the present and discuss plans for the future, it's time to learn how to talk about things that happened in the past. To do this, you will be using what's called the preterite tense. As with the present tense, in the preterite, Spanish verbs follow a pattern according to whether they end in -ar, -er, or -ir. Let's first take a look at regular verbs ending in -ar, like **estudiar**.

yo estudié	nosotros/as estudiamos
tú estudiaste	vosotros/as estudiasteis
él/ella/usted estudió	ellos/ellas/ustedes estudiaron

You might have noticed that the conjugation of **-ar** verbs in the first person plural (**nosotros/as**) is the same in the present and in the preterite. Thus, **estudiamos** can mean *we speak* or *we spoke*; the context should always make it clear whether it is present or past.

Ayer hablé con mis padres por teléfono.
Yesterday, I spoke to my parents over the phone.

La semana pasada viajamos a París.
Last week we traveled to Paris.

Viajamos a las Bahamas para nuestras vacaciones.
We travel to the Bahamas on our vacation.

Ella terminó el informe anoche.
She finished the report last night.

Here are some useful time expressions you can use with the preterite.

ayer	*yesterday*
anoche	*last night*
la semana pasada	*last week*
el mes pasado	*last month*
el año pasado	*last year*

luego	*then*
entonces	*then*
después	*afterwards*
más tarde	*later*
una vez	*once*

Hablamos por teléfono y después tomamos un café.
We talked on the phone and then had a cup of coffee.

Caminamos por el parque y luego desayunamos en el hotel.
We walked through the park and then had breakfast at the hotel.

Even though the verb **estar** is an **-ar** verb, it follows an irregular pattern.

estar (*to be*)

yo estuve	nosotros/as estuvimos
tú estuviste	vosotros/as estuvisteis
él/ella/usted estuvo	ellos/ellas/ustedes estuvieron

PRACTICE 2
Change the following sentences to the preterite.

1. Tú caminas mucho.
2. Ella saborea el vino tinto.
3. Ella toca el piano.
4. Ustedes hablan por teléfono con su jefe.

5. Vosotros escucháis música clásica.

6. Él está en Nueva York.

7. Hoy estamos en un restaurante italiano.

8. Esta semana contestamos sus preguntas.

Culture note

Shopping for food can sometimes be an adventure, for not in every country will you find **supermercados** (*supermarkets*) like in the United States. Many times you will find that there are **plazas de mercado** (*outdoor markets*) where you can find just about anything from fruits and vegetables to cleaning products and even clothes. Going to the market is not only about buying; it's about socializing and interacting with other people. Of course, there are also food stores, and many of them tend to be smaller stores that specialize in a particular category of food.

la panadería	*bread bakery*
la pastelería	*bakery (for pastries, etc.)*
la lechería	*dairy store*
la carnicería	*butcher shop*
la pescadería	*fish shop, fish market*
la tienda	*convenience store*
la charcutería	*delicatessen*

ANSWERS

PRACTICE 1: 1. bien; **2.** tristemente; **3.** mucho; **4.** rápidamente; **5.** tarde; **6.** nada; **7.** menos; **8.** peor.

PRACTICE 2: 1. Tú caminaste mucho. **2.** Ella saboreó el vino tinto. **3.** Ella tocó el piano. **4.** Ustedes hablaron por teléfono con su jefe. **5.** Vosotros escuchasteis música clásica. **6.** Él estuvo en Nueva York. **7.** Ayer estuvimos en un restaurante italiano. **8.** La semana pasada contestamos sus preguntas.

SENTENCE LIST 1

¿Cuál es el plato del día?	*What is the special of the day?*
¿Qué desea (usted) pedir?	*What would you like to order?*
¿Qué me recomienda?	*What do you recommend?*
¿Me podría traer la cuenta, por favor?	*Could you please bring me the check?*
¿Está incluida la propina en la cuenta?	*Is the tip included in the bill?*
¿Qué ingredientes tiene este plato?	*What ingredients are in this dish?*
¿Cómo quiere la carne?	*How would you like the meat?*
La quiero termino medio, por favor.	*I want it medium-rare, please.*
La quiero termino tres cuartos, por favor.	*I want it medium, please.*
La quiero bien asada, por favor.	*I want it well-done, please.*

NUTS & BOLTS 1

THE PRETERITE OF -ER AND -IR VERBS

Now let's look at the preterite of **-er** and **-ir** verbs, which follow the same pattern.

comer (*to eat*)

yo comí	nosotros/as comimos
tú comiste	vosotros/as comisteis
él/ella/usted comió	ellos/ellas/ustedes comieron

escribir (*to write*)

yo escribí	nosotros/as escribimos
tú escribiste	vosotros/as escribisteis
él/ella/usted escribió	ellos/ellas/ustedes escribieron

Take a look at how the verb **oír** (*to hear*) is conjugated in the preterite.

oír (*to hear*)

yo oí	nosotros/as oímos
tú oíste	vosotros/as oísteis
él/ella/usted oyó	ellos/ellas/ustedes oyeron

You already know that there are several verbs that are irregular in the present tense, and, in fact, you've already learned the conjugation of **estar** in the preterite, which is also irregular. We'll take a look at a few irregular verbs in the preterite over the next couple of lessons. Just keep in mind that a verb's being irregular in the present does not necessarily mean that it will be irregular in the preterite. The verbs **despertar(se), volver, almorzar,** and **salir** are examples of this. They have some irregularity in the present, but they're perfectly regular in the preterite.

Yo me despierto a las ocho todos los días.

I get up at eight every day.

Yo me desperté a las nueve ayer.

Yesterday, I got up at nine.

Ellos vuelven esta tarde.
They come back this afternoon.

Ellos volvieron ayer por la noche.
They came back yesterday evening.

Tú almuerzas a la misma hora siempre.
You always have lunch at the same time.

Tú almorzaste más temprano ayer.
You had lunch earlier yesterday.

Yo salgo de la oficina a las tres.
I leave the office at three.

Ayer salí a las cinco.
Yesterday, I left at five.

PRACTICE 1
Rewrite the following sentences in the preterite. Use the clues given in parentheses when necessary.

1. Yo bebo café y jugo de naranja con el desayuno.

2. Ella te escribe una carta todos los días. (ayer)

3. Vosotros coméis tostadas con mermelada.

4. Él duerme pocas horas.

5. Mañana vamos a salir tarde de la oficina. (ayer)

6. Ella come chocolate todo el día.

7. Yo no oigo nada.

8. Ellas parten para México.

SENTENCE LIST 2

¿En qué puedo servirle?	*How may I help you?*
Necesito un litro de leche.	*I need a liter of milk.*

¿Me puede dar un kilo de patatas?	*Could you give me a kilo of potatoes?*
¿Cuántas naranjas quiere?	*How many oranges do you want?*
Póngame dos chuletas de cordero, por favor.	*Give me two lamb chops, please.*
¿Quiere usted algo más?	*Would you like anything else?*
Eso es todo.	*That's all.*
¿Cuánto pesan las chuletas?	*How much do the chops weigh?*
¿Cómo están las papayas?	*How are the papayas?*
Deme tres botellas de vino tinto.	*Give me three bottles of red wine.*
¿Cuánto le debo?	*How much do I owe you?*

NUTS & BOLTS 2

The preterite of SER, IR, TENER, and HACER

As we mentioned before, there are a few verbs that are irregular in the preterite. The verbs **ser** (*to be*) and **ir** (*to go*) take identical forms in the preterite.

ser (*to be*)/**ir** (*to go*)

yo fui	nosotros/as fuimos
tú fuiste	vosotros/as fuisteis
él/ella/usted fue	ellos/ellas/ustedes fueron

It is easy to distinguish **ser** from **ir** by context.

Ella fue profesora de inglés. (ser)
She was an English teacher.

Ella fue a Chile de vacaciones. (ir)
She went to Chile on vacation.

The verbs **tener** and **hacer** are also irregular in the preterite.

tener (*to have*)

yo tuve	nosotros/as tuvimos
tú tuviste	vosotros/as tuvisteis
él/ella/usted tuvo	ellos/ellas/ustedes tuvieron

hacer (*to do, to make*)

yo hice	nosotros/as hicimos
tú hiciste	vosotros/as hicisteis
él/ella/usted hizo	ellos/ellas/ustedes hicieron

Tuvimos que esperar cuatro horas en el aeropuerto.
We had to wait four hours at the airport.

Yo hice un viaje muy largo.
I took (lit., made) a very long trip.

PRACTICE 2
Fill in the blanks with the correct form of the preterite of **ser, hacer, ir,** or **tener.**

1. Yo _____ al supermercado esta mañana.

2. Tú _____ una familia pequeña.

3. Ellos _____ una presentación muy buena.

4. Ella _____ una cantante famosa.

5. Él _____ una llamada por teléfono al exterior.

6. Ellos _____ felices.

7. Ustedes _____ un apartamento en Nueva York.

8. Vosotros _____ a Costa Rica de vacaciones.

Culture note

In the Spanish-speaking world, eating habits are a bit different from those in the United States. In most countries, people follow the European way of eating; that is, they don't switch the fork from the left to the right hand when eating; the right hand is not kept on the lap, but rather on the table; and people usually wish each other **¡Buen provecho!** (*Enjoy your meal!*) before beginning to eat. Another custom is known as **la sobremesa,** or *after-dinner conversation.* Usually people stay seated around the table after lunch or dinner to chat while having a drink or a cup of coffee.

ANSWERS

PRACTICE 1: 1. Yo bebí café y jugo de naranja con el desayuno. **2.** Ella te escribió una carta ayer. **3.** Vosotros comisteis tostadas con mermelada. **4.** Él durmió pocas horas. **5.** Ayer salimos tarde de la oficina. **6.** Ella comió chocolate todo el día. **7.** Yo no oí nada. **8.** Ellas partieron para México.

PRACTICE 2: 1. fui; **2.** tuviste; **3.** hicieron; **4.** fue; **5.** hizo; **6.** fueron; **7.** tuvieron; **8.** fuisteis.

—————————— Lesson 32 (conversations) ——————————

CONVERSATION 1

Roberto is travelling through Colombia. He is now in Villa de Leyva, at a local restaurant, ordering something for lunch.

Mesero: Buenas tardes, ¿qúe desea pedir?
Roberto: ¿Cuál es el plato del día?
Mesero: Como entrada tenemos un ceviche de pescado; el plato principal es ajiaco con pollo, y de postre le podemos ofrecer arroz con leche, natilla o cuajada con melado.

Roberto:	¿Qué ingredientes tiene el ajiaco?
Mesero:	El ajiaco es una sopa espesa a base de pollo, diferentes tipos de papa, y guascas, una hierba típica de la región. Se sirve con mazorca y aguacate.
Roberto:	Bueno, suena muy bien. Tráigame el ajiaco solamente.
Mesero:	¿Y de postre?
Roberto:	¿Cuál me recomienda?
Mesero:	La cuajada con melado está muy buena.
Roberto:	Muy bien.
Mesero:	¿Algo más?
Roberto:	Una cerveza, por favor.

Waiter:	Good afternoon, what would you like to order?
Roberto:	What's the special of the day?
Waiter:	As an appetizer we have ceviche de pescado; the main dish is ajiaco con pollo, and as a dessert we can offer you arroz con leche, natilla, or cuajada con melado.
Roberto:	What are the ingredients in ajiaco?
Waiter:	Ajiaco is a type of thick soup with chicken, different kinds of potatoes, and guascas, a typical herb of the region. It's served with corn and avocado.
Roberto:	Well, it sounds good. Bring me the ajiaco by itself.
Waiter:	And for dessert?
Roberto:	Which one do you recommend?
Mesero:	The cuajada con melado is very good.
Roberto:	Very good.
Mesero:	Anything else?
Roberto:	A beer, please.

Notes

Villa de Leyva is probably one of the finest colonial towns in Colombia. It is located in Boyacá, a department in the center of the country. Founded in 1572, Villa de Leyva has a very small population—not more than 4,500 inhabitants—and is considered a national monument to colonial architecture. It is a popular recreational destination for people living in Bogotá because it is only a couple of hours away by car.

NUTS & BOLTS 1
Spelling changes in the preterite

Most of the time, irregularities in the preterite have to do with spelling changes. For example, verbs ending in **-car** change the **c** to **qu** before **e**; verbs ending in **-gar** change the **g** to **gu** before **e**; and verbs ending in **-zar** change the **z** to **c** before **e**.

sacar (*to take out*)

yo saqué	**nosotros/as sacamos**
tú sacaste	**vosotros/as sacasteis**
él/ella/usted sacó	**ellos/ellas/ustedes sacaron**

llegar (*to arrive*)

yo llegué	**nosotros/as llegamos**
tú llegaste	**vosotros/as llegasteis**
él/ella/usted llegó	**ellos/ellas/ustedes llegaron**

empezar (*to begin*)

yo empecé	**nosotros/as empezamos**
tú empezaste	**vosotros/as empezasteis**
él/ella/usted empezó	**ellos/ellas/ustedes empezaron**

Spanish doesn't allow three consecutive vowels in a word; therefore, **i** is often changed to **y**.

leer (*to read*)

yo leí	nosotros/as leímos
tú leíste	vosotros/as leísteis
él/ella/usted leyó	ellos/ellas/ustedes leyeron

creer (*to believe*)

yo creí	nosotros/as creímos
tú creíste	vosotros/as creísteis
él/ella/usted creyó	ellos/ellas/ustedes creyeron

The verbs **decir** (*to say*) and **traer** (*to bring*) take a **j** between the vowels.

decir (*to say*)

yo dije	nosotros/as dijimos
tú dijiste	vosotros/as dijisteis
él/ella/usted dijo	ellos/ellas/ustedes dijeron

traer (*to bring*)

yo traje	nosotros/as trajimos
tú trajiste	vosotros/as trajisteis
él/ella/usted trajo	ellos/ellas/ustedes trajeron

¿Llegaste a tiempo a tu cita?
Did you get to your appointment on time?

Leyó el periódico y se marchó al trabajo.
She/He read the newspaper and left for work.

Le dije la verdad a él.
I told him the truth.

Nos trajeron un vino excelente.
They brought us an excellent wine.

PRACTICE 1
Change the sentence using the pronoun given in parentheses.

1. Marqué las cajas con nuestros nombres y dirección. (usted)

2. No creí lo que dijo. (vosotros)

3. Ellas dijeron la verdad. (nosotras)

4. Pagamos la cuenta. (yo)

5. ¿Trajeron lápiz y papel para tomar nota? (usted)

6. Él apagó la luz muy tarde. (ellas)

7. Ustedes comenzaron a estudiar italiano. (él)

8. No leísteis el periódico esta mañana. (tú)

CONVERSATION 2
Roberto has decided to help his friend Marisa, who is busy working, with grocery shopping. He's at a local grocery store, getting a few things.

Tendero: ¿En qué puedo servirle?
Roberto: Necesito dos litros de leche.
Tendero: ¿Entera o descremada?
Roberto: Entera. También quiero un kilo de naranjas, una lata de atún, una bolsa de papas, y un manojo de zanahorias.
Tendero: ¿Algo más?
Roberto: Las papayas tiene buena pinta.

Tendero:	Sí, están muy dulces. ¿Quiere llevar una?
Roberto:	Sí, pero no muy grande.
Tendero:	¿Qué le parece ésta?
Roberto:	Sí, se ve bien. ¿Cuanto le debo?
Tendero:	Son diez mil trescientos pesos.
Roberto:	Aquí tiene. Muchas gracias. Hasta luego.

Shopkeeper:	*How may I help you?*
Roberto:	*I need two liters of milk.*
Sho keeper:	*Whole or skim milk?*
Roberto:	*Whole. I also want a kilo of oranges, a can of tuna, a bag of potatoes, and a handful of carrots.*
Shopkeeper:	*Anything else?*
Roberto:	*The papayas look good.*
Shopkeeper:	*Yes, they're very sweet. Would you like to take one?*
Roberto:	*Yes, but not a very big one.*
Shopkeeper:	*How about this one?*
Roberto:	*Yes, it looks good. How much do I owe you?*
Shopkeeper:	*That's ten thousand, three hundred pesos.*
Roberto:	*Here you are. Thanks. Good-bye.*

NOTES

The metric system is generally, but not always, used in the Spanish-speaking world. So you will hear people buying things like:

cuatro onzas de queso	*four ounces of cheese*
media libra de naranjas	*a half pound of oranges*
dos litros de leche	*two liters of milk*
cien gramos de crema	*a hundred grams of cream*
una libra de arroz	*a pound of rice*
un kilo de patatas	*a kilo of potatoes*

NUTS & BOLTS 2
IRREGULAR VERBS IN THE PRETERITE

The following verbs follow a slightly different pattern of conjugation in the preterite.

poder (to be able)	poner (to put)	saber (to know)	querer (to want)	andar (to walk)	venir (to come)
pude	puse	supe	quise	anduve	vine
pudiste	pusiste	supiste	quisiste	anduviste	viniste
pudo	puso	supo	quiso	anduvo	vino
pudimos	pusimos	supimos	quisimos	anduvimos	vinimos
pudisteis	pusisteis	supisteis	quisisteis	anduvisteis	vinisteis
pudieron	pusieron	supieron	quisieron	anduvieron	vinieron

Él no pudo comer.
He couldn't eat.

Ella puso el pollo en agua caliente.
She put the chicken in hot water.

Ayer supimos la noticia.
Yesterday we learned the news.

Nosotros no quisimos pagar la cuenta.
We didn't want to pay the bill.

Anduviste por todo el museo.
You walked through the entire museum.

Mi esposo vino a casa tarde.
My husband came home late.

PRACTICE 2

Fill in the blanks with the correct Spanish preterite form of the English verb in parentheses.

1. ¿Dónde _____ él mi suéter? (to put)

2. Ella no _____ llamar a sus padres. (to want)

3. Usted no _____ completar el cuestionario. (to be able)

4. Él _____ de Argentina. (to come)

5. Yo no _____ comer en ese restaurante. (to be able)

6. Ayer nosotros _____ dos horas por el parque. (to walk)

7. ¿Vosotros _____ cómo llegar a la casa de Juan? (to know)

8. Ellos _____ ayer por la noche. (to come)

Culture note

Many people think that food in all of the Spanish-speaking world is hot and spicy. Well, that is perhaps the case in Mexico and a few other countries in Central America. But the truth is, the cuisines of Spanish-speaking countries are as varied as the people who enjoy them. In Spain, you will find **paella** (a saffron-spiced rice with different kinds of meat and seafood) and the traditional **tortilla de patatas** (potato omelet). Argentina is known for the excellent quality of its beef; steaks are usually served with **chimichurri**, a green sauce of herbs and chilies, and **empanadas** (meat and cheese pastries) are very popular for lunch. In Venezuela and Colombia, **arepas** (baked cornmeal cakes) are traditionally served with breakfast, and, on the Caribbean coast, **arroz con coco** (coconut rice) is a typical side dish. Popular desserts in Colombia are **arroz con leche** (rice pudding), **cuajada con melado** (soft cheese with melted sugar), and **natilla** (soft custard). And in Peru, **ceviche** (raw fish marinated in spices and lime juice) is one of the country's staple dishes.

ANSWERS

PRACTICE 1: 1. Usted marcó las cajas con nuestros nombres y dirección. **2.** No creísteis lo que dijo. **3.** Nosotras dijimos la verdad. **4.** Pagué la cuenta. **5.** ¿Trajo lápiz y papel para tomar nota? **6.** Ellas apagaron la luz muy tarde. **7.** Él comenzó a estudiar italiano. **8.** No leíste el periódico esta mañana.

PRACTICE 2: 1. puso; **2.** quiso; **3.** pudo; **4.** vino; **5.** pude; **6.** anduvimos; **7.** Supisteis; **8.** vinieron.

UNIT 8 ESSENTIALS

Les voy a servir una paella.

I'm going to serve them a paella.

Le dijimos la verdad a él.

We told him the truth.

¿Me enviaste el paquete a mí o a Juan?

Did you send the package to me or to Juan?

Ellos trabajan lentamente.

They work slowly.

Ella canta clara y melódicamente.

She sings clearly and melodiously.

Tú dibujas muy bien.

You draw very well.

Estuvimos en Madrid la semana pasada.

We were in Madrid last week.

Estamos en Madrid ahora.

We're in Madrid now.

Vieron una película muy cómica.

They saw a very funny movie.

Ella fue cantante de ópera.

She was an opera singer.

Ella fue a Lima por negocios.
She went to Lima on business.

Tuvieron un apartamento en Brasilia.
They had an apartment in Brasilia.

Ella hizo unos postres deliciosos.
She made some delicious desserts.

Llegué muy tarde por la noche.
I arrived very late in the evening.

La reunión empezó a las tres y media.
The meeting started at 3:30.

No supimos la respuesta.
We didn't know the answer.

No quisieron pagar la cuenta.
They didn't want to pay the bill.

UNIT 9
School and work

In this unit, you'll learn more about expressing the past. You will also learn lots of useful vocabulary related to school and work.

──────────── Lesson 33 (words) ────────────

WORD LIST 1

la materia	*school subject*
la(s) matemática(s)	*mathematics*
la historia	*history*
la literatura	*literature*
la ciència	*science*
la biología	*biology*
la química	*chemistry*
la geografía	*geography*
la filosofía	*philosophy*
la asignatura	*course*
los estudios	*studies*
la beca	*scholarship*
matricularse	*to register*
la biblioteca	*library*
la sala de conferencias	*lecture hall*
graduarse	*to graduate*
los derechos de matrícula	*tuition*
la tesis	*dissertation*
la licenciatura	*master's degree*
el título académico	*academic degree*

NUTS & BOLTS 1
MORE IRREGULAR VERBS IN THE PRETERITE

Here are the irregular preterite forms of **dar** (*to give*), **pedir** (*to ask for*), and **ver** (*to see*).

dar	pedir	ver
di	pedí	vi
diste	pediste	viste
dio	pidió	vio
dimos	pedimos	vimos
disteis	pedisteis	visteis
dieron	pidieron	vieron

Ella nos dio una noticia muy buena.
She gave us very good news.

Él me pidió mi número de teléfono.
He asked me for my phone number.

Vimos una película romántica.
We saw a romantic movie.

In Spanish, we use the verb **haber** to say *there is/there are*. In the present tense, the form is **hay,** and in the preterite, it is **hubo.**

Hubo mucha gente en la fiesta de anoche.
There were a lot of people at last night's party.

Hubo solamente una película extranjera en el festival de cine.
There was only one foreign movie in the film festival.

PRACTICE 1

Fill in the blank with the correct preterite form of **dar, pedir, ver,** or **haber.**

1. Ella nos _____ disculpas.

2. Tú me _____ un libro muy interesante para leer.

3. _____ una reunión extraordinaria ayer.

4. Ustedes _____ el accidente.

5. _____ cinco personas para la entrevista.

6. Ella le _____ una carta de referencia.

7. Yo no _____ al ladrón.

8. Nosotros te _____ la carta la semana pasada.

WORD LIST 2

la cita	*appointment*
la reunión	*meeting*
la sala de conferencias	*conference room*
el contrato	*contract*
el/la empleado/a	*employee*
el sindicato	*union*
el seguro	*insurance*
la entrevista	*interview*
la cualificación	*qualification*
la hoja de vida/el historial de trabajo/el currículum vítae	*résumé*
las referencias	*references*
el/la jubilado/a	*retired person*

NUTS & BOLTS 2
DOUBLE OBJECT PRONOUNS

In Units 7 and 8, you learned about direct and indirect object pronouns. They are basically not much different from one another, except for the third person singular and plural.

Indirect object pronouns	Direct object pronouns
me (. . . a mí)	me
te (. . . a ti)	te
le (. . . a él/ella/usted)	lo/la
nos (. . . a nosotros/as)	nos
os (. . . a vosotros/as)	os
les (. . . a ellos/ellas/ustedes)	los/las

Just as in English, it's possible to have both a direct object pronoun and an indirect object pronoun in the same sentence in Spanish. In that case, the indirect object pronoun comes first. To avoid the awkward repetition of the same sounds, use **se** instead of **le** or **les** preceding **lo(s)/la(s)**. In order to clarify the meaning of **se**, use **a él/a ella/a usted/a ellos/a ellas/a ustedes**.

Ellos me dan un libro (a mí).

They give me a book.

Ellos me lo dan (a mí).

They give it to me.

Nosotros le entregamos el informe a ella.

We gave the report to her.

Nosotros se lo entregamos a ella.

We gave it to her.

Yo les envié un correo electrónico a ellos.
I sent an email to them.

Yo se los envié a ellos.
I sent it to them.

When the pronouns appear in sentences with more than one verb, they can be placed either before the verbs or attached to the end of the main verb.

Él está entregando su examen al profesor.
He is giving his test to the teacher.

Él se lo está entregando.
He is giving it to him.

Él está entregándoselo.
He is giving it to him.

Vosotros vais a dar una sorpresa a Juan.
You are going to give Juan a surprise.

Vosotros se la vais a dar.
You are going to give it to him.

Vosotros vais a dársela.
You are going to give it to him.

PRACTICE 2
Replace the direct object in these sentences with the corresponding direct object pronoun.

1. Ella nos está vendiendo una radio.

2. El estudiante hace el trabajo.

3. Yo me compré unos pantalones negros.

4. Vosotros os tomáis una medicina.

5. Él le va a decir la verdad a Sofía.

6. Ellas le trajeron un regalo.

7. Él no puede comer carne.

8. Ellos le están enviando un correo a su jefe.

ANSWERS

PRACTICE 1: **1.** pidió; **2.** diste; **3.** Hubo; **4.** vieron; **5.** Hubo; **6.** pidió; **7.** vi; **8.** dimos.

PRACTICE 2: **1.** Ella nos la está vendiendo. **2.** El estudiante lo hace. **3.** Yo me los compré. **4.** Vosotros os la tomáis. **5.** Él se la va a decir. **6.** Ellas se lo trajeron. **7.** Él no la puede comer. **8.** Ellos se lo están enviando.

—————— Lesson 34 (phrases) ——————

PHRASE LIST 1

aprobar un curso	*to pass a course*
tomar un examen	*to take a test*
aprobar/suspender un examen	*to pass/fail a test*
escribir un trabajo de investigación	*to write a research paper*
estudiante a tiempo completo	*full-time student*

estudiante a tiempo parcial	*part-time student*
especializarse en . . .	*to major in . . .*
sacar buenas/malas notas	*to get good/bad grades*
el horario de clases	*class schedule*
me interesa(n) . . .	*I'm interested in . . .*
No estoy seguro todavía.	*I'm not sure yet.*
¿Qué te parece . . . ?	*What do you think of . . . ?*
Y tú, ¿qué piensas?	*And how about you? What do you think?*

NUTS & BOLTS 1

EXPRESSING PAST ACTIONS WITH HACE AND ACABAR DE

The verb **acabar** means *to finish* something. But you will hear it often in the expression **acabar de** + infinitive, which is equivalent to saying *to have just* in English. It refers to something that happened recently. Here are a few examples of how it is used.

Acabo de terminar el informe.
I have just finished the report.

Ella acaba de hacer una llamada a Ecuador.
She has just made a phone call to Ecuador.

Nosotros acabamos de terminar la entrevista.
We've just finished the interview.

To express an action that began in the past and continues into the present, use **hace** + time + **que** + present tense. Note that the verb in Spanish is in the present tense, but in English, it's translated as the present perfect progressive (*have/has been doing*).

Hace un año que estudio español.
I've been studying Spanish for a year.

Hace cinco años que ella trabaja aquí.
She's been working here for five years.

¿Cuánto hace que estudia arquitectura?

How long have you been studying architecture?

To express *ago*, use **hace** + time + **que** + preterite. In this case, the verb tense in both languages is the simple past.

Hace un año que estudié español.

I studied Spanish a year ago.

Hace cinco años que ella trabajó aquí.

She worked here five years ago.

¿Cuánto hace que estudió arquitectura?

How long ago did you study architecture?

PRACTICE 1
Use the English translations to help fill in the blanks.

1. Hace tres semanas que _____ en el informe. (*She's been working on the report for three weeks.*)

2. _____ mi matrícula hace un mes. (*I paid my tuition a month ago.*)

3. Ella _____ aquí hace dos años. (*She worked here two years ago.*)

4. María acaba de _____ un libro. (*María has just read a book.*)

5. Ellos acaban de _____ una nueva computadora. (*They've just bought a new computer.*)

6. Nosotros _____ hace una hora. (*We ate an hour ago.*)

7. Hace tres meses que _____ español. (*I've been studying Spanish for three months.*)

8. Acaban de _____ de vacaciones. (*They've just left on vacation.*)

PHRASE LIST 2

la solicitud de empleo	*job application*
La jornada es de treinta y siete horas.	*It is a thirty-seven-hour workweek.*

¿Cuándo comienzo?	When do I start?
Hay un período de prueba de seis meses.	There's a probationary period of six months.
un mes de vacaciones	a month's vacation
¿Hay incentivos?	Are there any incentives?
No tengo referencias.	I don't have references.
contribuciones a la pensión y el seguro	pension and insurance contributions
Domino el francés.	I speak French fluently.
¿Cuántos años de experiencia tiene?	How many years of experience do you have?

NUTS & BOLTS 2
EXPRESSING OBLIGATION OR NECESSITY

In English, when you want to express obligation or strong necessity, you use *to have to*, *must*, or *should*. In Spanish, use **tener que** + infinitive or **deber** + infinitive, as you learned in Lesson 21. You can also use the construction **hay que** + infinitive, which is a bit more impersonal.

Ella tiene que estudiar para el examen.
She has to study for the test.

Debemos hacer una lista de invitados.
We must make a guest list.

Hay que hablar claramente.
It is necessary to speak clearly.

PRACTICE 2
Fill in the blanks with the appropriate form of the verb in parentheses.

1. Ellos _____ tomar en cuenta la situación. (deber)

2. Yo _____ que vender mi apartamento. (tener)

3. Ella no _____ venir a la oficina hoy. (deber)

4. _____ que consultar con un abogado. (haber)

5. Él _____ que llamar al hospital. (tener)

6. _____ que llamar a Juan inmediatamente. (haber)

7. Nosotros _____ hacer una excepción en este caso. (deber)

8. Ellos _____ que enviar el informe lo antes posible. (tener)

Tip!

Take a look at the following words. They are all related to an amount of money, but they are not necessarily synonyms.

el sueldo	*pay*
el salario	*salary*
el jornal/la paga	*wage*
el pago	*payment*
la retribución	*repayment*
los honorarios	*fees*
el ingreso	*earnings*

ANSWERS

PRACTICE 1: 1. trabaja; **2.** Pagué; **3.** trabajó; **4.** leer; **5.** comprar; **6.** comimos; **7.** estudio; **8.** partir.

PRACTICE 2: 1. deben; **2.** tengo; **3.** debe; **4.** Hay; **5.** tiene; **6.** Hay; **7.** debemos; **8.** tienen.

—————————— Lesson 35 (sentences) ——————————

SENTENCE LIST 1

¿**Cuál es tu carrera?**	*What is your major?*
¿**Cuál es tu especialidad?**	*What is your major?*
¿**En qué año estás?**	*What year are you in?*
Se gradúa el año que viene.	*He/She graduates next year.*
¿**Qué clases tomas este semestre?**	*What classes are you taking this semester?*

¿Qué notas sacaste?	*What grades did you get?*
¿Qué planes tienes para el futuro?	*What are your plans for the future?*
Pienso ser periodista.	*I'm thinking about being a journalist.*
Acaba de graduarse en medicina.	*He/She just graduated in medicine.*
Tenemos que escribir un trabajo de investigación.	*We have to write a research paper.*

NUTS & BOLTS 1

THE IMPERFECT OF -AR VERBS

So far, you've learned how to express actions that happened in the past with the preterite tense. There is, however, another past tense, called the imperfect, which is used to describe actions in the past that do not have a clear beginning or end, but rather are part of a routine or habit. The imperfect often corresponds to the English habitual past, with *used to* + verb, or to the past progressive *was/were* + *-ing*.

Durante el verano, me levantaba a las nueve.
During the summer, I used to get up at nine.

Después del desayuno, caminaba por la playa.
After breakfast, I would walk along the beach.

To form the imperfect of **-ar** verbs, simply take the root of the verb and add the following endings.

pagar (*to pay*)

yo pagaba	nosotros/as pagábamos
tú pagaabas	vosotros/as pagabais
él/ella/usted pagaba	ellos/ellas/ustedes pagaban

PRACTICE 1
Complete the following paragraph with the verbs in the imperfect tense.

Cuando tenía nueve años 1me_____ (yo/gustar) jugar con mis amigos en el parque. A veces 2_____ (nosotros/montar) en bicicleta, otra veces 3_____ (nosotros/jugar) fútbol. El tiempo 4_____ (pasar) muy rápido porque nos divertíamos mucho. Cuando 5_____ (llegar) la noche, 6_____ (nosotros/jugar) a las escondidas. En el verano, 7_____ (nosotros/acostarse) muy tarde y 8_____ (nosotros/levantarse) muy tarde también.

SENTENCE LIST 2

¿En qué trabaja?	*What do you do for a living?*
Le ofrecemos un contrato por un año.	*We're offering you a one-year contract.*
Hay que trabajar horas extras.	*You have to work overtime.*
Tengo una especialización en farmacia clínica.	*I have a master's degree in clinical pharmacy.*
¿Cuál es su objetivo en solicitar este puesto?	*What is your aim in applying for this job?*
Su oferta es muy interessante.	*Your offer is very interesting.*
¿Cuándo comienzo?	*When do I start?*
¿Qué otras cualificaciones posee?	*What other qualifications do you have?*
Soy bueno trabajando en equipo.	*I'm good at working on a team.*
Sé trabajar bajo presión.	*I know how to work under pressure.*

NUTS & BOLTS 2
THE IMPERFECT OF -ER AND -IR VERBS
The same set of endings is used in the imperfect of **-er** and **-ir** verbs.

vender (*to sell*)

yo vendía	nosotros/as vendíamos
tú vendías	vosotros/as vendíais
él/ella/usted vendía	ellos/ellas/ustedes vendían

escribir (*to write*)

yo escribía	nosotros/as escribíamos
tú escribías	vosotros/as escribíais
él/ella/usted escribía	ellos/ellas/ustedes escribían

The imperfect doesn't always correspond to habitual or progressive past actions. Sometimes it's translated as the simple past when it describes a number of conditions and qualities, such as physical appearance, age, occupation, traits or characteristics, mental and emotional states, location, beliefs, opinions, and wishes. Notice that all of these conditions and qualities are things that you can think of as "background" information—not some action that happened at a specific point in time in the past, but rather, characteristics that lasted over a period.

Ella tenía el pelo rojo y largo.
She had long red hair.

Mi abuelo tenía setenta años, estaba triste, y no quería hablar.
My grandfather was seventy years old, he was sad, and he didn't want to talk.

Su casa estaba lejos de las montañas y estaba en mal estado.
His house was far away from the mountains and in bad shape.

PRACTICE 2

Fill in the blanks with the verb(s) given in the imperfect.

1. Ella _____ siempre tarde del trabajo. (salir)

2. Mi tío Alfonso _____ una casa cerca al mar. (tener)

3. Ella _____ en Brasil. (vivir)

4. Ella _____ cincuenta años pero _____ más vieja. (tener/parecer)

5. Ellos _____ novelas rosa. (escribir)

6. Vosotros _____ hasta tarde los fines de semana. (dormir)

7. Nosotros _____ que ella no _____ dinero. (saber/tener)

8. Yo no _____ lo que _____. (creer/oír)

Culture note

Some universities in Latin America and Spain are quite different from those in the United States. There may be no on-campus housing, because students generally live at home with their parents or rent and share apartments or houses with other students. Even though students do play a number of different sports, there are often no teams associated with any one university, nor are there scholarships offered to these athletes. Furthermore, there are no fraternities or sororities; students meet more informally at cafés or at home.

ANSWERS

PRACTICE 1: 1. gustaba; **2.** montábamos; **3.** jugábamos; **4.** pasaba; **5.** llegaba; **6.** jugábamos; **7.** nos acostábamos; **8.** nos levantábamos.

PRACTICE 2: 1. salía; **2.** tenía; **3.** vivía; **4.** tenía/parecía; **5.** escribían; **6.** dormíais; **7.** sabíamos/tenía; **8.** creía/oía.

CONVERSATION 1

Isabel and Olga have been friends since high school, but they haven't seen each other in months. They've just bumped into each other at the university bookstore.

Isabel: ¡Hola, Olga! ¡Qué sorpresa! ¿Cómo estás?

Olga: ¡Lo mismo digo! ¿Cómo te ha ido? ¡No sabía que estudiabas en esta universidad también!

Isabel: Sí, decidí especializarme en ingeniería mecánica y me gané una beca para estudiar aquí. Y tú, ¿cuál es tu carrera?

Olga: ¡Felicitaciones! Estoy estudiando pediatría.

Isabel: ¿En qué año estás?

Olga: Me gradúo en dos años. Pero no estoy segura si voy a continuar.

Isabel: ¿Por qué no? Siempre te gustó trabajar con niños.

Olga: Ya lo sé. Pero estoy pensando especializarme en sicología infantil. Y a ti, ¿cuánto te falta?

Isabel: Tres semestres más. Ya estoy lista para empezar a trabajar.

Olga: Sí, te entiendo. Bueno, y ¿qué te parece está universidad?

Isabel: Me gusta mucho. Estoy muy contenta aquí.

Isabel: Hi, Olga! What a surprise! How are you?

Olga: Same here! How have you been? I didn't know that you studied here as well!

Isabel: Yes, I decided to major in mechanical engineering and I was awarded a scholarship to study here. And you, what's your major?

Olga: Congratulations! I'm studying to be a pediatrician.

Isabel: What year are you in?

Olga: *I'll graduate in two years. But I'm not sure whether I am going to continue.*

Isabel: *Why not? You always liked working with kids.*

Olga: *I know. But I am thinking about majoring in child psychology. And you, how much more do you have to go?*

Isabel: *Three more semesters. I'm ready to start working.*

Olga: *Yes, I understand. Well, so, what do you think of the university?*

Isabel: *I like it a lot. I'm very happy here.*

NOTES

More and more women in Latin America and Spain are studying to go into fields that were once associated with men only, such as engineering or physics. Despite this, employment opportunities are not the same, varying from country to country and across social backgrounds.

NUTS & BOLTS 1

IR, SER, AND VER IN THE IMPERFECT

The good news about the imperfect tense is that there are only three irregular verbs.

ir (*to go*)

yo iba	nosotros/as íbamos
tú ibas	vosotros/as ibais
él/ella/usted iba	ellos/ellas/ustedes iban

ser (*to be*)

yo era	nosotros/as éramos
tú eras	vosotros/as érais
él/ella/usted era	ellos/ellas/ustedes eran

ver (*to see*)

yo veía	nosotros/as veíamos
tú veías	vosotros/as veíais
él/ella/usted veía	ellos/ellas/ustedes veían

Here are some examples of these three irregular verbs in sentences. Note that the imperfect in each of the examples below describes a background setting against which the main events of a story take place.

Eran las once de la noche y nevaba.
It was eleven at night and it was snowing.

Era un día de invierno y no se veía a nadie en la calle.
It was a winter day and there was no one to be seen on the street.

Estaba nublado e iba a llover.
It was cloudy and it was going to rain.

PRACTICE 1
Change the underlined phrases using the pronoun given in parentheses.

1. Era viernes por la noche y <u>Miguel estaba</u> en una fiesta. (nosotros)

2. Eran las once de la mañana y <u>yo tenía</u> mucho frío. (tú)

3. Una vez cuando <u>nadabamos</u> en la piscina . . . (ellos)

4. Era un día muy bonito y <u>ellos querían</u> ir al campo. (nosotros)

5. Una noche, cuando <u>caminaba</u> a casa . . . (vosotros)

6. Era tarde y <u>ella caminaba</u> sola. (ellos)

CONVERSATION 2

Hernando is applying for a job as a pharmacist and is being interviewed for the position by the head of pharmacology of a well-known hospital in Buenos Aires.

Doctor: Su hoja de vida es impresionante. Está muy cualificado. ¿Cuál es su objetivo en solicitar este puesto?

Hernando: Quiero vincularme con un hospital prestigioso para desarrollarme profesionalmente.

Doctor: Y, ¿qué es lo que nos ofrece usted a nosotros?

Hernando: Gran capacidad para el trabajo. Sé manejar situaciones estresantes, y soy bueno trabajando en equipo.

Doctor: ¿Domina el inglés?

Hernando: Claro que sí. Tengo una especialización en farmacia clínica de la universidad de Brighton en Inglaterra. Además hablo francés e italiano.

Doctor: Bueno, le podemos ofrecer un contrato por un año con jornada de treinta y siete horas y un mes de vacaciones.

Hernando: Su oferta es muy interesante. ¿Cuándo comienzo?

Doctor: Nos gustaría que empezara tan pronto como sea posible.

Hernando: Estoy disponible a partir del quince de este mes, ¿le parece bien?

Doctor: Perfecto. ¡Bienvenido a bordo!

Doctor: *Your résumé is impressive. You're very well qualified. What's your aim in applying for this job?*

Hernando: *I want to join a prestigious hospital in order to advance professionally.*

Doctor: *And, what do you offer us?*

Hernando: *Great work capacity. I know how to handle stressful situations, and I'm a good team worker.*

Doctor: *Do you speak English?*

Hernando:	Yes, of course. I have a master's degree in clinical pharmacy from Brighton University in England. Plus, I speak French and Italian.
Doctor:	Well, we can offer you a one-year contract with a thirty-seven-hour workweek and a month of vacation.
Hernando:	Your offer is very interesting. When do I start?
Doctor:	We would like you to start as soon as possible.
Hernando:	I'm available as of the fifteenth of this month. How does that sound?
Doctor:	Perfect! Welcome aboard!

NOTES

There are a number of English words that the Royal Academy of Spanish Language has accepted into the Spanish language. Today these words are so common that Spanish speakers might not even realize that they're borrowed from English. This misimpression is made easier by the spelling of the words, which has often been adapted for the Spanish language.

estresante	*stressing*
fútbol	*soccer*
parqueadero	*parking lot*
computadora	*computer*

NUTS & BOLTS 2
USING THE PRETERITE AND THE IMPERFECT

You can use the imperfect to express two or more actions that were going on at the same time. Simultaneous actions are often linked with words like **mientras** (*while*) or **mientras tanto** (*meanwhile*).

Ella leía el periódico mientras yo cocinaba.
She read the newspaper while I cooked.

Mientras nosotros mirábamos televisión, ellos se vestían.
While we watched television, they got dressed.

To indicate that two or more actions happened sequentially, use the preterite.

Ella desayunó y luego fue a trabajar.
She had breakfast and then went to work.

Yo leí el periódico, tomé mi café y miré la tele.
I read the newspaper, drank my coffee, and watched TV.

In cases when you have an ongoing action that is interrupted by another action, use the imperfect to describe the action that was in progress and the preterite to describe the action that interrupted it.

Yo dormía cuando sonó el teléfono.
I was sleeping when the phone rang.

Empezó a llover cuando jugabamos en el parque.
It began to rain while we were playing in the park.

PRACTICE 2
Form sentences using the preterite and/or the imperfect following the clues given:

1. Ella/leer/una novela/minetras/yo/jugar/a las cartas. (simultaneous actions)

2. Ellos/trabajar/en el jardín/después/ir/de compras. (one action happens after the other)

3. Nosotros/cocinar/cuando/ella/llamar/por teléfono. (one action interrupts the other)

4. Él/tomar/el examen/y luego/tomar/un café/con sus amigos. (one action happens after the other)

5. Mientras/yo/dormir/vosotros/mirar/la tele. (simultaneous actions)

6. Vosotros/almorzar/luego/ir de compras. (one action happens after the other)

7. Ella/llorar/él/gritar. (simultaneous actions)

8. Yo/cantar/cuando/ellos/llamar a la puerta. (one action interrupts the other)

Tip!

Back in Lesson 12, we touched on accent marks and how they're used in Spanish. Now that you have some more experience under your belt, let's take a closer look. If a word ends in a vowel (**a, e, i, o, u**) or the letters **n** or **s**, and the stress falls on the last syllable, an accent mark is required.

caminó	*(he/she) walked*
dormí	*I slept*
canción	*song*
verás	*you will see*

If the word ends in a consonant other than **n** or **s** and the stress falls on the next-to-last syllable, an accent mark is also required.

lápiz	*pencil*
difícil	*difficult*
cárcel	*prison*
mártir	*martyr*

Sometimes, accent marks are used only to differentiate between words that would otherwise look identical.

él—el	*he—the*
qué—que	*what—that*
más—mas	*more—but*
tú—tu	*you—your*
sé—se	*I know—himself/herself, etc.*
sí—si	*yes—if*

Remember that question words have an accent when used in a question but the corresponding relative pronouns or connecting words do not.

¿cómo?	how?	como	as, like
¿cuál?	which?	cual	which, as
¿cuándo?	when?	cuando	when
¿dónde?	where?	donde	where
¿qué?	what?	que	which, that
¿quién?	who/whom?	quien	who, whom
¿cuánto?	how much?	cuanto	as much, as many

For example, in the first sentence below, **¿cómo?** is a question word, and in the second, **como** is a relative pronoun, introducing another sentence within the main one.

¿Cómo funciona?
How does it work?

No funciona como yo me imaginaba.
It doesn't work like (lit, how) I thought.

Demonstrative pronouns (**éste, ése, áquel**) have an accent, while demonstrative adjectives (**este, ese, aquel**) don't. Of course, if all of this is a bit overwhelming, don't worry. As with everything else, the more you read and write in Spanish, the easier this will become, and you'll get used to seeing certain words with an accent mark.

ANSWERS

PRACTICE 1: 1. Era viernes por la noche y nosotros estábamos en una fiesta. **2.** Eran las once de la mañana y tú tenías mucho frío. **3.** Una vez cuando nadaban en la piscina . . . **4.** Era un día muy bonito y queríamos ir al campo. **5.** Una noche, cuando caminabais a casa . . . **6.** Era tarde y ellos caminaban solos.

PRACTICE 2: 1. Ella leía una novela mientras yo jugaba a las cartas. **2.** Ellos trabajaron el el jardín y después fueron de compras. **3.** Nosotros cocinábamos cuando ella llamó por teléfono. **4.** Él tomó el examen y luego tomó un café con sus amigos. **5.** Mientras yo dormía, vosotros mirabais la tele. **6.** Vosotros almorzasteis y luego fuisteis de compras. **7.** Ella lloraba y él gritaba. **8.** Yo cantaba cuando ellos llamaron a la puerta.

UNIT 9 ESSENTIALS

Ella nos dio una noticia muy buena.

She gave us very good news.

Hubo mucha gente en la fiesta.

There were a lot of people at the party.

Hubo una película interesante.

There was one interesting film.

Nosotros le entregamos el informe a él.

We give him the report.

Nosotros se lo entregamos.

We give it to him.

Acabo de terminar el informe.

I have just finished the report.

Hace un año que estudio espanol.

I have been studying Spanish for a year.

Hace un año que estudié español.

I studied Spanish a year ago.

Ella tiene que estudiar para el examen.

She has to study for the test.

Debemos hacer una lista de invitados.

We have to make a guest list.

Hay que hablar claramente.
It is necessary to speak clearly.

Después del desayuno, caminaba por la playa.
After breakfast, I used to walk along the beach.

Cuando la conocí, ella tenía el pelo rojo y largo.
When I met her, she had long red hair.

Estaba nublado e iba a llover.
It was cloudy and it was going to rain.

Yo dormía cuando sonó el teléfono.
I was sleeping when the phone rang.

UNIT 10
Sports and hobbies

In this unit, you'll learn how to express doubt, denial, and conditions in Spanish. You'll also learn how to talk about the hobbies you have and the sports you enjoy.

—————————— Lesson 37 (words) ——————————

WORD LIST 1

la afición	*hobby*
el/la aficionado/a	*fan*
el pasatiempos	*hobby*
el tiempo libre	*free time*
coleccionar	*to collect*
la artesanía	*craft*
la fotografía	*photography*
la música	*music*
la pintura	*panting*
el baile	*dancing*
la filatelia	*stamp collecting*
las antigüedades	*antiques*
la cocina	*cooking*
la costura	*sewing*
la lectura	*reading*

NUTS & BOLTS 1
THE CONDITIONAL

The present conditional is used to express the probability or possibility that something would happen, depending on specific circumstances. In most cases where *would* is used in English, the conditional is used in Spanish. To form the conditional, simply add the following endings to the infinitive form of the verb: **-ía, -ías, -ía, -íamos, -íais, -ían.**

hablar (*to talk*)	ser (*to be*)	abrir (*to open*)
hablaría (*I would talk*)	sería (*I would be*)	abriría (*I would open*)
hablarías	serías	abrirías
hablaría	sería	abriría
hablaríamos	seríamos	abriríamos
hablaríais	seríais	abriríais
hablarían	serían	abrirían

The following verbs have irregular stems.

saber	sabría	*to know*
tener	tendría	*to have*
salir	saldría	*to go out*
poder	podría	*to be able to*
hacer	haría	*to make*
decir	diría	*to say*
haber	habría	*there is/there are*
querer	querría	*to want*
venir	vendría	*to come*

Let's look at some examples of the conditional.

Yo estudiaría ruso, pero no tengo tiempo.
I would study Russian, but I don't have time.

En tu caso, yo no diría nada.
In your case, I wouldn't say anything.

Con más dinero, ella haría maravillas.
With more money, she would perform miracles.

PRACTICE 1
Form sentences with the verbs in parentheses, using the conditional.

1. Nosotros _____ algo pero no hay nada en la nevera. (comer)

2. Yo _____ medicina pero no me gusta ver sangre. (estudiar)

3. Nadie _____ en esa casa tan vieja. (vivir)

4. Ella _____ la verdad, pero no puede. (decir)

5. Ellos _____ temprano, pero tienen que terminar el informe. (salir)

6. Los chicos _____ su tarea, pero olvidaron sus libros. (hacer)

7. Vosotros _____ al cine, pero ya es muy tarde. (ir)

8. Tú _____ una computadora, pero no tienes el dinero. (comprar)

WORD LIST 2

el deporte	*sport*
el atleta	*athlete*
el deportista	*person who plays sports*
el jugador	*player*
el ciclismo	*biking, cycling*
el fútbol	*soccer*
el béisbol	*baseball*

la natación	*swimming*
el buceo	*diving*
la equitación	*horseback riding*
la caza	*hunting*
el baloncesto	*basketball*
el ajedrez	*chess*

NUTS & BOLTS 2
IMPERSONAL SE

In English, we can make general statements with words like *you*, *people*, or *one*: *You shouldn't drink in public. In Spain, people eat supper very late. One shouldn't swim right after eating.* In all of these sentences, words like *you*, *people*, and *one* are used to mean *people in general*, rather than any particular person. These sentences are impersonal because we don't have anyone specific in mind. In Spanish, the impersonal **se** is used in front of verbs to make general statements like these. Generally, you use **se** with either the third person singular or the third person plural of the verb.

Se dice que va a llover.

They say it's going to rain.

En España, se cena muy tarde.

In Spain, people eat supper very late.

Las oficinas se cierran a las tres.

The offices close at three.

¿Cómo se dice "helado" en francés?

How do you say "ice cream" in French?

No se debe comer a prisa.

One shouldn't eat quickly.

PRACTICE 2

Form sentences using the impersonal **se**. Conjugate the verb in the present tense.

1. En ese lugar no (poder) pagar con tarjetas de crédito.

2. En la universidad no (deber) llegar tarde a una clase.

3. En Cuba (conseguir) buenos cigarros.

4. Para sacar buenas notas (tener) que estudiar mucho.

5. (Pensar) que aprender otro idioma es importante.

6. (Decir) que es mala suerte viajar en martes trece.

7. ¿Cómo (decir) "buenos días" en ruso?

8. ¿Cómo (escribir) esa palabra?

Tip!

Reading newspaper and magazine articles in Spanish might turn out to be a frustrating experience at first because of the number of new words and expressions. Some of the tips described in this course will help you decipher the meanings of many words without having to look them up in the dictionary. However, there will be times, especially when a word or expression keeps coming up in the text, that you'll need to look it up. When looking up words in a dictionary, it's important to remember that verbs are listed in the infinitive form, not the conjugated form. Don't always take the first definition you find listed; many words have multiple meanings and functions. You need to decide which one is the best for the context of the sentence. And a very important rule when dealing with two languages is to be extremely suspicious of word-for-word translations. Idiomatic expressions are often completely different across languages (and sound funny when translated literally!), but even "regular" expressions can be constructed in very different ways with very different words. So, don't abuse your dictionary; it is a tool that can provide you with a wealth of information, but it can lead you astray if you use it in the wrong way.

ANSWERS
PRACTICE 1: 1. comeríamos; **2.** estudiaría; **3.** viviría; **4.** diría; **5.** saldrían; **6.** harían; **7.** iríais; **8.** comprarías.

PRACTICE 2: 1. En ese lugar no se puede pagar con tarjetas de crédito. **2.** En la universidad no se debe llegar tarde a una clase. **3.** En Cuba se consiguen buenos cigarros. **4.** Para sacar buenas notas se tiene que estudiar mucho. **5.** Se piensa que aprender otro idioma es importante. **6.** Se dice que es mala suerte viajar en martes trece. **7.** ¿Cómo se dice "buenos días" en ruso? **8.** ¿Cómo se escribe esa palabra?

─────────── Lesson 38 (phrases) ───────────

PHRASE LIST 1

The following phrases will help you describe what you enjoy doing in your free time.

coleccionar objetos de arte	*to collect pieces of art*
visitar tiendas de antigüedades	*to visit antique shops*
asistir a una subasta	*to attend an auction*
descansar	*to rest*
tener un pasatiempos costoso	*to have an expensive hobby*
pasar el día en la piscina	*to spend the day at the swimming pool*
ser perezoso	*to be lazy*
escuchar música	*to listen to music*
practicar un deporte	*to play a sport*
hacer ejercicio	*to do exercise*
llevar un diario	*to keep a diary*

NUTS & BOLTS 1
THE SUBJUNCTIVE

Up to this point, you've been studying ways to express facts related to time (present, past, and future) in what is known as the *indicative mood*. All this means is that you have been learning how to present information in a factual and objective way; you're *in-*

dicating how things are (or how you think they are). However, there are ways of expressing things that aren't necessarily part of the world as it is. These may include things like emotions, persuasion, doubt, denial, and uncertainty. In the next few lessons, we'll be looking at the *subjunctive mood,* a way to express things or events that are not factual or concrete, but rather, hypothetical or subjective. In Spanish, the subjunctive is usually introduced by **que.** Take a look at these examples.

Espero que mi equipo gane el partido.
I hope my team wins the match.

Ojalá que no llueva hoy.
I hope it doesn't rain today.

Both examples express a hope for something that may or may not turn out to be true or to happen, so the subjunctive is used instead of the indicative. To form the present subjunctive of regular verbs, take the conjugation of the verb in the first person singular (**yo**) of the present tense, drop the final **-o,** and add the following endings. Note the use of opposite vowels: **-ar** verbs use **-e** endings, and **-er** and **-ir** verbs use **-a** endings.

comprar (*to buy*)	comer (*to eat*)	escribir (*to write*)
compre	coma	escriba
compres	comas	escribas
compre	coma	escriba
compremos	comamos	escribamos
compréis	comáis	escribáis
compren	coman	escriban

Verbs with an irregular stem in the **yo** form keep that stem in all forms of the present subjunctive, such as the following verbs.

tener (yo tengo)	tenga	*to have*
hacer (yo hago)	haga	*to make*
venir (yo vengo)	venga	*to come*
salir (yo salgo)	salga	*to go out*
poner (yo pongo)	ponga	*to put*
decir (yo digo)	diga	*to say*
traer (yo traigo)	traiga	*to bring*
conocer (yo conozco)	conozca	*to know*

Verbs with a stem change in the present indicative have the same kind of stem change in the present subjunctive. In **-ar** and **-er** verbs, the stem change occurs in all persons except **nosotros(as)** and **vosotros(as).** On the other hand, **-ir** verbs undergo the stem change in all persons. Here are three examples.

pensar (*to think*)	poder (*to be able to*)	servir (*to serve*)
piense	pueda	sirva
pienses	puedas	sirvas
piense	pueda	sirva
pensemos	podamos	sirvamos

penséis	podáis	sirváis
piensen	puedan	sirvan

PRACTICE 1
Give the corresponding subjunctive form of the following verbs.

1. que tú (querer)
2. que él (oír)
3. que yo (venir)
4. que nosotros (salir)
5. que ellas (saber)

6. que vosotras (dormir)
7. que ustedes (pedir)
8. que él (hablar)
9. que usted (partir)
10. que ella (sentir)

PHRASE LIST 2
The following phrases will help you when talking about a game such as soccer.

ganar un partido	*to win a game*
perder un partido	*to lose a game*
llenar un estadio	*to fill up a stadium*
el número de espectadores	*the number of spectators*
marcar/hacer/anotar un gol	*to make a goal*
intercambiar camisetas	*to exchange T-shirts*
comprar boletos en la taquilla	*to buy tickets at the gate*
quedar empatados	*to be tied*
hacer una cola/fila	*to stand in line*
el medio tiempo	*halftime*
vitorear a un equipo	*to cheer for a team*
el campeonato mundial de fútbol	*the world soccer championship*

NUTS & BOLTS 2
USING THE SUBJUNCTIVE

So, how do you use the subjunctive? Whenever you want to express a request, a desire, or a demand, or give advice, you will be using the subjunctive mood. Usually, when the verb in the main clause of the sentence expresses any of these, the verb that comes after (in the dependent **que** clause) must be in the subjunctive. The following verbs and phrases are usually followed by another verb in the subjunctive.

aconsejar que . . .	*to advise that/to* . . .
querer que . . .	*to want that/to* . . .
desear que . . .	*to wish that* . . .
pedir que . . .	*to request that* . . .
insistir que . . .	*to insist that* . . .
recomendar que . . .	*to recommend that* . . .
sugerir que . . .	*to suggest that* . . .
preferir que . . .	*to prefer that* . . .
prohibir que . . .	*to forbid that/to* . . .
Es preferible que . . .	*It's preferable that* . . .
Es mejor que . . .	*It's better that* . . .
Es necesario que . . .	*It's necessary that* . . .

Here are a few examples to illustrate how the subjunctive is used:

Quiero que se vaya inmediatamente.
I want him to leave right now.

Te prohíbo que hables con ellos.
I forbid you to talk to them.

Es preferible que nos llame mañana.
It is preferable that you call us tomorrow.

Ella desea que tú vuelvas pronto.
She wishes that you come back soon.

Ustedes sugieren que se cambie la fecha.
You suggest that the date be changed.

Notice that where Spanish uses the subjunctive, English often uses infinitives, such as *I want him to leave now* or *I want you to talk to them.* But English also has a subjunctive, as shown in the last three examples: *that he call us, that you come back,* and *that the date be changed* are all examples of the English subjunctive. It may sound stuffy and formal in English, because the subjunctive is dying out in English. But in Spanish, it's alive and well, and it doesn't sound overly formal.

PRACTICE 2
Fill in the blanks with the correct form of the verb in the subjunctive mood.

1. Es mejor que tú _____ (venir) más temprano.

2. Le recomiendo a usted que _____ (traer) los documentos necesarios.

3. Yo insisto en que los niños _____ (comer) todas sus verduras.

4. Nosotros preferimos que ellos _____ (salir) de viaje el lunes.

5. Te aconsejo que no _____ (mirar) tanta televisión.

6. Les sugerimos que _____ (llamar) antes de venir.

7. Te prohíbo que _____ (fumar).

8. Les pedimos que _____ (escribir) una carta.

Tip!

A good way of learning the subjunctive is to remember that it is always introduced by the word **que.** When you ask a Spanish speaker how to conjugate a verb in this mood, they will always respond by using **que** plus the verb. It simply sounds correct and it is an easier way to remember how to conjugate the verbs.

ANSWERS

PRACTICE 1: 1. que tú quieras; **2.** que él oiga; **3.** que yo venga; **4.** que nosotros salgamos; **5.** que ellas sepan; **6.** que vosotras durmáis; **7.** que ustedes pidan; **8.** que él hable; **9.** que usted parta; **10.** que ella sienta.

PRACTICE 2: 1. Es mejor que tú vengas más temprano. **2.** Le recomiendo a usted que traiga los documentos necesarios. **3.** Yo insisto en que los niños coman todas sus verduras. **4.** Nosotors preferimos que ellos salgan de viaje el lunes. **5.** Te aconsejo que no mires tanta televisión. **6.** Les sugerimos que llamen antes de venir. **7.** Te prohíbo que fumes. **8.** Les pedimos que escriban una carta.

──────── Lesson 39 (sentences) ────────

SENTENCE LIST 1

Los discos de vinilo tienen su encanto.	*LPs have a certain charm.*
¿Eres un aficionado al fútbol?	*Are you a soccer fan?*
Me gusta el sonido que hace la aguja.	*I like the sound the needle makes.*
Tengo una colección enorme.	*I have a huge collection.*
Lo cual quiere decir que no te gusta mi música.	*Which means you don't like my music.*
Prefiero la música clásica.	*I prefer classical music.*
Tenemos gustos muy diferentes.	*We have very different tastes.*

Es el deporte que menos me gusta.	It's the sport that I like the least.
La tecnología nos permite escuchar la música de forma tan clara.	Technology allows us to listen to music in such a clear way.

NUTS & BOLTS 1
IRREGULAR VERBS IN THE SUBJUNCTIVE

A few verbs have an irregular present subjunctive form.

estar (*to be*)	ser (*to be*)	saber (*to know*)	dar (*to give*)	ir (*to go*)
esté	sea	sepa	dé	vaya
estés	seas	sepas	des	vayas
esté	sea	sepa	dé	vaya
estemos	seamos	sepamos	demos	vayamos
estéis	seáis	sepáis	deis	vayáis
estén	sean	sepan	den	vayan

Es mejor que todos sepan los resultados del examen.
It is better that everyone know the results of the test.

Ella prefiere que estemos en su casa a las ocho.
She prefers us to be at her house at eight.

Te sugiero que seas más puntual.
I suggest you be more punctual.

The present subjunctive of the verb **haber** (*there is/there are*) is **haya**.

Es mejor que haya suficiente comida.
It is better that there be enough food.

Sugiero que haya más invitados.
I suggest there be more guests.

Verbs ending in **-car,** **-gar,** and **-zar** undergo small spelling changes in all persons of the present subjunctive.

buscar (*to look for*)	pagar (*to pay*)	comenzar (*to begin*)
busque	pague	comience
busques	pagues	comiences
busque	pague	comience
busquemos	paguemos	comencemos
busquéis	paguéis	comencéis
busquen	paguen	comiencen

Te recomiendo que busques tu pasaporte.
I recommend that you look for your passport.

Es mejor que pagues esa cajetilla de cigarrillos.
It is better that you pay for that pack of cigarettes.

Nos sugieren que comencemos de inmediato.
They suggest that we begin immediately.

PRACTICE 1
Fill in the blanks with the correct form of the present subjunctive of the verbs in parentheses.

A mí me gusta coleccionar violines, pero mi esposa me prohíbe que los 1_____ (poner) en la sala de nuestra casa. Ella prefiere que 2_____ (ellos–estar) en el sótano. Ella me prohíbe que 3_____ (yo–comprar) más violines. Insiste en que 4_____ (yo–buscar) otra afición. Ella me sugiere que 5_____ (yo–coleccionar) algo más pequeño y fácil de guardar. Deseo que nosotros 6_____ (ganar) la lotería para comprar una casa muy grande donde pueda poner mis violines. Pero es mejor que yo 7_____ (ser) más real, y 8_____ (comenzar) a buscar otra afición. Voy a sugerirle que 9_____ (nosotros–ir) al Museo de Historia Natural. Tal vez ella prefiera que 10_____ (yo–saber) más de fósiles y los empiece a coleccionar.

SENTENCE LIST 2

¡Ni lo sueñes!	*Don't even dream about it!*
No nos lo podemos perder.	*We can't miss it.*
¿Quieres ir al partido del sábado?	*Would you like to go to Saturday's game?*
Es mejor que pase por tu apartamento más tarde.	*It is better that I drop by your apartment later on.*
Te apuesto a que el Boca gana.	*I bet you Boca will win.*
El marcador va a ser dos a cero.	*The score will be two to zero.*
¿Quieres que te recoja en tu casa?	*Would you like me to pick you up at your place?*
Tengo unos boletos para el partido.	*I have a few tickets for the game.*
Soy un hincha de ese equipo.	*I'm a fan of that team.*

NUTS & BOLTS 2
VERBS FOLLOWED BY THE SUBJUNCTIVE

The subjunctive mood is also used to express feelings, emotions, and personal perceptions. Here are a few verbs and expressions that require the use of the subjunctive. They're all followed by the word **que** + the verb in the subjunctive mood (notice that some verbs are reflexive).

sentir que . . .	*to regret that . . .*
esperar que . . .	*to hope that . . .*
tener miedo de que . . .	*to be afraid that . . .*
gustar que . . .	*to like (it) that . . .*
enfadarse que . . .	*to be angry that . . .*
alegrarse de que . . .	*to be glad that . . .*
preocuparse que . . .	*to worry that . . .*
sorprenderse que . . .	*to be surprised that . . .*
molestarse que . . .	*to be bothered that . . .*
Es una lástima que . . .	*It's a pity that . . .*
Es triste que . . .	*It's sad that . . .*
Es bueno que . . .	*It's good that . . .*

Let's take a look at some examples, and again, notice the different ways that the subjunctive can be translated into English.

Nos enfada que (ellas) lleguen tarde.
We're angry that they arrive late.

Me preocupa que (él) viaje de noche.
It worries me that he travels at night.

Le gusta que lo despierten temprano.
He likes to be woken up early.

Tengo miedo de que (ella) sepa la verdad.
I'm afraid of her learning the truth.

Es una lástima que (ustedes) no esten aquí.

It's a pity that you aren't here.

Notice in the above examples, that subject pronouns (for both the indicative and the subjunctive verbs) are usually omitted. Because most sentences occur in a context, it's easy to know who the subject of each verb is. The subject pronoun is specified only when it's necessary to make the meaning clear.

PRACTICE 2
Answer the following questions using the words provided.

1. ¿De qué te alegras? Yo/alegrarse/tú/estar aquí.

2. ¿Qué le preocupa a Martín? Él/preocuparse/no haber/boletos para el cine.

3. ¿Qué espera usted que ella haga? Yo/esperar/ella/llegar temprano.

4. ¿Qué le sorprende a ella de él? Ella/sorprenderse/él/coleccionar rocas.

5. ¿Qué temen ellos? Ellos/temer/su equipo/perder/el partido.

6. ¿Qué alegra a tus padres? Ellos/alegrarse/yo/llamarlos por teléfono.

7. ¿Qué os molesta de Enrique? Nosotros/molestarse/él/fumar.

8. ¿Qué te enfada? Yo/enfadarse/la gente/decir/mentiras.

Discovery activity

Explore the internet to find more examples of the subjunctive at work. In a search engine, type the phrases **que él sea** or **que ella vaya** or any other examples of the subjunctive. Collect three or four sentences and see if you can figure out why the subjunctive is used. What is the speaker conveying? Is it emotion, doubt, uncertainly, desire, etc.? The more examples of the subjunctive you see, the easier it will be for you to master it.

ANSWERS

PRACTICE 1: 1. ponga; 2. estén; 3. compre; 4. busque;
5. coleccione; 6. ganemos; 7. sea; 8. comience; 9. vayamos;
10. yo sepa.

PRACTICE 2: 1. Me alegro de que estés aquí. 2. Le preocupa
que no hayan boletos para el cine. 3. Espero que ella llegue
temprano. 4. A ella le sorprende que él coleccione rocas.
5. Ellos temen que su equipo pierda el partido. 6. Les alegra
que yo los llame por teléfono. 7. Nos molesta que él fume.
8. Me enfada que la gente diga mentiras.

——————— Lesson 40 (conversations) ———————

CONVERSATION 1

Clarisa is on a date with Manuel. They are getting to know each
other and are talking about each other's interests.

Clarisa: **Tengo una colección enorme de discos de
vinilo.**

Manuel: **Es un poco extraño hoy en día en que la
tecnología nos permite escuchar la música de
una forma más clara con los discos compactos.**

Clarisa: **Para mí, los discos de vinilo tienen su encanto.
Me encanta escuchar el sonido que hace la
aguja cuando se termina el disco. No sé . . . me
parece que hoy todo tiene que ser tan perfecto,
que las cosas pierden su gracia.**

Manuel: **¿Y coleccionas toda clase de música?**

Clarisa: **No, no toda. Me gusta mucho la música clásica
y me encanta el jazz. También tengo discos de
los años cicuenta y sesenta.**

Manuel: **Lo cual quiere decir que no te gusta la música
más moderna.**

Clarisa: **No, no mucho . . . Y a ti, ¿que música te gusta?**

Manuel: **Bueno, pues yo tengo una colección de
guitarras eléctricas.**

Clarisa: Así que te gusta el "heavy metal".

Manuel: Sí, así es. Tenemos gustos muy diferentes en cuanto a música.

Clarisa: No me dirás que también eres un aficionado al fútbol, porque es el deporte que menos me gusta.

Manuel: Mmm . . . ¿Te gustaría otro martini?

Clarisa: I have an enormous collection of LPs.

Manuel: That's a bit strange, because today, technology gives us the possibility of listening to music in such a clear way with CDs.

Clarisa: LPs have a certain charm for me. I love to hear the sound the needle makes once the record is over. I don't know . . . I think that today, everything has to be so perfect that things lose their appeal.

Manuel: Do you collect all kinds of music?

Clarisa: No, not all. I like classical music very much and I love jazz. I also have records from the fifties and sixties.

Manuel: So, that means you don't like more modern music.

Clarisa: No, not really . . . And you, what kind of music do you like?

Manuel: I have a collection of electric guitars.

Clarisa: So you like heavy metal.

Manuel: Yes, that's right. We have very different tastes regarding music.

Clarisa: Don't tell me that you're a soccer fan, because it's the sport I like the least.

Manuel: Mmm . . . Would you like another martini?

NOTES

Soccer, or **fútbol** in Spanish, is a multibillion-dollar business in Latin America and throughout the world, and it moves millions of fans to follow their teams whereever they go. Brazil, Argentina, and Uruguay are the Latin American countries with the longest soccer traditions. Regardless of the political instability of some countries and the deep economic and social differences that exist, soccer has the power to bring people closer together like no other sport or event.

When you talk about **fútbol,** you can't help but talk about great athletes who once had a dream and have made it come true. Players like Pelé (Edson Arantes do Nascimento), also known as the King of Soccer in Brazil, the country's top goal scorer; Diego Armando Maradona, Argentina's greatest soccer player and perhaps one of the most controversial; the Brazilians' Ronaldo, who now plays for the AC Milan; and Ronaldinho, who plays for the FC Barcelona; and others like the Colombian goalkeeper Huiguita and el Pibe Valderrama are every kid's role model and every adult's hero. Soccer is played on neighborhood streets, parks, and beaches all over Latin America. It's a sport that knows no social class, race, or age. It can bring people together in a way that no other sport can, filling up stadiums the size of the Estadio Maracana in Rio de Janeiro, which, in the 1950 World Championship, held 199,548 fans to see the last game between Uruguay and Brazil. To learn more about **fútbol,** and to practice your Spanish, check out:

www.fifa.com/es/index.html

NUTS & BOLTS 1
THE SUBJUNCTIVE VS. THE INDICATIVE
The subjunctive is also used to express disbelief, doubt, denial, and uncertainty.

Dudo que nuestro equipo gane.
I doubt our team will win.

Es posible que me trasladen a Nueva York.
It's possible that I'll be transferred to New York.

However, if the verb in the main clause expresses certainty, belief, or affirmation, the indicative is used.

Creo que nuestro equipo va a ganar.
I believe our team will win.

Es verdad que me han trasladado a Nueva York.
It's true that I've been transferred to New York.

The following verbs and phrases are commonly used to express disbelief, doubt, denial, and uncertainty.

no creer que . . .	*not to believe that . . .*
no pensar que . . .	*not to think that . . .*
Es posible que . . .	*It is possible that . . .*
dudar que . . .	*to doubt that . . .*
No es verdad que . . .	*It is not true that . . .*
No es cierto que . . .	*It is not true that . . .*
Es imposible que . . .	*It is imposible that . . .*
No hay nada que . . .	*There's nothing that . . .*
No hay nadie que . . .	*There's no one who . . .*
No hay ningún . . . que . . .	*There's no (thing) that . . . / (person) who . . .*
negar que . . .	*to deny that . . .*

PRACTICE 1
Change the following sentences using the clues given.

Ex. Creo que van a comprar un apartamento en Lima. (yo no creer que)

No creo que vayan a comprar un apartamento en Lima.

1. Es cierto que Ana está embarazada. (No es cierto que)

2. Vamos a sacar una buena nota en el examen. (Es posible que)

3. Es seguro que el equipo está retrasado. (Es posible que)

4. Es verdad que en esa compañía pagan un sueldo muy alto. (No es verdad que)

5. Ellos están buscando trabajo. (yo dudar)

6. Estoy seguro de que va a llover. (yo no creer)

7. Hay otro deporte más exigente que el fútbol. (nosotros dudar)

8. Todo en esta vida es difícil. (yo negar)

CONVERSATION 2

Carlos and Manuel are making plans for the weekend and are talking about their favorite sport.

Carlos: Oye, Manuel, ¿quieres ir al partido del sábado?

Manuel: ¡Me encantaría! ¿Tienes boletos?

Carlos: Sí, precisamente tengo dos boletos para el partido entre Boca Juniors y el Atlético River Plate.

Manuel: Bueno, pues es un partido que no nos lo podemos perder. Tú sabes que yo soy un hincha del Boca. ¿A qué hora juegan?

Carlos: El partido empieza a las siete de la noche. ¿Quieres que te recoja en tu casa a eso de las cinco y media?

Manuel: No, creo que estaré en la oficina trabajando. Es mejor que me pase por tu apartamento cuando termine.

Carlos: Está bien. Y . . . ¿cómo van a ser nuestras apuestas esta vez?

Manuel: Te apuesto a que el Boca gana uno a cero en los primeros treinta minutos de juego.

Carlos: ¡Ni lo sueñes! El River Plate está jugando muy bien y creo que va a ganar. Te apuesto a que el marcador va a ser dos a cero. Además, tu equipo tiene un portero pésimo.

Manuel: Bueno, ya veremos. Nosotros vamos a llegar a la Copa Libertadores. Hasta el sábado.

Carlos: *Listen, Manuel, would you like to go to the soccer game on Saturday?*

Manuel: *I'd love to! Do you have tickets?*

Carlos: *Yes, I have two tickets for the game between Boca Juniors and Atlético River Plate.*

Manuel: *Well, it's a game we can't miss. You know I'm a big fan of Boca. What time do they play?*

Carlos: *The game starts at seven in the evening. Do you want me to pick you up at your place at around five thirty?*

Manuel: *No, I think I'll be at work. I'll drop by your apartment when I'm done.*

Carlos: *Okay. So what are our bets going to be this time?*

Manuel: *I bet you Boca will win one to nothing in the first thirty minutes of the game.*

Carlos: *In your dreams! River Plate is playing very well and I think they'll win. I bet you the score will be two to zero. Plus, your team has a terrible goalkeeper.*

Manuel: *We'll see. We'll make it to the Copa Libertadores. See you Saturday.*

NOTES

The soccer club **Atlético Boca Juniors** is one of the most popular and successful in Argentina. It's located in **La Boca,** a neighborhood in Buenos Aires. This club, along with its rival, **Atlético River Plate,** can fill up entire stadiums in Argentina. The **Boca Juniors** have won several soccer cups, including the International Cup in 1978, 2000, and 2003; and the **Copa Libertadores** in 1977, 1978, 2000, 2001, and 2003. To read more about both clubs, check out *www.bocajuniors.com.ar* and *www.cariverplate.com.ar.*

NUTS & BOLTS 2
RELATIVE PRONOUNS AND CLAUSES

Relative pronouns, such as *that, which,* and *who(m),* are used to refer back to a previous noun in a sentence. They introduce relative clauses, which are mini-sentences that give more information about that previous noun: *The book that I read is very interesting. The team that I like the most just won.* In many cases in English, we can even omit relative pronouns like *who* and *that.* In Spanish, however, relative pronouns cannot be left out, and there is a wider variety to choose from.

The two most common relative pronouns are **que** and **quien.** **Que** is used to refer to both people and things. **Quien** (plural form **quienes**) is used only to refer to people, and it's preceded by the prepositions **a, con, para,** or **de.**

El equipo que acaba de ganar es mi favorito.

The team that has just won is my favorite.

El jugador con quien hablaste es muy famoso.

The player you talked to is very famous.

El hombre que está afuera es su esposo.

The man who's outside is her husband.

Las mujeres a quienes entrevistaste son atletas profesionales.

The women you interviewed are professional athletes.

When the relative pronoun must specify one among several previously mentioned nouns, a compound form using the definite article (**el, la, los, las**) + **que** or **cual(es)** is used. They are generally used after prepositions, such as **en, sin, por,** and **para.** Notice that the definite article agrees in number and gender with the noun it refers to.

No es el auto en el que viajé la semana pasada.

It's not the car that I traveled in last week. (. . . in which I traveled last week.)

Es la calle por la que caminamos ayer.
It's the street we walked along yesterday. (. . . along which we walked yesterday.)

Son los sueños en los cuales siempre piensas.
They are the dreams that you always think of. (. . . in which you always think.)

Es la mujer de la cual está enamorado.
She's the woman he's in love with. (. . . with whom he's in love.)

Cuyo (cuya, cuyos, cuyas) is also a relative pronoun but looks more like an adjective, because it agrees in gender and number with the person or thing possessed, not with the person or thing it refers to.

El autor, cuyo nombre no recuerdo, vivió en esta ciudad.
The author, whose name I don't remember, lived in this city.

Los niños, cuyas manos están sucias, no quieren lavarse.
The children, whose hands are dirty, don't want to wash up.

PRACTICE 2
Choose the relative pronoun that best completes the sentence.

1. Los pasajes _____ compré son solamente de ida. (los cuales, que, los que)

2. La cantante, _____ fama es mundial, viene a finales de septiembre. (que, quien, cuya)

3. El apartamento en _____ quiero vivir está en el último piso de ese edificio. (la cual, el cual, los cuales)

4. Las mujeres _____ nos visitaron eran espías. (quienes, que, cuyas)

5. Los chicos, _____ nombres desconozco, son los hijos de nuestra vecina. (cuyos, que, quienes)

6. Esos son los documentos con _____ te debes presentar ante el juez. (quienes, los cuales, cuyos)

7. El hombre con _____ nos encontramos, era el esposo de Maura. (los cuales, quienes, quien)

8. Las estampillas _____ compré son para mi colección. (la cual, quien, que)

Culture note

One of the most prestigious soccer trophies is without doubt **La Copa Libertadores de América.** It's an international cup organized by **CONMEBOL (Confederación Sudaméricana de Fútbol)** and is played for by the leading clubs in South America. Argentina has been the champion twenty times, followed by Brazil, which has won the trophy thirteen times. For more information, check out *www.conmebol.com.*

The **Copa América** is another important national competition in South America. It's played every two years. Twelve countries participate: Argentina, Brazil, Bolivia, Chile, Colombia, Ecuador, Paraguay, Peru, Uruguay, and Venezuela, along with two additional guests from other soccer confederations.

ANSWERS
PRACTICE 1: 1. No es cierto que Ana esté embarazada. **2.** Es posible que saquemos una buena nota en el examen. **3.** Es posible que el equipo esté retrasado. **4.** No es verdad que en esa compañía paguen un sueldo muy alto. **5.** Dudo que ellos estén buscando trabajo. **6.** No creo que vaya a llover. **7.** Nosotros dudamos que haya otro deporte más exigente que el fútbol. **8.** Niego que todo en esta vida sea difícil.

PRACTICE 2: 1. que; **2.** cuya; **3.** el cual; **4.** que; **5.** cuyos; **6.** los cuales; **7.** quien; **8.** que.

UNIT 10 ESSENTIALS
Yo estudiaría italiano, pero no tengo tiempo.
I would study Italian, but I don't have time.

En tu caso, yo no diría nada.
In your case, I wouldn't say anything.

En España se cena muy tarde.
In Spain, people eat supper very late.

¿Cómo se dice "helado" en ruso?
How do you say "ice cream" in Russian?

Espero que mi equipo gane el partido.
I hope my team wins the game.

Ojalá que no llueva hoy.
I hope it doesn't rain today.

Es mejor que tú vengas más temprano.
It is better that you come earlier.

Le recomiendo que traiga los documentos.
I advise you to bring the documents.

Ella prefiere que estemos en la oficina a las siete.
She prefers that we be at the office at seven.

Es mejor que haya suficiente comida.
It is better that there be enough food.

Sugiero que haya más invitados.
I suggest there be more guests.

Es una lástima que ustedes no estén aquí.
It's a pity that you aren't here.

Dudo que nuestro equipo gane.
I doubt that our team will win.

No es el auto en el cual viajé la semana pasada.
It is not the car that I traveled in last week.

El autor, cuyo nombre no recuerdo, vivió en esta ciudad.
The author, whose name I don't remember, lived in this city.

A. RESERVATION FORM
Reservaciones en línea
Hotel Camino Real
Ciudad: Cancún
Estado: Quintana Roo

INFORMACIÓN PERSONAL
Apellido: _____
Nombre: _____
Teléfono: _____
E-mail: _____
País: _____
Ciudad: _____
Dirección: _____

DETALLES DE LA RESERVACIÓN
Fecha de llegada (Día/Mes/Año): _____
Fecha de salida (Día/Mes/Año): _____
Hora de llegada (Día/Mes/Año): _____

HABITACIONES
Habitación sencilla con baño compartido: _____
Habitación sencilla con baño privado: _____
Habitación sencilla de lujo: _____
Habitación doble con baño compartido: _____
Habitación doble con baño privado: _____
Habitación doble de lujo: _____
Habitación triple con baño privado: _____
Suite de lujo: _____
Favor de indicar aquí sus peticiones especiales al hotel: _____
Pulse aquí para enviar la reservación.

ONLINE RESERVATIONS
HOTEL CAMINO REAL
City: Cancún
State: Quintana Roo

PERSONAL INFORMATION
First Name: _____
Last Name: _____
Telephone: _____
E-mail: _____
Country: _____
City: _____
Address: _____

RESERVATION DETAILS
Arrival Date (Day/Month/Year): _____
Departure Date (Day/Month/Year): _____
Time of Arrival (Day/Month/Year): _____

ROOMS
Single room with shared bathroom: _____
Single room with private bathroom: _____
Single luxury room: _____
Double room with shared bathroom: _____
Double room with private bathroom: _____
Double luxury room: _____
Triple room with private bathroom: _____
Luxury suite: _____
Please indicate any special requests for the hotel here: _____
Click here to send the reservation.

B. E-mail

Fecha: 7 de julio de 2009
Para: enmon@muchocorreo.es
De: cpermar@muchocorreo.es
Asunto: Planes de vacaciones
Querido Enrique:
Ya por fin te podemos escribir con nuestros planes para el fin del verano. Viajaremos a Venecia, vía Barcelona, el 24 de julio. Estaremos allí tres días y el 27 nos vamos a Croacia. Regresaremos a Barcelona el día 7 de agosto y nos quedaremos una semana. La hora prevista de llegada de nuestro vuelo es a las 6 de la tarde. Si todo sale bien, sobre las 8 de la noche estaremos instalados en nuestro hotel que se llama Hotel Oriente Husa, al lado del Liceo, en Las Ramblas, teléfono: 93–3022558 y la reserva está a nombre de María Jesús. Nuestro teléfono móvil es el 838831007. Quizás tú llegarás más tarde o más temprano y estés muy cansado de tu viaje. Ya nos dirás el teléfono y el nombre de tu hotel y si no podemos cenar juntos, al menos podremos tomar algo después. En cualquier caso, tenemos el día siguiente para vernos. Hacer coincidir el viaje con el tuyo, que esta vez diseñamos enteramente por Internet, fue bastante complicado, pero, al fin, parece resuelto. Y es que después de saber que estuviste en Londres sin nosotros saberlo cuando estábamos allí, no queríamos que por unas horas nos quedásemos sin la posibilidad de vernos otra vez. Ya nos dirás si tus fechas siguen como estaban. Si es posible, por favor envíanos tu itinerario. Nos podrías adjuntar tu itinerario con todos tus vuelos cuando respondas a este mensaje. ¡Tenemos muchas ganas de verte!

Cariños,
César y María Jesús

Date: July 7, 2009
To: enmon@muchocorreo.es
From: cpermar@muchocorreo.es
Subject: Vacation Plans
Dear Enrique:

We can finally write to you with our final summer plans. We are flying to Venice, via Barcelona, on July 24th. We will spend three days there, and on the 27th, we're off to Croatia. We will be back in Barcelona on August 7th, where we'll stay for an extra week. Our flight is expected to arrive at 6 P.M. If everything goes as planned, by 8 P.M. we will have checked into our hotel, which is called Hotel Oriente Husa, next the the Lyceum on Las Ramblas, telephone: 93-3022558. The reservation is under Maria Jesus's name. Our cell phone number is 838831007. You might arrive earlier or later than that, and you might be very tired after your flight. Let us know the name of your hotel and your phone number; if we can't have dinner together, at least we'll have a drink later that night. In any case, we have the next day to see each other. It was very difficult to make our schedule coincide with yours; we planned everything on the internet, and everything seems to be finalized and set. You see, after knowing that we were in London at the same time and we didn't know about it, we didn't want to miss the opportunity to see each other again. Let us know if your dates are still the same. If it's possible, please send us your itinerary. You could attach your itinerary with all your flight information when you reply to this message. We are so much looking forward to seeing you!

Love,
César and María Jesús

C. Business Letter

Envíos Rápidos
Calle Segovia 552
La Paz, Asunción

Sr. Ricardo Hernández
Calle Ensenada 445
La Paz, Asunción

2 de junio de 2010

Estimado Sr. Hernández:

Me dirijo a usted en respuesta a su carta del 17 de mayo en la cual afirma que, debido a la suma pendiente de mi cuenta, procederá contra mí a menos que salde por completo la deuda dentro de un plazo de siete días.

Su carta me ha sorprendido porque llevamos haciendo negocios durante 12 años y en el pasado siempre he pagado a tiempo. Lamento que haya optado por esta vía y le pido una prórroga del plazo para pagar. Le comuniqué en mi última carta que mis propios acreedores se están retrasando últimamente, lo cual explica las dificultades que estoy experimentando en estos momentos.

Le aseguro que tengo la intención de abonar la totalidad de la cuenta dentro de un plazo de treinta días, y como prueba de mi buena fe le adjunto un cheque para cubrir una parte del saldo.

Con la confianza de poder llegar a un acuerdo amistoso, le saluda cordialmente,
Ricardo García

Envíos Rápidos
552 Segovia Street
La Paz, Asunción

Sr. Ricardo Hernández
445 Ensenada Street
La Paz, Asunción

June 2, 2010

Dear Mr. Hernández

I am writing in reply to your letter of May 17th, in which you state that due to the outstanding amount on my account, you will be taking action against me unless full settlement is made within seven days.

The letter surprised me, because I have been doing business with you for twelve years now, and in the past I have always paid on time. I regret that you should adopt this line of action and ask you and allow me an extension. I informed you in my last letter that my own creditors have been holding back payments recently, and this explains the difficulties I am experiencing at the moment.

I would like to assure you that I intend to make full payment within thirty days, and as evidence of my good faith, I have enclosed a check to cover part of the balance.

Sincerely,
Ricardo García

D. RECIPE
Tortilla de papas

6 porciones
4 papas medianas, peladas y cortadas en cubitos de 1/2 pulgada (1 cm.)
1 cebolla picada
1 cubito de caldo concentrado de pollo
1/2 taza de agua
2 paquetes de sustituto de huevo líquido
8 claras de huevo (opcional)
2 cdtas. de aceite de oliva
1/4 cdta. de polvo de hornear
1/4 cdta. de pimienta
sal al gusto

Hierva las papas unos minutos sin que lleguen a ablandarse totalmente. En una sartén honda de material antiadherente, disuelva el cubito con el agua. Eche la cebolla y cuando esté blanda, agregue las papas, y revuelva ocasionalmente. Retire del fuego. Con una espumadera saque las papas y cebolla para que escurran y ponga aparte. Bata las claras con el polvo de hornear a punto de merengue e incorpore el sustituto de huevo, las papas, las cebollas, la pimienta y la sal. Una la mezcla con movimientos suaves y envolventes. Eche una cucharadita de aceite en una sartén de material antiadherente cuando esté bien caliente. Vierta la mezcla y baje a fuego mediano, moviendo la sartén para que no se queme. Cuando los bordes se hayan despegado de la sartén y la superficie se haya asentado, levante con cuidado un borde, si la parte de abajo ha empezado a dorarse, ya está lista para virar. Tape la sartén con un plato grande y vírela sobre el plato. Eche la otra cucharadita de aceite a la sartén y deslice la tortilla en la misma. Cocine unos minutos más moviendo la sartén hasta que la tortilla se dore por debajo.

Potato tortilla

6 servings
4 medium potatoes, peeled and cut into 1/2-inch cubes
1 minced onion
1 cube of concentrated chicken broth
1/2 cup water
2 packets of liquid egg replacer
8 egg whites (optional)
2 tsp. olive oil
1/4 tsp. baking powder
1/4 tsp. pepper
salt to taste

Boil the potatoes for a few minutes without letting them completely soften. Dissovle the cube in the water in a deep nonstick frying pan. Add in the onion, and when it's soft, add the potatoes, stirring occasionally. Remove from heat. Take out the potatoes and onion with a skimmer so that they drain, and set them aside. Beat the egg whites with the baking powder until stiff, and add in the egg replacer, the potatoes, the onions, the pepper, and the salt. Gently combine by stirring around the outside of the mixture. Put a teaspoonful of olive oil in a well-heated nonstick frying pan. Pour in the mixture and lower the heat to medium, moving the pan so that it doesn't burn. When the edges have separated from the pan and the top has settled, carefully lift one side, and if the bottom has begun to brown, it's ready to be turned. Cover the pan with a large plate and turn it over, turning the tortilla out onto the plate. Put the other teaspoonful of olive oil in the pan and slide the tortilla into it. Cook for a few more minutes while moving the pan until the bottom of the tortilla browns.

SUPPLEMENTAL VOCABULARY

1. WEATHER

el tiempo	*weather*
Está lloviendo.	*It's raining.*
Está nevando.	*It's snowing.*
Está granizando.	*It's hailing.*
Hace viento.	*It's windy.*
Hace calor.	*It's hot.*
Hace frío.	*It's cold.*
Hace sol.	*It's sunny.*
Está nublado.	*It's cloudy.*
Hace muy buen tiempo.	*It's beautiful.*
la tormenta	*storm*
el viento	*wind*
el sol	*sun*
el trueno	*thunder*
el relámpago	*lightening*
el huracán	*hurricane*
la temperatura	*temperature*
el grado	*degree*
la lluvia	*rain*
la nieve	*snow*
la nube	*cloud*
la niebla	*fog*
la niebla tóxica/el smog	*smog*
el paraguas	*umbrella*

2. FOOD

la comida	*food*
la cena	*dinner*

el almuerzo	*lunch*
el desayuno	*breakfast*
la carne	*meat, beef*
el pollo	*chicken*
la carne de cerdo	*pork*
el pescado	*fish*
el camarón/la gamba	*shrimp*
la langosta	*lobster*
el pan	*bread*
el huevo	*egg*
el queso	*cheese*
el arroz	*rice*
la verdura/el vegetal	*vegetable*
la lechuga	*lettuce*
el tomate	*tomato*
la zanahoria	*carrot*
el pepino	*cucumber*
el pimiento	*pepper*
la fruta	*fruit*
la manzana	*apple*
la naranja	*orange*
el plátano/la banana	*banana*
la pera	*pear*
las uvas	*grapes*
la bebida	*drink*
el agua	*water*
la leche	*milk*
el jugo/el zumo	*juice*
el café	*coffee*
el té	*tea*
el vino	*wine*
la cerveza	*beer*

el refresco	*soft drink, soda*
la sal	*salt*
la pimienta	*pepper*
el azúcar	*sugar*
la miel	*honey*
frío/caliente	*hot/cold*
dulce/amargo	*sweet/sour*

3. PEOPLE

la gente	*people*
la persona	*person*
el hombre	*man*
la mujer	*woman*
el adulto/la adulta	*adult*
el niño/la niña	*child*
el niño/el chico	*boy*
la niña/la chica	*girl*
el adolescente	*teenager*
alto/bajo	*tall/short*
viejo/joven	*old/young*
gordo/delgado	*fat/thin*
simpático/antipático	*friendly/unfriendly*
alegre/triste	*happy/sad*
bonito/feo	*beautiful/ugly*
enfermo/saludable	*sick/healthy*
fuerte/débil	*strong/weak*
famoso	*famous*
inteligente	*intelligent*
dotado	*talented*

4. AT HOME

en casa	*at home*
la casa	*house*

el apartamento	*apartment*
la habitación	*room*
la sala	*living room*
el comedor	*dining room*
la cocina	*kitchen*
el dormitorio	*bedroom*
el baño	*bathroom*
el vestíbulo	*hall*
el armario	*closet*
la ventana	*window*
la puerta	*door*
la mesa	*table*
la silla	*chair*
el sofá	*sofa, couch*
la cortina	*curtain*
la alfombra	*carpet*
el televisor	*television*
el lector de cd	*CD player*
la lámpara	*lamp*
el lector de dvd	*DVD player*
el sistema de sonido	*sound system*
la pintura/el cuadro	*painting, picture*
el estante	*shelf*
las escaleras	*stairs*
el techo	*ceiling*
la pared	*wall*
el suelo	*floor*
pequeño/grande	*big/small*
nuevo/viejo	*new/old*
madera/de madera	*wood/wooden*
plástico/hecho de plástico	*plastic/made of plastic*

5. THE HUMAN BODY

el cuerpo humano	*the human body*
la cabeza	*head*
la cara	*face*
la frente	*forehead*
el ojo	*eye*
la ceja	*eyebrow*
las pestañas	*eyelashes*
la oreja	*ear*
la nariz	*nose*
la boca	*mouth*
el diente	*tooth*
la lengua	*tongue*
la mejilla	*cheek*
la barbilla	*chin*
el pelo	*hair*
el cuello	*neck*
el pecho	*chest*
el pecho/el seno	*breast*
los hombros	*shoulders*
el brazo	*arm*
el codo	*elbow*
la muñeca	*wrist*
la mano	*hand*
el estómago/el abdomen	*stomach/abdomen*
el pene	*penis*
la vagina	*vagina*
la pierna	*leg*
la rodilla	*knee*
el tobillo	*ankle*
el pie	*foot*

el dedo	*finger*
el dedo del pie	*toe*
la piel	*skin*
la sangre	*blood*
el cerebro	*brain*
el corazón	*heart*
los pulmones	*lungs*
el hueso	*bone*
el músculo	*muscle*
el tendón	*tendon*

6. TRAVEL AND TOURISM

viaje y turismo	*travel and tourism*
el turista	*tourist*
el hotel	*hotel*
el hostal	*youth hostel*
la recepción	*reception desk*
registrarse	*to check in*
pagar la cuenta	*to check out*
la reserva/la reservación	*reservation*
el pasaporte	*passport*
el recorrido por autobús	*tour bus*
la visita guiada	*guided tour*
la cámara	*camera*
el centro de información	*information center*
el mapa/el plano	*map*
el folleto	*brochure*
el monumento	*monument*
visitar los lugares de interés	*to go sightseeing*
hacer una foto	*to take a picture*
¿Puedes hacernos una foto?	*Can you take our picture?*

7. IN THE OFFICE

en la oficina	*in the office*
la oficina/el despacho	*office*
el escritorio	*desk*
la computadora/el ordenador	*computer*
el teléfono	*telephone*
el fax	*fax machine*
el estante	*bookshelf*
el armario	*filing cabinet*
la carpeta/el archivo	*file*
el jefe/la jefa	*boss*
el colega/la colega	*colleague*
el empleado/la empleada	*employee*
el personal/la plantilla	*staff*
la compañía	*company*
el negocio	*business*
la fábrica	*factory*
la sala de conferencias	*meeting room*
la reunión	*meeting*
la cita	*appointment*
el salario	*salary*
el trabajo	*job*
ocupado	*busy*
trabajar	*to work*
ganar	*to earn*

8. AT SCHOOL

en la escuela	*at school*
la escuela	*school*
la universidad	*university*
el aula	*classroom*
el curso	*course*

el maestro/la maestra	*teacher*
el profesor/la profesora	*professor*
el estudiante/la estudiante	*student*
la asignatura	*subject*
el cuaderno	*notebook*
el libro de texto	*textbook*
las matemáticas	*math*
la historia	*history*
la química	*chemistry*
la biología	*biology*
la literatura	*literature*
la lengua/el idioma	*language*
el arte	*art*
la música	*music*
la gimnasia	*gym*
el receso	*recess*
el examen/la prueba	*test*
la nota	*grade*
las calificaciones	*report card*
el diploma	*diploma*
el título	*degree*
difícil/fácil	*difficult/easy*
estudiar	*to study*
aprender	*to learn*
aprobar	*to pass*
suspender	*to fail*

9. SPORTS AND RECREATION

deportes y recreo	*sports and recreation*
el fútbol/el fútbol americano	*soccer/football*
el baloncesto	*basketball*
el béisbol	*baseball*

el hockey	*hockey*
el tenis	*tennis*
el juego/el partido	*game*
el equipo	*team*
el estadio	*stadium*
el entrenador/la entrenadora	*coach*
el jugador/la jugadora	*player*
el campeón/la campeona	*champion*
la pelota/el balón	*ball*
hacer excursionismo/hacer senderismo	*to go hiking*
ir de camping	*to go camping*
hacer un deporte	*to play a sport*
jugar un partido	*to play a game*
ganar	*to win*
perder	*to lose*
empatar	*to draw, to tie*
los naipes/las cartas	*cards*
el billar	*pool, billiards*

10. NATURE

la naturaleza	*nature*
el árbol	*tree*
la flor	*flower*
el bosque	*forest*
la montaña	*mountain*
el campo	*field*
el río	*river*
el lago	*lake*
el océano	*ocean*
el mar	*sea*
la playa	*beach*

el desierto	*desert*
la roca	*rock*
la arena	*sand*
el cielo	*sky*
el sol	*sun*
la luna	*moon*
la estrella	*star*
el agua	*water*
la tierra	*land*
la planta	*plant*
el cerro/la colina	*hill*
el estanque	*pond*

11. COMPUTERS AND THE INTERNET

las computadoras y la Internet	*computers and the internet*
la computadora/el ordenador	*computer*
el teclado	*keyboard*
el monitor/la pantalla	*monitor/screen*
la impresora	*printer*
el ratón	*mouse*
el módem	*modem*
la memoria	*memory*
el cd rom	*CD-ROM*
el lector de cd rom	*CD-ROM drive*
el archivo	*file*
el documento	*document*
el cable	*cable*
línea de suscriptor/abonado digital (dsl)	*DSL*
la Internet	*internet*
el sitio web	*website*

la página web	*webpage*
el correo electrónico	*e-mail*
el espacio para charla/el chat	*chat room*
el registro del web	*weblog (blog)*
el mensaje instantáneo	*instant message*
el documento adjunto	*attachment*
enviar un correo electrónico/ correo-e	*to send an e-mail*
enviar un documento adjunto	*to send an attachment*
pasar/retransmitir	*to forward*
contestar	*to reply*
eliminar	*to delete*
guardar un documento	*to save a document*
abrir un documento	*to open a file*
cerrar un documento	*to close a file*
adjuntar un documento	*to attach a file*

12. FAMILY AND RELATIONSHIPS

familia y relaciones	*family and relationships*
la madre	*mother*
el padre	*father*
el hijo	*son*
la hija	*daughter*
la hermana	*sister*
el bebé	*baby*
el hermano	*brother*
el esposo/marido	*husband*
la esposa/mujer	*wife*
la tía	*aunt*
el tío	*uncle*
la abuela	*grandmother*
el abuelo	*grandfather*

el primo/la prima	*cousin*
la suegra	*mother-in-law*
el suegro	*father-in-law*
la madrastra	*stepmother*
el padrastro	*stepfather*
el hijastro	*stepson*
la hijastra	*stepdaughter*
el novio	*boyfriend*
la novia	*girlfriend*
el prometido/la prometida	*fiancé(e)*
el amigo/la amiga	*friend*
el/la pariente	*relative*
querer/amar	*to love*
conocer	*to know (a person)*
encontrarse con	*to meet*
casarse con	*to marry*
divorciarse de	*to divorce (someone)*
divorciarse	*to get a divorce*
heredar	*to inherit*

13. ON THE JOB

empleos	*jobs*
el policía/la mujer policía	*policeman/policewoman*
el abogado/la abogada	*lawyer*
el doctor/la doctora	*doctor*
el ingeniero/la ingeniera	*engineer*
el hombre de negocios/ la mujer de negocios	*businessman/businesswoman*
el vendedor/la vendedora	*salesman/saleswoman*
el maestro/la maestra	*teacher*
el profesor/la profesora	*professor*
el banquero/la banquera	*banker*

el arquitecto/la arquitecta	*architect*
el veterinario/la veterinaria	*veterinarian*
el dentista/la dentista	*dentist*
el carpintero/la carpintera	*carpenter*
el obrero/la obrera	*construction worker*
el taxista/la taxista	*taxi driver*
el artista/la artista	*artist*
el escritor/la escritora	*writer*
el fontanero/la fontanera	*plumber*
el electricista/la electricista	*electrician*
el periodista/la periodista	*journalist*
el actor/la actriz	*actor/actress*
el músico	*musician (m. or f.)*
el granjero/la granjera	*farmer*
el secretario/la secretaria	*secretary*
la asistente/el asistente	*assistant*
desempleado/desempleada	*unemployed*
jubilado/jubilada	*retired*
a tiempo completo	*full-time*
a tiempo parcial	*part-time*
el trabajo fijo	*steady job*
el trabajo de verano	*summer job*

14. CLOTHING

la ropa	*clothing*
la camisa	*shirt*
los pantalones	*pants*
los vaqueros/los tejanos	*jeans*
la camiseta	*T-shirt*
los zapatos	*shoes*
los calcetines	*socks*
el cinturón	*belt*

las zapatillas deportivas	*sneakers, tennis shoes*
el vestido	*dress*
la falda	*skirt*
la blusa	*blouse*
el traje	*suit*
el sombrero	*hat*
los guantes	*gloves*
la bufanda	*scarf*
la chaqueta	*jacket*
el abrigo	*coat*
el pendiente	*earring*
la pulsera	*bracelet*
el collar	*necklace*
las gafas	*eyeglasses*
las gafas de sol	*sunglasses*
el reloj	*watch*
el anillo	*ring*
los calzoncillos	*underpants*
la camisilla/la camiseta	*undershirt*
el bañador	*bathing trunks*
el traje de baño	*bathing suit*
el pijama	*pajamas*
el algodón	*cotton*
el cuero	*leather*
la seda	*silk*
la talla	*size*
llevar/vestir/calzar	*to wear*

15. IN THE KITCHEN

en la cocina	*in the kitchen*
la nevera	*refrigerator*
el fregadero	*(kitchen) sink*

el mostrador	*counter*
la cocina	*stove*
el horno	*oven*
el microondas	*microwave*
el aparador	*cupboard*
el cajón	*drawer*
el plato	*plate*
la taza	*cup*
el cuenco/tazón	*bowl*
el vaso	*glass*
la cuchara	*spoon*
el cuchillo	*knife*
la lata	*can*
la caja	*box*
la botella	*bottle*
el bote/cartón	*carton*
la cafetera	*coffeemaker*
la tetera	*teakettle*
la batidora	*blender*
la plancha	*iron*
la tabla de planchar	*ironing board*
la escoba	*broom*
el lavaplatos	*dishwasher*
la lavadora	*washing machine*
la secadora	*dryer*
cocinar	*to cook*
lavar los platos	*to do the dishes*
lavar la ropa	*to do the laundry*
el detergente de vajilla	*dishwashing detergent*
el detergente de ropa	*laundry detergent*
la lejía	*bleach*
limpio/sucio	*clean/dirty*

16. IN THE BATHROOM

en el baño	*in the bathroom*
el inodoro	*toilet*
el lavabo	*sink (wash basin)*
la bañera	*bathtub*
la ducha	*shower*
el espejo	*mirror*
el botiquín	*medicine cabinet*
la toalla	*towel*
el papel higiénico	*toilet paper*
el champú	*shampoo*
el jabón	*soap*
el gel de baño	*bath gel*
la crema de afeitar	*shaving cream*
la navaja de afeitar	*razor*
lavarse	*to wash onself*
ducharse/bañarse	*to take a shower/bath*
afeitarse	*to shave*
la colonia	*cologne*
el perfume	*perfume*
el desodorante	*deodorant*
el vendaje	*bandage*
el polvo	*powder*

17. AROUND TOWN

por la ciudad	*around town*
el pueblo	*town*
la ciudad	*city*
la aldea	*village*
el carro/el coche/ el automóvil	*car*
el autobús	*bus*

el tren	train
el taxi	taxi
el subterráneo/el metro	subway/metro
el tráfico	traffic
el edificio	building
el edificio de apartamentos	apartment building
la biblioteca	library
el restaurante	restaurant
la tienda	store
la calle	street
el parque	park
la estación de ferrocarril	train station
el aeropuerto	airport
el avión	airplane
la intersección	intersection
la farola	lamppost
la luz de la calle	streetlight
el banco	bank
la iglesia	church
el templo	temple
la mezquita	mosque
la acera	sidewalk
la panadería	bakery
la carnicería	butcher shop
la cafetería	café, coffee shop
la farmacia	drugstore, pharmacy
el supermercado	supermarket
el mercado	market
la zapatería	shoe store
la tienda de ropa	clothing store
la tienda de electrodomésticos	appliance and electronics store

la librería	*bookstore*
la tienda por departamentos	*department store*
el alcalde	*mayor*
el ayuntamiento/la alcaldía	*city hall/municipal building*
comprar	*to buy*
ir de compras	*to go shopping*
cerca/lejos	*near/far*
urbano	*urban*
suburbano	*suburban*
rural	*rural*

18. ENTERTAINMENT

el entretenimiento	*entertainment*
la película	*movie, film*
ir al cine	*to go to the movies*
ver una película	*to see a movie*
el teatro	*theater*
ver una obra de teatro	*to see a play*
la ópera	*opera*
el concierto	*concert*
el club	*club*
el circo	*circus*
la entrada/el boleto	*ticket*
el museo	*museum*
la galería	*gallery*
la pintura	*painting*
la escultura	*sculpture*
el programa de televisión	*television program*
mirar la televisón	*to watch television*
la comedia	*comedy*
el documental	*documentary*
la obra dramática	*drama*

el libro	*book*
la revista	*magazine*
leer un libro	*to read a book*
leer una revista	*to read a magazine*
escuchar música	*to listen to music*
la canción	*song*
la banda/el conjunto	*band*
las noticias	*the news*
el programa de entrevistas	*talk show*
cambiar de canales	*to change channels*
divertirse	*to have fun*
estar aburrido	*to be bored*
gracioso	*funny*
interesante	*interesting*
emocionante	*exciting*
espantoso	*scary*
fiesta	*party*
restaurante	*restaurant*
ir a una fiesta	*to go to a party*
tener una fiesta	*to have a party*
bailar	*to dance*

The following is a list of Spanish language websites that students of Spanish will find interesting and useful.

www.livinglanguage.com	Living Language's site offers online courses, descriptions of supplemental learning material, resources for teachers and librarians, and much more.
cvc.cervantes.es	A site that promotes Spanish language and culture, with a lot of resources for students.
telemundo.yahoo.com	Yahoo! and Telemundo's web-portal for Spanish speakers in the U.S.
es.yahoo.com	Yahoo! for users in Spain.
mx.yahoo.com	Yahoo! for users in Mexico.
ar.yahoo.com	Yahoo! for users in Argentina.
www.google.com/intl/es	Google in the Spanish language.
news.google.es	Google news in Spanish.
www.onlinenewspapers.com	A site that will link you to newspapers from all around the world.
www.cnn.com/espanol	CNN en Español. This website contains international news from CNN in Spanish.

www.bbcmundo.com	BBC en Español. This site provides news in Spanish with a strong emphasis on international coverage.
latino.msn.com	MSN's Latin American portal.
www.terra.com	This is a major portal in many Spanish and Portuguese speaking countries.
www.diccionarios.com	This online dictionary gives synonyms and antonyms as well as translations from Spanish into several other languages, including English, and vice versa.
www.hola.com	This website's focus is on celebrities and European royalty, like the British magazine *Hello*.
espndeportes.espn.go.com	This is the Spanish version of the ESPN sports website.
www.canal13.cl	TV stations from Chile.

SUMMARY OF SPANISH GRAMMAR

1. THE ALPHABET

a	a	*j*	jota	*r*	ere
b	be	*k*	ka	*s*	ese
c	c	*l*	ele	*t*	te
d	de	*m*	eme	*u*	u
e	e	*n*	ene	*v*	ve
f	efe	*ñ*	eñe	*w*	doble ve
g	ge	*o*	o	*x*	equis
h	hache	*p*	pe	*y*	i griega
i	i	*q*	cu	*z*	zeta

The letters *ch, ll,* and *rr* were until recently considered separate letters.

2. PUNCTUATION
There are several differences between Spanish and English.

2.1. Inverted exclamation points and question marks precede exclamations and questions.

¿Adónde va usted?	*Where are you going?*
¡Hombre! ¿Adónde va Ud.?	*Man! Where are you going?*
¡Venga!	*Come!*
¡Qué hermoso día!	*What a beautiful day!*

2.2. The question mark is placed before the question part of the sentence.

Juan, ¿adónde vas?	*Juan, where are you going?*
Usted conoce al Sr. Díaz, ¿no es verdad?	*You know Mr. Díaz, don't you?*

2.3. Dashes are often used to show direct quotation.

Muchas gracias—dijo.	*"Thanks a lot," he said.*
Esta mañana—dijo—fui al centro.	*"This morning," he said, "I went downtown."*
—¿Cómo está usted?	*"How are you?"*
—Muy bien, gracias.	*"Very well, thank you."*

2.4. Capitals are not used as frequently as in English. They are only used at the beginning of sentences and with proper nouns. The pronoun *yo* (I), adjectives of nationality, the days of the week, and the months are not capitalized.

Somos americanos.	*We're Americans.*
Él no es francés sino inglés.	*He's not French but English.*
Vendré el martes o el miércoles.	*I'll come Tuesday or Wednesday.*
Hoy es el primero de febrero.	*Today is the first of February.*

2.5. Ellipses (. . .) are used frequently to indicate interruption, hesitation, etc.

3. ACCENT MARKS

3.1. The accent mark is used to show an irregularly stressed syllable or to distinguish between two words that are pronounced identically.

América (*America*)	precaución (*precaution*)
sí (*yes*)	si (*if*)
el (*the*)	él (*he*)

3.2. The tilde (~) is used over the letter *n* to indicate the *ni* sound in *onion* or *ny* in *canyon*.

español (*Spanish*)	mañana (*tomorrow*)
muñeca (*doll*)	año (*year*)

3.3. The dieresis (¨) is used over *u* in the combination *gu* to indicate the pronunciation *gw*. The combination *gu* without the dieresis is pronounced as *k*.

vergüenza (*shame*)   pingüino (*penguin*)
guitarra (*guitar*)   guía (*guide*)

4. THE DEFINITE ARTICLE
4.1. THE FORMS OF THE DEFINITE ARTICLE ARE:

	Singular	Plural
Masculine	el	los
Feminine	la	las

el muchacho (*the boy*)   los muchachos (*the boys*)
la muchacha (*the girl*)   las muchachas (*the girls*)

El is used before a feminine noun beginning with stressed *a* (or *ha*).

el agua (*the water*)   las aguas (*the waters*)
el hacha (*the axe*)   las hachas (*the axes*)

The article *lo* is used before parts of speech other than nouns when they are used as nouns.

lo malo (*what's bad, the bad part*)   lo difícil (*the difficult thing*)
lo hecho (*what's done*)   lo posible (*what's possible*)
lo dicho (*the thing that's said*)   lo necesario (*what's necessary*)
lo útil (*the useful thing*)   lo único (*the only thing*)

4.2. THE DEFINITE ARTICLE IS USED
a. with abstract nouns:

La verdad vale más que las riquezas.   *Truth is worth more than riches.*

b. with nouns referring to a class:

los soldados (*soldiers*) los generales (*generals*)

c. with names of languages, except immediately after common verbs, such as *hablar, saber, aprender, estudiar,* etc., or the prepositions *en* or *de*:

El español no es difícil.	*Spanish is not difficult.*
Ella habla bien el portugués.	*She speaks Portuguese well.*
Dígalo Ud. en inglés.	*Say it in English.*
Hablo español.	*I speak Spanish.*

d. in expressions of time:

Es la una de la mañana.	*It's 1:00 A.M.*
Son las dos de la tarde.	*It's 2:00 P.M.*
Llegan a las diez de la noche.	*They're getting here at 10:00 P.M.*

e. with the days of the week:

Abren los domingos a las dos y media.	*They open Sundays at 2:30 P.M.*
Partimos el lunes próximo.	*We leave next Monday.*

f. with the year, seasons, etc.:

Nos conocimos en el año 2007.	*We met in 2007.*
Vino el año pasado.	*He came last year.*
La primavera es muy hermosa.	*Spring is very beautiful.*
En el invierno hace frío.	*It's cold in winter.*

g. with certain geographical names:

El Brasil (*Brazil*)	El Uruguay (*Uruguay*)
El Canadá (*Canada*)	El Ecuador (*Ecuador*)
El Perú (*Peru*)	El Japón (*Japan*)

h. with parts of the body and articles of clothing instead of possessives:

Me duele la cabeza.	*My head hurts.*
Quítese el abrigo.	*Take your coat off.*

5. THE INDEFINITE ARTICLE

5.1. THE FORMS OF THE INDEFINITE ARTICLE ARE:

	Singular	Plural
Masculine	un	unos
Feminine	una	unas

un hombre (*a man*)	unos hombres (*men, some men, a few men*)
una mujer (*a woman*)	unas mujeres (*women, some women, a few women*)

Unos (unas) is often used to mean "some" or "a few."

unos días (*a few days*)	unas páginas (*a few pages*)

5.2. THE INDEFINITE ARTICLE IS *NOT* USED

a. before rank, profession, trade, nationality, etc.:

Soy capitán.	*I'm a captain*
Soy médico.	*I'm a doctor.*
Soy abogado.	*I'm a lawyer.*
Es profesor.	*He's a teacher.*
Soy norteamericano.	*I'm an American.*
Ella es española.	*She's Spanish.*

b. before *ciento/cien* (hundred), *cierto* (certain), or *mil* (thousand):

cien hombres	*a hundred men*
cierto hombre	*a certain man*
mil hombres	*a thousand men*

c. after the preposition *sin* (without):

Salió sin sombrero.   *He left without a hat.*

6. CONTRACTIONS

6.1. *de + el = del*

del hermano (*from the brother, of the brother*)   del puerto (*from the port, of the port*)

6.2. *a + el = al*

al padre (*to the father*)   al país (*to the country*)

7. THE DAYS OF THE WEEK

The days of the week are masculine and are not capitalized. The article is usually necessary, except after *ser*.

el domingo	*Sunday*
el lunes	*Monday*
el martes	*Tuesday*
el miércoles	*Wednesday*
el jueves	*Thursday*
el viernes	*Friday*
el sábado	*Saturday*

El domingo es el primer día de la semana.   *Sunday is the first day of the week.*

Van a visitarlos el domingo.   *They're going to pay them a visit on Sunday.*

Mañana es sábado.   *Tomorrow is Saturday.*

Notice that "on Sunday," "on Monday," and so on, are *el domingo, el lunes,* etc., whereas "on Tuesdays" is *los martes.*

8. THE MONTHS OF THE YEAR

The names of the months are masculine and are not capitalized. They are usually used without the definite article.

enero	*January*
febrero	*February*

marzo	March
abril	April
mayo	May
junio	June
julio	July
agosto	August
septiembre	September
octubre	October
noviembre	November
diciembre	December

9. THE SEASONS

el invierno	winter
la primavera	spring
el verano	summer
el otoño	fall

The names of seasons are usually not capitalized. They're used with the definite article, but after *de* and *en*, the article may or may not be used.

| Hace frío en (el) invierno. | *It's cold in (the) winter.* |
| Trabajo durante los meses de verano. | *I work during the summer months.* |

10. GENDER

10.1. NATURAL GENDER

Nouns referring to males are masculine, and nouns referring to females are feminine. Masculine nouns usually end in -*o*, and feminine nouns usually end in -*a*. Nouns that end in -*e* may be of either gender.

el padre (*the father*)	la madre (*the mother*)
el hijo (*the son*)	la hija (*the daughter*)
el hombre (*the man*)	la mujer (*the woman*)
el toro (*the bull*)	la vaca (*the cow*)
el gato (*the tomcat*)	la gata (*the female cat*)

The masculine plural of certain nouns stands for both genders.

los padres	*the parents, the father and mother*
los reyes	*the king and queen*
mis hermanos	*my brothers and sisters, my siblings*

10.2. GRAMMATICAL GENDER

All Spanish nouns, including inanimates and abstract concepts, have grammatical gender.

a. Nouns ending in -*o* are usually masculine.

el cuerpo (*the body*)	el cielo (*the sky*)
el dinero (*the money*)	el radio (*the radius*)

Two common exceptions are *la mano* (the hand) and *la radio* (the radio).

b. Nouns ending in -*r*, -*n*, and -*l* are generally masculine.

el calor (*the heat*)	el pan (*the bread*)
el sol (*the sun*)	el rincón (*the corner*)

c. Names of trees, days of the week, months, oceans, rivers, mountains, and other parts of speech used as nouns are generally masculine.

el álamo (*the poplar*)	el Tajo (*the Tagus River*)
el martes (*Tuesday*)	los Andes (*the Andes*)
el Atlántico (*the Atlantic Ocean*)	el ser joven (*the state of being young*)

d. Nouns ending in -*a* are usually feminine.

la cabeza (*the head*)	la mesa (*the table*)
la farmacia (*the drugstore*)	la ventana (*the window*)

Some common exceptions are:

el día (*the day*)	el mapa (*the map*)
el drama (*the drama*)	el clima (*the climate*)
el problema (*the problem*)	el poeta (*the poet*)

e. Nouns ending in -*dad, -tad, -tud, -ción, -sión, -ez,* and -*umbre* are usually feminine.

la ciudad (*the city*) la cantidad (*quantity*)
la libertad (*liberty*) la virtud (*virtue*)
la condición (*the condition*) la costumbre (*the custom*)
la tensión (*tension*) la madurez (*maturity*)

f. Names of cities, towns, and fruits are generally feminine.

Barcelona es muy bonita. *Barcelona is very nice.*
Comí una naranja y una *I ate an orange and an apple.*
manzana.

g. Note the following contrasts:

el orden (*order, arrangement*) la orden (*order, command*)
el capital (*capital, money*) la capital (*capital city*)
el cura (*priest*) la cura (*cure*)
el radio (*radius*) la radio (*radio*)

11. THE PLURAL

a. Nouns ending in an unstressed vowel or diphthong add -*s*.

el libro (*the book*) los libros (*the books*)
la puerta (*the door*) las puertas (*the doors*)
el agua (*the water*) las aguas (*the waters*)

b. Nouns ending in a stressed vowel or diphthong add -*es*.

el rubí (*the ruby*) los rubíes (*the rubies*)
la ley (*the law*) las leyes (*the laws*)

A few common exceptions are *las mamás* (mommies), *los papás* (daddies), and *los pies* (feet).

c. Nouns ending in a consonant add -*es*.

el avión (*the airplane*) los aviones (*the airplanes*)
el comedor (*the dining room*) los comedores (*the dining rooms*)
la canción (*the song*) las canciones (*the songs*)

d. Nouns ending in -z change the z to c and then add -es.

la luz (*the light*)   las luces(*the lights*)

el lápiz (*the pencil*)   los lápices (*the pencils*)

e. Some nouns are unchanged in the plural.

los martes (*Tuesdays*)   los Martínez (*the Martínez family*)

12. THE POSSESSIVE

Possession is shown by the preposition *de*.

el libro de Juan (*Juan's book*)   los amigos de los niños (*the boys' friends*)

las ventanas de la casa (*the windows of the house*)   la computadora del profesor (*the teacher's computer*)

13. ADJECTIVES

Adjectives agree with the nouns that they modify in both gender and number.

un muchacho alto (*a tall boy*)   una muchacha alta (*a tall girl*)

dos muchachos altos (*two tall boys*)   dos muchachas altas (*two tall girls*)

a. If the masculine singular ending is -o, the feminine singular is -a, the masculine plural is -os, and the feminine plural is -as.

Masc. Sing.	Fem. Sing.	Masc. Pl.	Fem. Pl.
alto (*tall*)	alta	altos	altas
rico (*rich*)	rica	ricos	ricas
bajo (*low*)	baja	bajos	bajas

b. If the masculine singular ending is not -o, there is no change in the feminine singular, and both genders take -es in the plural.

Masc. Sing.	Fem. Sing.	Masc. Pl.	Fem. Pl.
grande (*big*)	grande	grandes	grandes
pobre (*poor*)	pobre	pobres	pobres
azul (*blue*)	azul	azules	azules
cortés (*polite*)	cortés	corteses	corteses
útil (*useful*)	útil	útiles	útiles
triste (*sad*)	triste	tristes	tristes

c. There are four exceptions to this rule: adjectives of nationality that end in a consonant, adjectives that end in -*án*, adjectives that end in -*ón*, and adjectives that end in -*or*. In these cases, the feminine singular ends in -*a*, the masculine plural in -*es*, and the feminine plural in -*as*.

Masc. Sing.	Fem. Sing.	Masc. Pl.	Fem. Pl.
español (*Spanish*)	española	españoles	españolas
francés (*French*)	francesa	franceses	francesas
inglés (*English*)	inglesa	ingleses	inglesas
holgazán (*lazy*)	holgazana	holgazanes	holgazanas
burlón (*joker*)	burlona	burlones	burlonas
preguntón (*inquisitive*)	preguntona	preguntones	preguntonas

Masc. Sing.	Fem. Sing.	Masc. Pl.	Fem. Pl.
encantador (*charming*)	encantadora	encantadores	encantadoras
fascinador (*fascinating*)	fascinadora	fascinadores	fascinadoras

d. A few adjectives drop the final -*o* when they come before a masculine singular noun.

uno (*one*)   bueno (*good*)
malo (*bad*)   alguno (*some*)
ninguno (*none*)   primero (*first*)
tercero (*third*)   último (*last*)

Eres un buen amigo.   *You're a good friend.*
Hoy es el primer día del mes. *Today's the first day of the month.*

e. *Grande* becomes *gran* when it comes before a singular noun of either gender, *ciento* becomes *cien* before nouns and the number *mil,* and *Santo* becomes *San* before any name that doesn't begin with *To-* or *Do-*.

un gran amigo (*a great friend*) un gran poeta (*a great poet*)
una gran mujer (*a great woman*) una gran obra (*a great work*)
cien dólares (*a hundred dollars*) cien mil personas (*one hundred thousand people*)
San Juan   San Luis
Santo Tomás   Santo Domingo

14. POSITION OF ADJECTIVES
Descriptive adjectives usually follow the noun.
un libro blanco   *a white book*
una casa blanca   *a white house*

mi sombrero nuevo	*my new hat*
dinero mexicano	*Mexican money*
un hombre inteligente	*an intelligent man*
huevos frescos	*fresh eggs*

Exceptions are adjectives that describe an inherent quality.

un buen muchacho	*a good boy*

Articles, numbers, possessives, and quantitatives usually precede the noun.

muchas personas	*many persons*
poca gente	*few people*
cuatro huevos	*four eggs*
mis libros	*my books*

Some descriptive adjectives can come either before or after the noun.

una niña pequeña *or* una pequeña niña	*a little girl*
un día hermoso *or* un hermoso día	*a nice (beautiful) day*
una linda muchacha *or* una muchacha linda	*a pretty girl*

Other common adjectives used this way are *bueno* (good), *malo* (bad), and *bonito* (pretty).

A few adjectives have one meaning when they come before a noun and another when they follow one.

un hombre pobre	*a poor man (lacking money)*
¡Pobre hombre!	*Poor (unfortunate) man!*
un hombre grande	*a large (tall) man*
un gran hombre	*a great (important) man*
un libro nuevo	*a new (recent) book*
un nuevo hombre	*a new (different) man*
cierto hombre	*a certain man*
una noticia cierta	*a true piece of news*

15. COMPARISON

The regular comparitive is formed with *más* (more) or *menos* (less), and the regular superlative is formed with the definite article + *más* (the most) or *menos* (the least).

fácil	*easy*
más fácil	*easier*
menos fácil	*less easy*
el más fácil	*the easiest*
el menos fácil	*the least easy*

Certain common adjectives have irregular forms.

bueno (*good*)	mejor (*better, best*)
malo (*bad*)	peor (*worse, worst*)
mucho (*much*)	más (*more, most*)
poco (*little*)	menos (*less, least*)
grande (*big*)	mayor (*older*), más grande (*bigger*)
pequeño (*small*)	menor (*younger*), más pequeño (*smaller*)

Esta mesa es más grande que aquélla.	*This table is larger than that one.*
Pedro es mayor que Juan.	*Peter is older than Juan.*

"More . . . than" is expressed as *más . . . que,* and "less . . . than" is expressed as *menos . . . que.*

Mi hermana es más alta que mi madre.	*My sister is taller than my mother.*
Es más inteligente de lo que parece.	*He's more intelligent than he looks.*

"As . . . as" is expressed as *tan . . . como* before an adjective or adverb, and *tanto . . . como* before a noun.

Tan fácil como . . .	*As easy as . . .*
Él habla español tan bien como yo.	*He speaks Spanish as well as I do.*

Tiene tanto dinero como Ud.

He has as much money as you.

"The more/less . . . the more/less" is expressed as *cuanto más/menos . . . tanto más/menos . . .*

Cuanto más le trate tanto más le agradará.

The more you get to know him (deal with him), the more you like him.

The ending *-ísimo* is the absolute superlative, which can be translated as "extremely," "most," etc.

Es muy útil.

It's very useful.

Es utilísimo.

It's most/extremely useful.

16. PRONOUNS
16.1. SUBJECT PRONOUNS

yo (*I*)	nosotros (*we*, masc.)
	nosotras (*we*, fem.)
tú (*you*)	vosotros (*you*, masc.)
	vosotras (*you*, fem.)
él (*he*)	ellos (*they*, masc.)
ella (*she*)	ellas (*they*, fem.)
usted (*you*, polite)	ustedes (*you*, polite)

The subject pronouns are usually dropped unless special emphasis or clarity is required. The singular *tú* form is informal, while *usted* is formal or polite. The plural forms *vosotros* and *vosotras* are not used in Latin America and are replaced by *ustedes*. The masculine plural forms are used to refer to mixed groups.

(yo) hablo	*I speak*
(tú) hablas	*you speak* (infml.)
(él) habla	*he speaks*
(ella) habla	*she speaks*
(usted) habla	*you speak* (polite)
(nosotros) hablamos	*we speak* (masc. or mixed)
(nosotras) hablamos	*we speak* (fem.)

(vosotros) habláis	*you speak* (masc. or mixed)
(vosotras) habláis	*you speak* (fem.)
(ellos) hablan	*they speak* (masc. or mixed)
(ellas) hablan	*they speak* (fem.)
(ustedes) hablan	*you speak* (polite)

16.2. DIRECT OBJECT PRONOUNS

me (*me*)	nos (*us*)
te (*you*, fam.)	os (*you*, fam.)
la (*her, you, it*, fem.)	las (*them, you*, fem.)
lo (*him, you, it*, masc.)	los(*them, you*, polite)

Direct object pronouns come before the conjugated verb. They may either come before or be attached to an infinitive or a participle.

Carlos no te conoce.	*Carlos doesn't know you.*
Los oigo pero no los veo.	*I hear them, but I don't see them.*
Nosotros no la olvidamos.	*We don't forget her.*
Nosotros no queremos olvidarla.	*We don't want to forget her.*
Nosotros no la queremos olvidar.	*We don't want to forget her.*

16.3. INDIRECT OBJECT PRONOUNS

me (*to me*)	nos (*to us*)
te (*to you*, fam.)	os (*to you*, fam.)
le (*to him, to her, to you,* polite)	les (*to them, to you*, polite)

Indirect object pronouns come before the conjugated verb. They may either come before or be attached to an infinitive or a participle.

Les voy a ofrecer champaña.	*I'm going to offer them champagne.*
Le voy a regalar una guitarra.	*I'm going to give him a guitar.*

Margarita le está dando el plato.	*Margarita is giving him/her the dish.*
Margarita está dándole el plato.	*Margarita is giving him/her the dish.*

A prepositional phrase with *a* (to) is often added to clarify the meaning of *le* or *les*.

Le voy a regalar una guitarra a él.	*I'm going to give him a guitar.*
Margarita le está dando el plato a Marta.	*Margarita is giving Marta the dish.*
Le escribí a María ayer.	*I wrote to Maria yesterday.*

16.4. Pronouns used after Prepositions
After prepositions such as *para* (for), most of the pronouns used are identical to subject pronouns, except for *mí* (me) and *ti* (you).

para mí (*for me*)	para nosotros/as (*for us*)
para ti (*for you*, fam.)	para vosotros/as (*for you*)
para él (*for him*)	para ellos (*for them*, masc.)
para ella (*for her*)	para ellas (*for them*, fem.)
para usted (*for you*, polite)	para ustedes (*for you*, polite)

The special forms *conmigo* (with me), *contigo* (with you), and *consigo* (with him/her) also exist.

No puede vivir conmigo.	*He/She can't live with me.*
Necesito reunirme contigo urgentemente.	*I need to meet with you urgently.*

16.5. Reflexive Pronouns
Reflexive pronouns are used when a person or thing does something to himself, herself, or itself—for example, "I wash myself."

me (*myself*)	nos (*ourselves*)
te (*yourself,* fam.)	os (*yourselves,* fam.)
se (*himself, herself, yourself,* polite)	se (*themselves, yourselves,* polite)

They come directly before the conjugated verb. Many verbs that are reflexive in Spanish are not reflexive in English.

¿Cómo se llama usted?	*What's your name?*
Nos vemos en el espejo.	*We see ourselves in the mirror.*

16.6. Position of Pronouns

When there are both direct and indirect object pronouns in a sentence, the indirect object pronoun precedes the direct object pronoun. If both begin with *l*, the indirect (*le, les*) becomes *se*.

Me lo dan.	*They give it to me.*
Se lo diré.	*I will tell it to him/her/you.*

When *se* is present, it comes before the other object pronouns. *Se* may denote an impersonal action or a personal object that may or may not be reflexive.

Se dice.	*It is said.*
Se te dijo.	*It was told to you.*
Se la trató bien.	*She was treated well.*
Se lo dice.	*He says it to him/her./He says it to himself./She says it to herself.*

Object pronouns come before the verb. They may come after an infinitive or a present participle.

Lo veo.	*I see him.*
Se lo da.	*He gives it to him.*
tenerlo	*to have it*
dárselo	*to give it to him*
Quiero verlo.	*I want to see him.*
Voy a verlo.	*I'm going to see him.*
teniéndolo	*having it*
diciéndolo	*saying it*
Estoy mirándolo.	*I am looking at him.*

Object pronouns follow affirmative commands but come before negative commands.

Tómalo.	*Take it.*
Dígamelo Ud.	*Tell it to me.*
No me lo diga Ud.	*Don't tell me.*

17. CONJUNCTIONS

y	*and*
o	*or*
pero	*but*
más	*but*
que	*that*
pues	*since, as*
si	*if*
sino	*but*
por qué	*why*
porque	*because*
ni . . . ni	*neither . . . nor*

The conjunction *y* (and) becomes *e* before a word beginning with *i-* or *hi-*. The conjunction *o* (or) becomes *u* before a word beginning with *o-* or *ho-*. *Más* may be used in place of *pero* (but) in very formal or literary language, and in the negative, *pero* becomes *sino*.

Roberto y Juan son hermanos.	*Roberto and Juan are brothers.*
María e Isabel son primas.	*María and Isabel are cousins.*
Madre e hija.	*Mother and daughter.*
Cinco o seis pesos.	*Five or six pesos.*
Voy con mi hermano o con mi hermana.	*I'm going with my brother or with my sister.*
siete u ocho horas	*seven or eight hours*
cinco u ocho meses	*five or eight months*
Quiero venir pero no puedo.	*I want to come but I can't.*

Pensé que vendría más no pudo.	*I thought he would come, but he wasn't able to.*
No es francés sino inglés.	*He's not French but English.*
No viene hoy sino mañana.	*He isn't coming today, but tomorrow.*

18. INTERROGATIVES

The most common interrogatives are as follows. Notice that they're written with an accent.

¿Qué?	*What?*
¿Qué dice usted?	*What are you saying?*
¿Por qué?	*Why?*
¿Por qué dice usted eso?	*Why do you say that?*
¿Cómo?	*How?*
¿Cómo se dice en español esto?	*How do you say this in Spanish?*
¿Cómo se llama usted?	*What's your name? (lit., How do you call yourself?)*
¿Cuánto?	*How much?/How many?*
¿Cuánto dinero necesita usted?	*How much money do you need?*
¿Cuántas casas hay?	*How many houses are there?*
¿Cuánto hay de Madrid a Barcelona?	*How far is it from Madrid to Barcelona?*
¿Cuál?	*What?/Which one?*
¿Cuál es su nombre?	*What's your name?*
¿Cuál quiere usted?	*Which one do you want?*
¿Quién?	*Who?*
¿Quién vino con usted?	*Who came with you?*
¿Quién tiene eso?	*Who has that?*
¿Dónde?	*Where?*
¿Dónde está su amigo?	*Where is your friend?*
¿Cuándo?	*When?*
¿Cuándo se marcha Ud.?	*When are you going (leaving)?*
¿Cuándo ocurrió eso?	*When did that happen?*

19. ADVERBS

The Spanish suffix *-mente* corresponds to "-ly" in English. It is added to the feminine form of the adjective.

desfortunadamente	*unfortunately*
exclusivamente	*exclusively*

When there are two adverbs, the ending *-mente* is added only to the last one.

clara y concisamente	*clearly and concisely*

Adverbs are compared like adjectives.

alegremente	*cheerfully*
más alegremente	*more cheerfully*
lo más alegremente	*most cheerfully*

There are some irregular comparative forms of adverbs.

bien (*well*)	mejor (*better, best*)
mal (*poorly, badly*)	peor (*worse, worst*)
mucho (*much, a lot*)	más (*more, most*)
poco (*little*)	menos (*less, least*)

Many adverbs act as prepositions when *de* is added.

después	*afterward*
después de las cinco	*after five o'clock*
además	*besides*
¿Qué hay además de eso?	*What is there apart from this?*

When *de que* is added, adverbs act as conjunctions.

Después de que venga . . .	*After he comes . . .*

Common adverbs of time include:

hoy	*today*
ayer	*yesterday*
mañana	*tomorrow*

temprano	*early*
tarde	*late*
a menudo	*often*
siempre	*always*
nunca	*never*
jamás	*never*
luego	*afterward*
rápido	*quickly*
despacio	*slowly*
antes	*before*
después	*afterward*

Common adverbs of place include:

aquí	*here*
acá	*here (more common in Latin America)*
ahí	*there*
allí	*there (farther away)*
adelante	*forward, on*
atrás	*behind*
dentro	*inside*
arriba	*up, above*
fuera	*outside*
abajo	*down, below*
cerca	*near*
lejos	*far*

Common adverbs of quantity include:

muy	*very*
mucho	*much*
poco	*little*
más	*more*
menos	*less*
además	*besides*

cuánto	how much
tan	so much
tanto	so much
demasiado	too much
apenas	scarcely

Adverbs expressing affirmation include:

sí	yes
verdaderamente	truly
cierto	certainly
ciertamente	certainly
claro	of course
desde luego	of course
por supuesto	of course

Adverbs expressing negation include:

no	no, not
nunca	never
jamás	never
nunca jamás	never/ever (more emphatic)
ya no	no more, not now
todavía no	not yet
tampoco	neither, either
no tal	no indeed
ni	nor
ni . . . ni	neither . . . not
ni siquiera	not even

19.1. HERE AND THERE

Aquí (here) refers to something near the speaker, and *ahí* (there) refers to something near the person spoken to.

Tengo aquí los libros.	*I have the books here.*
¿Qué tiene Ud. ahí?	*What do you have there?*
¿Está Ud. ahí?	*Are you there?*

Acá (here) expresses motion toward the speaker, and *allá* (there) indicates motion away from the speaker. Both are more common in Latin America.

¡Venga Ud. acá!	*Come here!*
¡Vaya Ud. allá!	*Go there!*
Va allá.	*He's/She's going there.*

Allí (there) refers to something remote from both speaker and listener.

Vienen de allí.	*They come from there.*
Viví en Sudamérica por varios años.	*I've lived in South America for several years.*
¿Ha estado Ud. allí?	*Have you ever been there?*

20. DIMINUTIVES AND AUGMENTATIVES

The endings *-ito* (*-cito*, *-ecito*), *-illo* (*-cillo*, *-ecillo*), and *-uelo* (*-zuelo*, *-ezuelo*) imply smallness. In addition, *-ito* often implies attractiveness or admiration, whereas *-illo* and *-uelo* imply unattractiveness or deprecation. (They should be used with care.)

chico (*boy*)	chiquillo (*little boy*)
señora (*lady, Mrs., Ms.*)	señorita (*young lady, Miss*)
un poco (*a little*)	un poquito (*a little bit*)
pedazo (*piece*)	pedacito (*a little piece*)
gato (*cat*)	gatito (*kitten*)
papá (*papa*)	papito (*daddy*)
cuchara (*tablespoon*)	cucharita (*teaspoon*)
cigarro (*cigar*)	cigarrillo (*cigarette*)
autor (*author*)	autorcillo (*unimportant author*)

The endings *-ón* (*-ona*) and *-ote* indicate largeness (often awkwardness and unattractiveness, as well).

tonto (*foolish*)	tontón (*big fool, silly fool*)
silla (*chair*)	sillón (*big chair*)
cuchara (*spoon*)	cucharón (*ladle*)
hombre (*man*)	hombrón (*he-man*)

21. DEMONSTRATIVES

21.1. DEMONSTRATIVE ADJECTIVES

Masculine	Feminine	
este	esta	*this*
ese	esa	*that*
aquel	aquella	*that (farther removed)*
estos	estas	*these*
esos	esas	*those*
aquellos	aquellas	*those (farther removed)*

Spanish demonstrative adjectives usually precede the nouns they modify and always agree in gender and number.

este muchacho	*this boy*
aquellos vecinos	*those neighbors (over there)*

Ese and *aquel* both mean "that." *Aquel* points out a thing removed in space or time from the speaker or from the person spoken to.

Esa señora es muy amable.	*That lady is very kind.*
Aquel señor llegó el mes pasado.	*That gentleman arrived last month.*

21.2. DEMONSTRATIVE PRONOUNS

Masculine	Feminine	
éste	ésta	*this (one)*
ése	ésa	*that (one)*

Masculine	Feminine	
aquél	aquélla	*that (one)*
éstos	éstas	*these*
ésos	ésas	*those*
aquéllos	aquéllas	*those*

Neuter	
esto	*this (one), this thing*
eso	*that (one), that thing*
aquello	*that (one), that thing*

The same difference exists between the pronouns *ése* and *aquél* as between the adjectives *ese* and *aquel*.

No quería éste sino aquél.	*I didn't want this one, but the one over there.*

Éste and *aquél* also mean "the latter" and "the former."

Acaban de llegar el embajador y su secretario.	*The ambassador and his secretary just arrived.*
Éste es joven y aquél es viejo.	*The former is old and the latter is young.*

Notice that the Spanish order is the opposite of the English: *éste . . . aquél* (the latter . . . the former).

The neuter demonstrative pronouns *esto, eso,* and *aquello* refer to an idea previously stated and not to a specific thing.

Me dijo que aquello fue horrible.	*He told me that that was horrible.*

22. INDEFINITE ADJECTIVES AND PRONOUNS

todos	*all*
tal	*such*
ni uno	*not one*
otro	*other*
alguien	*someone*
nadie	*nobody*
algo	*something, anything*
ninguno	*no one, none*
alguno	*someone*
varios	*several*
nada	*nothing*
cualquiera	*whatever, whoever*
quienquiera	*whoever*

Alguien llama por teléfono.	*Somebody's calling on the phone.*
Nadie habla italiano aquí.	*No one here speaks Italian.*
No sabe nada.	*He/She doesn't know anything.*

23. NEGATION

No (not) comes before the verb:

No veo.	*I don't see.*
Él no habla.	*He isn't speaking.*

There are two forms for "nothing," "never," "no one," etc., both with and without *no*:

No veo nada.	Nada veo.	*I see nothing.*
No voy nunca.	Nunca voy.	*I never go.*
No viene nadie.	Nadie viene.	*No one is coming*

24. WORD ORDER

The usual order is subject-verb-adverb-object.

Juan vio allí a sus amigos.	*Juan saw his friends there.*

The tendency in Spanish is to put the longer or emphasized phrase last.

Me dio una carta.	*He gave me a letter.*
¿Compró la casa su padre?	*Did your father buy the house?*
Han caído veinte soldados.	*Twenty soldiers were killed.*

As in English, questions sometimes have the same word order as statements, but with question intonation—in other words, with a rise in pitch at the end.

¿Juan va a ir allí?	*Juan is going to go there?*

However, the more usual way of asking a question is to put the subject after the verb.

¿Va a ir allí Juan?	*Is Juan going to go there?*
¿Viene su amigo?	*Is your friend coming?*
¿Ha comido Ud.?	*Have you eaten?*
¿Habla usted español?	*Do you speak Spanish?*
¿Tiene usted dinero?	*Do you have any money?*
¿Por qué volvió Ud.?	*Why did you return?*
¿Ha recibido Juan mi carta?	*Did Juan get my letter?*

Adjectives come right after *ser,* which may mean that the subject of a question comes last.

¿Es tarde?	*Is it late?*
¿Es bueno?	*Is it good?*
¿Es difícil la prueba?	*Is the test difficult?*
¿Es fácil el problema?	*Is the problem easy?*

25. VERBS

25.1. THE INDICATIVE/*EL INDICATIVO*

Spanish verbs are divided into three conjugations according to their infinitive endings.

-AR verbs	(Class I)	hablar (*to speak*)
-ER verbs	(Class II)	comer (*to eat*)
-IR verbs	(Class III)	vivir (*to live*)

25.2. The Present Tense/*El Presente*

To conjugate a verb in the present tense, take off the *-ar, -er,* or *-ir* of the infinitive, and add the following endings:

Pronoun	-AR	-ER	-IR
yo	-o	-o	-o
tú	-as	-es	-es
él, ella, Ud.	-a	-e	-e
nosotros/as	-amos	-emos	-imos
vosotros/as	-áis	-éis	-ís
ellos/as	-an	-en	-en

hablar (*to speak*)	comer (*to eat*)	vivir (*to live*)
hablo	como	vivo
hablas	comes	vives
habla	come	vive
hablamos	comemos	vivimos
habláis	coméis	vivís
hablan	comen	viven

Note that the *vosotros* forms (*-áis, -éis, -ís*) are not used in Latin America. Also note that there are a number of verbs with irregular present (and other) tense conjugations, which are covered at the end of this summary.

The Spanish present tense can be translated into English in several ways—as a simple present, a present progressive, or a present emphatic.

Hablo español.   *I speak Spanish./I am speaking Spanish./I do speak Spanish.*

25.3. THE PRESENT PROGRESSIVE/*EL PRESENTE PROGRESIVO*

The present progressive emphasizes that an action is taking place at the moment of speech. It is formed with the auxiliary verb *estar* (to be—*estoy, estás, está, estamos, estáis, están*) and the present participle of the main verb. To form the present participle of *-ar* verbs, take off the *-ar* and add *-ando* to the stem. For *-er* and *-ir* verbs, take off the *-er* or *-ir* and add *-iendo* to the stem.

Estás hablando por teléfono.   *You're talking on the phone.*

Está comiendo churros.   *He/She is eating churros.*

No están escribiendo cartas.   *They/You aren't writing letters.*

25.4. THE PRETERITE/*EL PRETÉRITO*

To form the preterite, or simple past, take off the infinitive ending and add:

	-AR	-ER and -IR
yo	-é	-í
tú	-aste	-iste
él, ella, Ud.	-ó	-ió
nosotros/as	-amos	-imos

	-AR	-ER and -IR
vosotros/as	-asteis	-isteis
ellos/as	-aron	-ieron

The preterite expresses an action that began and ended in the past. It usually corresponds to the English simple past tense.

Él lo dijo.	*He said it.*
Habló conmigo.	*He spoke with me.*
Fui allí.	*I went there.*
Él nos vio.	*He saw us.*
Escribí una carta.	*I wrote a letter.*
Llovió todo el día.	*It rained all day.*
El tren se paró.	*The train stopped.*
Pasó tres años allí.	*He spent three years there.*
Lo vi.	*I saw him/it.*

Note that many common verbs have irregular preterite forms. Refer to the table of irregular verbs for more information.

25.5. THE IMPERFECT/*EL IMPERFECTO*
To form the imperfect, take off the infinitive ending and add:

	-AR	-ER and -IR
yo	-aba	-ía
tú	-abas	-ías
él, ella, Ud.	-aba	-ía
nosotros/as	-ábamos	-íamos

	-AR	-ER and -IR
vosotros/as	-abais	-íais
ellos/as	-aban	-ían

The imperfect is used to indicate continued or customary action in the past, or to refer to a "background" state or activity that was happening when some other action interrupted.

Cuando yo estaba en Madrid, siempre visitaba los teatros. — *When I was in Madrid, I always used to visit the theaters.*

Le encontraba todos los días. — *I used to meet him every day.*

Después del desayuno, corría por la playa. — *After breakfast, I would jog along the beach.*

Eran las once de la noche y nevaba. — *It was eleven at night and it was snowing.*

Él escribía cuando ella entró. — *He was writing when she entered.*

Empezó a llover cuando jugábamos en el parque. — *It began to rain while we were playing in the park.*

The following are the only Spanish verbs that are irregular in the imperfect:

ser (*to be*)	era, eras, era, éramos, érais, eran
ir (*to go*)	iba, ibas, iba, íbamos, íbais, iban
ver (*to see*)	veía, veías, veía, veíamos, veíais, veían

25.6. The Future/*El Futuro*

The future tense of regular verbs is formed by adding the ending -*é*, -*ás*, -*á*, -*emos*, -*éis*, or -*án* to the full infinitive.

hablar (*to speak*)	comer (*to eat*)	vivir (*to live*)
hablaré	comeré	viviré
hablarás	comerás	vivirás
hablará	comerá	vivirá
hablaremos	comeremos	viviremos
hablaréis	comeréis	viviréis
hablarán	comerán	vivirán

A few common verbs have irregular future stems: *diré* (I will say), *haré* (I will do), *podré* (I will be able to), *querré* (I will like), *sabré* (I will know), *saldré* (I will leave), *tendré* (I will have), *pondré* (I will put), and *vendré* (I will come).

The future tense generally expresses a future action, corresponding to the future with *will* in English.

| Lo compraré. | *I'll buy it.* |
| Iré mañana. | *I'll go tomorrow.* |

The future tense can also be used to express probability or conjecture.

¿Qué hora será?	*What time can it be?/What time do you think it must be?*
Será la una.	*It must be almost one.*
Estará comiendo ahora.	*He's probably eating now.*

25.7. The Present Perfect/*El Pretérito Perfecto*

The present perfect is formed with the auxiliary verb *haber* (*he, has, ha, hemos, habéis, han*) and the past participle of the main verb.

To form the past participle, take off the -ar ending of the infinitive and add -ado, or take off the -er or -ir ending and add -ido. The present perfect is used to indicate a past action that continues into the present or that has ended only recently.

Ha venido con su amigo.	*He has come with his friend.*
Hoy ella no ha comido.	*Today she hasn't eaten.*
¿Has estado en su casa?	*Have you been in his/her/their house?*

25.8. THE PAST PERFECT/*EL PLUSCUAMPERFECTO*

The past perfect, also known as the pluperfect, is formed with the imperfect of the auxiliary *haber (había, habías, había, habíamos, habíais, habían)* and the past participle of the main verb. It is equivalent to the English past perfect, and it refers to an action that happened before another point of reference in the past.

Ya habían llegado.	*They had already arrived.*
Yo había siempre querido conducir un Mercedes.	*I had always wanted to drive a Mercedes.*
Mis padres no habían ido a Grecia.	*My parents hadn't gone to Greece.*

25.9. THE FUTURE PERFECT/*EL FUTURO PERFECTO*

The future perfect is formed with the future of the auxiliary *haber (habré, habrás, habrá, habremos, habréis, habrán)* and the past participle of the main verb. It indicates an action that will happen before another point of reference in the future, and it is equivalent to the English future perfect. It can also be used to indicate probability.

Habrán llegado para entonces.	*They will have arrived by then.*
Habrá ido a China.	*He/She might have gone to China.*
Habrán llegado ayer.	*They probably arrived yesterday.*
¿Se habrán divertido?	*I wonder if they had any fun.*

25.10. THE PRETERITE PERFECT/*EL PRETÉRITO ANTERIOR*

The preterite perfect, which is rather rare, is formed by adding the past participle to the preterite of *haber (hube, hubiste, hubo, hubi-*

mos, hubisteis, hubieron). It is used to indicate that something occurred immediately before some other action in the past. It is usually replaced by the past perfect (*pluscuamperfecto*).

Apenas hubo oído eso, se marchó.	*No sooner had he heard that than he left.*
Cuando hube terminado las tareas, pude salir.	*When I had finished the homework, I was able to go.*

26. THE CONDITIONAL/*EL CONDICIONAL*
26.1. THE SIMPLE CONDITIONAL/*EL CONDICIONAL SIMPLE*

The conditional of regular verbs is formed by adding the ending -*ía, -ías, -ía, -íamos, -íais,* or -*ían* to the infinitive. It translates into English as *would*.

-AR	-ER	-IR
hablar (*to speak*)	comer (*to eat*)	vivir (*to live*)
hablaría	comería	viviría
hablarías	comerías	vivirías
hablaría	comería	viviría
hablaríamos	comeríamos	viviríamos
hablaríais	comeríais	viriríais
hablarían	comerían	vivirían

The same verbs that are irregular in the future are irregular in the conditional: *diría* (I would say), *haría* (I would do), *podría* (I could), *querría* (I would like), *sabría* (I would know), *saldría* (I would leave), *tendría* (I would have), *pondría* (I would put), and *vendría* (I would come).

The conditional is used to express hypothetical states or actions. Sometimes it expresses probability or conjecture.

¿Qué harías?	*What would you do?*
Mis amigos no vendrían.	*My friends wouldn't come.*
Serían las dos cuando él llegó.	*It was probably about two o'clock when he arrived.*
¿Qué hora sería?	*What time could it have been?*

26.2. THE PERFECT CONDITIONAL / EL CONDICIONAL COMPUESTO

The perfect conditional is formed with the conditional of the auxiliary *haber* (*habría, habrías, habría, habríamos, habríais, habrían*) and the past participle of the main verb. It corresponds to the past conditional in English with "would have."

| Habría hablado. | *I would have spoken.* |
| Habríamos ido. | *We would have gone.* |

27. IF-SENTENCES

If a sentence contains a clause beginning with *si* (if), the tense of the verb in the if-clause is determined by the tense of the verb in the main clause.

If the main clause has a verb in the:	the if-clause has a verb in the:
present	present/future
future	present
imperfect	imperfect
preterite	preterite
conditional	imperfect subjunctive (*-ra* or *-se*)
past conditional	past perfect subjunctive (*hubiera* or *hubiese*)

Si está aquí, trabaja.	*If he's/she's here, he's/she's working.*
Si estaba aquí, trabajaba.	*If he/she was here, he/she was working.*
Si está aquí mañana, trabajará.	*If he's/she's here tomorrow, he'll/she'll be working.*
Si estuviera aquí, trabajaría.	*If he/she were here, he'd/she'd be working.*

| Si fueras rico, ¿dónde vivirías? | *If you were rich, where would you live?* |
| Si hubiéramos llamado más temprano ayer, habríamos cerrado el trato. | *If we had called earlier yesterday, we would have closed the deal.* |

If the subject of the main clause and the subject of the if-clause are the same, it's possible to replace a verb in the subjunctive with an infinitive. In this case, *si* is replaced by *de*.

| De ser rico, ¿dónde vivirías? | *If you were rich, where would you live?* |
| De haber llamado más temprano ayer, habríamos cerrado el trato. | *If we had called earlier yesterday, we would have closed the deal.* |

28. THE SUBJUNCTIVE/*EL SUBJUNTIVO*

The indicative simply makes a statement about the world as it is, was, or will be. The subjunctive indicates a certain attitude toward the statement—uncertainty, desire, emotion, etc. The subjunctive is used in subordinate clauses when the statement is unreal, doubtful, indefinite, subject to some condition, or affected by will or emotion.

28.1. THE PRESENT SUBJUNCTIVE/*EL PRESENTE DEL SUBJUNTIVO*

The present subjunctive is formed by adding a present subjunctive ending to the stem of the first person singular present indicative. The endings for -*ar* verbs are -*e, -es, -e, -emos, -éis,* and -*en.* The endings for both -*er* and -*ir* verbs are -*a, -as, -a, -amos, -áis,* and *an.*

-AR	-ER	-IR
hablar (*to speak*)	comer (*to eat*)	vivir (*to live*)
hable	coma	viva
hables	comas	vivas

-AR	-ER	-IR
hable	coma	viva
hablemos	comamos	vivamos
habléis	comáis	viváis
hablen	coman	vivan

28.2. THE IMPERFECT SUBJUNCTIVE/*EL IMPERFECTO DEL SUBJUNTIVO*

The imperfect subjunctive is formed by adding an imperfect subjunctive ending to the stem of the third person plural preterite. There are two sets of endings. For -*ar* verbs, the endings are either -*ara, -aras, -ara, -áramos, -arais,* and -*aran* or -*ase, -ases, -ase, -ásemos, -aseis,* and -*asen.* For -*er* and -*ir* verbs, the endings are either -*iera, -ieras, -iera, -iéramos, -ierais,* and -*ieran* or -*iese, -ieses, -iese, -iésemos, -ieseis,* and -*iesen.*

-AR	-ER	-IR
hablar (*to speak*)	comer (*to eat*)	vivir (*to live*)
hablara	comiera	viviera
hablaras	comieras	vivieras
hablara	comiera	viviera
habláramos	comiéramos	viviéramos
hablarais	comierais	vivierais
hablaran	comieran	vivieran

or

-AR	-ER	-IR
hablar (*to speak*)	comer (*to eat*)	vivir (*to live*)
hablase	comiese	viviese
hablases	comieses	vivieses
hablase	comiese	viviese
hablásemos	comiésemos	viviésemos
hablaseis	comieseis	vivieseis
hablasen	comiesen	viviesen

28.3. THE PRESENT PERFECT SUBJUNCTIVE/*EL PRESENTE PERFECTO DEL SUBJUNTIVO*

The present perfect subjunctive is formed with the subjunctive of the auxiliary *haber* (*haya, hayas, haya, hayamos, hayáis, hayan*) and the past participle of the main verb.

-AR	-ER	-IR
hablar (*to speak*)	comer (*to eat*)	vivir (*to live*)
haya hablado	haya comido	haya vivido
hayas hablado	hayas comido	hayas vivido
haya hablado	haya comido	haya vivido
hayamos hablado	hayamos comido	hayamos vivido
hayáis hablado	hayáis comido	hayáis vivido
hayan hablado	hayan comido	hayan vivido

28.4. The Past Perfect Subjunctive/*El Pluscuamperfecto del Subjuntivo*

The past perfect subjunctive is formed with the imperfect subjunctive of the auxiliary *haber* (*hubiera, hubieras, hubiera, hubiéramos, hubierais, hubieran,* or *hubiese, hubieses, hubiese, hubiésemos, hubieseis, hubiesen*) and the past participle of the main verb.

-AR	-ER	-IR
hablar (*to speak*)	comer (*to eat*)	vivir (*to live*)
hubiera/iese hablado	hubiera/iese comido	hubiera/iese vivido
hubieras/ieses hablado	hubieras/ieses comido	hubieras/ieses vivido
hubiera/iese hablado	hubiera/iese comido	hubiera/iese vivido
hubiéramos/iésemos hablado	hubiéramos/iésemos comido	hubiéramos/iésemos vivido
hubierais/ieseis hablado	hubierais/ieseis comido	hubierais/ieseis vivido
hubieran/iesen hablado	hubieran/iesen comido	hubieran/iesen vivido

28.5. Uses of the Subjunctive

a. The subjunctive is used with verbs of desire, request, suggestion, permission, approval and disapproval, judgment, opinion, uncertainty, emotion, surprise, fear, denial, and so on. It is often used in a dependent clause introduced by *que* (that).

Quisiera verlo.	*I'd like to see him.*
¡Ojalá que lo haga!	*I wish he would do it!*
¡Ojalá lo supiera!	*I wish I knew it!*

Temo que se lo diga a él.	*I'm afraid he/she may say it to him.*
No creo que él le haya visto.	*I don't believe he's seen him.*
Niega que le haya visto.	*He denies that he's seen him.*
Me sorprende mucho que él no lo haya hecho.	*I'm really surprised that he hasn't done it.*
Espero que no venga.	*I hope he/she doesn't come.*
Me alegro de que Ud. esté aquí.	*I'm glad you're here!*
Temo que esté enfermo.	*I'm afraid he may be sick.*
Temo que no llegue a tiempo.	*I'm afraid he/she won't (may not) come in time.*
Duda que lo hagamos.	*He/She doubts that we'll do it.*
Dudo que sea verdad.	*I doubt that it's true.*
Dudo que sea posible.	*I doubt it's possible.*
El doctor duda que yo haya tenido pulmonía.	*The doctor doubts that I've had pneumonia.*
No creo que lo sepa.	*I don't think he/she knows it.*
No creo que mi hermano haya estado aquí.	*I don't think that my brother has been here.*
Se lo digo para que lo sepa.	*I'm telling you so that you know it.*

b. The subjunctive forms are also used in affirmative or negative commands in the polite form, in negative commands in the familiar form, in "let's" suggestions, and in indirect or third person commands with "let (him/her/them)."

¡Abra usted la ventana!	*Open the window!*
¡No hablen ustedes ahora!	*Don't talk now!*
¡No me digas (tú)!	*Don't tell me!*
¡No habléis ahora!	*Don't talk now!*
¡Leamos!	*Let's read!*
¡Entremos!	*Let's go in!*
¡Que vaya él!	*Let him go!*
¡Viva España!	*Long live Spain!*
¡Que vengan!	*Let them come!*

| ¡Que entren! | *Let them come in!* |
| ¡Que no venga! | *Let him not come!* |

c. The subjunctive is often used in *si* (if) conditional clauses. In real conditionals, the indicative is used.

| Si estaba allí, yo no le vi. | *If he was there, I didn't see him.* |
| No iremos si llueve. | *If it rains, we won't go.* |

But in conditionals that are unreal or contrary to fact, the subjunctive is used. If the if-conditional refers to an unreal present or future time, the imperfect subjunctive is used. If the if-conditional refers to a past time, the past perfect subjunctive is used.

Si fuera él, lo haría.	*If I were him (he), I'd do it.*
Si fuera mío esto, lo vendería.	*If this were mine, I'd sell it.*
Si tuviera el dinero, lo compraría.	*If I had the money, I'd buy it.*
Aunque hubiese tenido dinero, no hubiera ido.	*Even if I had had the money, I wouldn't have gone.*
Si lo hubiera sabido, no habría venido.	*If I had known it, I wouldn't have come.*
Si hubiese estado aquí, habríamos ido.	*If he/she had been here, we would have gone.*
Aunque lo hubiese intentado, no hubiera podido hacerlo.	*Even if I would have tried, I wouldn't have been able to do it.*

d. The subjunctive is used after impersonal verbs that do not express certainty.

| Es importante que vengan. | *It's important that they come/for them to come.* |
| Es preciso que estén aquí. | *It's necessary that they be here/for them to be here.* |

Es necesario que Ud. venga.	*It's necessary that you come.*
Es posible que lo tenga.	*It's possible that he has it.*
Fue una lástima que no vinieran.	*It was a pity that they didn't come.*

e. The subjunctive is used after certain conjunctions that never introduce statements of accomplished fact.

antes (de) que	*before*
a condición de	*on the condition that*
aunque	*even if*
a (fin de) que/para que	*in order that, so that*
a menos que	*unless*
como si	*as if*
con tal (de) que/en caso de que	*provided that, providing*
dado que	*granted that, given*
no obstante que	*notwithstanding that*
suponiendo que	*supposing that*

Aunque él no lo quiera, se lo daré.	*I'll give it to him even though he may not want it.*
Lo compraré aunque me cueste mucho.	*I'll buy it even if it costs me a lot.*
Se lo digo para que lo sepa.	*I'm telling you so that you may know it.*
con tal de que llueva mañana	*provided that it rains tomorrow*
Se fue sin que lo supiésemos.	*He went away without us knowing it.*
Iré con Ud. en caso de que tenga tiempo.	*I'll go with you provided I have time.*
No vamos a poder ir a menos que él llegue ahora.	*We won't be able to go unless he arrives now.*

Other conjunctions may or may not introduce a statement of accomplished fact. When they do, they take the indicative; otherwise, they take the subjunctive.

a menos que	*unless*
a pesar de que	*in spite of, notwithstanding*
antes que	*before*
así que	*as soon as*
aunque	*although, even though*
con tal que	*provided (that)*
cuando	*when*
de manera que	*so that*
de modo que	*so that*
después (de) que	*after*
en cuanto	*as soon as*
hasta que	*until*
luego que	*as soon as*
mientras que	*as long as, while*
para que	*in order that, so that*
siempre que	*provided that, whenever*

Iremos aunque llueve.	*We'll go even though it's raining.*
Iremos aunque llueva.	*We'll go even if it rains (even if it should rain).*

f. The subjunctive is used to refer to indefinites like *ningún* (no one) or *alguien* (someone) when there's doubt about that person's existence.

No hay ningún hombre que entienda esto.	*There's no man who understands this.*
Busco a alguien que hable español.	*I'm looking for someone who might speak Spanish.*
No conozco a nadie que pueda hacerlo.	*I don't know anyone who can do it.*

g. The subjunctive is used after compounds with *-quiera* (-ever): *quienquiera* (whoever), *dondequiera* (wherever), *cualquiera* (whatever, whichever).

quienquiera que sea	*whoever he/she/it may be*
Él quiere hacer cualquier cosa que ella haga.	*He wants to do whatever she does.*
Él quiere ir donde quiera que ella vaya.	*He wants to go wherever she goes.*

29. THE IMPERATIVE

29.1. AFFIRMATIVE FAMILIAR COMMANDS

The familiar commands are the command forms used with people you would address as *tú* or *vosotros*. The singular (*tú*) command form in the affirmative is the same as the third person singular of the present indicative.

¡Habla (tú)!	*Speak!*
¡Come (tú)!	*Eat!*
¡Sube (tú)!	*Go up!*

The plural (*vosotros/as*) is formed by removing the *-r* of the infinitive and adding *-d*. Remember that this form is used only in Spain. In Latin American, the *ustedes* form is used.

¡Hablad (vosotros/as)!	*Speak!*
¡Comed (vosotros/as)!	*Eat!*
¡Subid (vosotros/as)!	*Go up!*

There are a few common irregular commands in the singular. Note that the plural is always regular.

	Singular	Plural
ser (*to be*)	sé	sed
decir (*to say*)	di	decid
ir (*to go*)	ve	id

	Singular	Plural
hacer (*to do*)	haz	haced
poner (*to put*)	pon	poned
tener (*to hold*)	ten	tened
venir (*to come*)	ven	venid

29.2. NEGATIVE FAMILIAR COMMANDS
Familiar commands in the negative are in the present subjunctive.

Singular	Plural	
¡No hables!	¡No habléis!	*Don't speak!*
¡No comas!	¡No comáis!	*Don't eat!*
¡No subas!	¡No subáis!	*Don't go up!*

29.3. AFFIRMATIVE POLITE COMMANDS
Polite commands are used with people you would address as *usted* or *ustedes*. Remember that in Latin America, all plural commands are in the *ustedes* form. Polite commands are formed like the subjunctive, with an *-e/-en* ending for *-ar* verbs, and an *-a/-an* ending for *-er* and *-ir* verbs.

Singular	Plural	
¡Hable!	¡Hablen!	*Speak!*
¡Coma!	¡Coman!	*Eat!*
¡Suba!	¡Suban!	*Go up!*

29.4. NEGATIVE POLITE COMMANDS

The negatives are simply the same forms, with *no* added.

Singular	Plural	
¡No hable!	¡No hablen!	*Don't speak!*
¡No coma!	¡No coman!	*Don't eat!*
¡No suba!	¡No suban!	*Don't go up!*

29.5. COMMANDS WITH PRONOUNS

Object pronouns follow and are attached to the affirmative imperative and precede the negative imperative. When pronouns are attached, accents are often added to preserve the stress pattern.

¡Léelo!	*Read it!*
¡Habladle!	*Speak to him!*
¡Háblame!	*Speak to me!*
¡Háblales!	*Speak to them!*
¡Véndamelo!	*Sell it to me!*
¡Dame . . . !	*Give me . . . !*
¡Dímelo!	*Tell it to me!*
¡Dígamelo!	*Tell it to me!*
¡Decídnoslo!	*Tell it to us!*
¡Cómalo!	*Eat it!*
¡Tómelo!	*Take it!*
¡Dígamelo!	*Tell it to me!*
¡Escríbame una carta!	*Write me a letter!*
¡Escríbamelo!	*Write it to me!*
¡No lo coma Ud.!	*Don't eat it!*
¡No me lo diga Ud.!	*Don't tell it to me!*
¡No me escriba Ud.!	*Don't write to me!*
¡No les hables!	*Don't speak to them!*

¡No me des . . . !	*Don't give me . . . !*
¡No me lo digas (tú)!	*Don't tell it to me!*
¡No me digas (tú) eso!	*Don't tell me that!*
¡No nos lo digáis!	*Don't tell it to us!*

29.6. INDIRECT OR THIRD PERSON COMMANDS

Indirect commands are in the subjunctive and are usually preceded by *que.*

¡Que entren!	*Let them come in!*
¡Que él lo haga!	*Let him do it!*
¡Que lo haga Juan!	*Let Juan do it!*
¡Que le hable María!	*Let Maria talk to him!*
¡Que venga!	*Let him come!*
¡Que vaya él!	*Let him go!*
¡Que no venga!	*Let him not come!*
¡Viva España!	*Long live Spain!*

29.7. FIRST PERSON PLURAL COMMANDS

First person plural (let's . . .) commands are expressed by the subjunctive.

¡Hablemos un rato!	*Let's talk awhile!*
¡No hablemos!	*Let's not talk!*
¡Esperemos!	*Let's wait!*

One slight irregularity is with *ir,* which uses a shortened form in the affirmative.

¡Vamos!	*Let's go!*
¡No vayamos!	*Let's not go!*

29.8. IMPERATIVE OF REFLEXIVE VERBS

With reflexives, the reflexive pronoun follows and is attached to the verb in the affirmative command, but precedes it in the negative. The final -*d* of the familiar plural is dropped before the reflexive -*os* is added. That is, *sentados* becomes *sentaos.*

Singular	Plural	
¡Cállate!	¡Callaos!	*Be quiet!*
¡No te calles!	¡No os calléis!	*Don't be quiet!*
¡Cállese!	¡Cállense!	*Be quiet!*
¡No se calle!	¡No se callen!	*Don't be quiet!*
¡Siéntate!	¡Sentaos!	*Sit down!*
¡No te sientes!	¡No os sentéis!	*Don't sit down!*
¡Siéntese Ud.!	¡Siéntense Uds.!	*Sit down!*
¡No se siente Ud.!	¡No se sienten!	*Don't sit down!*

30. PARTICIPLES

30.1. PRESENT PARTICIPLES

The present participle (also called the gerund) of -*ar* verbs is formed by dropping the -*ar* of the infinitive and adding -*ando*; the present participle of -*er* and -*ir* verbs is formed by dropping the -*er* or -*ir* and adding -*iendo*.

hablar–hablando   *to speak–speaking*
comer–comiendo   *to eat–eating*
vivir viviendo   *to live–living*

Object pronouns follow and are attached to the present participle, and an accent is added to retain the stress.

comprándolos   *buying them*
vendiéndomelo   *selling it to me*
dándoselo   *giving it to him*

The present participle is used in progressive tenses, with a form of the auxiliary *estar.*

Estoy caminando por el callejón.	*I'm walking along the alley.*
¿Está usted viendo televisión?	*Are you watching TV?*
No están escribiendo cartas.	*They/You aren't writing letters.*
¿Qué estabas diciendo?	*What were you saying?*

It's also used absolutely, to describe some action or state of being of the subject.

Durmiendo, no me oyeron.	*Because they were sleeping, they didn't hear me./They didn't hear me because they were sleeping.*
Estando cansados, dormían.	*Being tired, they were sleeping./They were taking a nap because they were tired.*

30.2. PAST PARTICIPLES

The past participle of *-ar* verbs is formed by dropping the *-ar* and adding *-ado*. The past participle of *-er* and *-ir* verbs is formed by dropping the *-er* or *-ir* and adding *-ido*.

hablar—hablado	*to speak—spoken*
comer—comido	*to eat—eaten*
vivir—vivido	*to live—lived*

The past participle is used with the auxiliary *haber* in all compound tenses: the present perfect, the past perfect, the preterite perfect, the future perfect, the past conditional, the present perfect of the subjunctive, and the past perfect subjunctive.

No han pedido nada especial.	*They haven't asked for anything special.*
Me habías mentido otra vez.	*You had lied to me again.*
No creo que él le haya visto.	*I don't believe he's seen him.*
Me sorprende mucho que él no lo haya hecho.	*I'm really surprised that he hasn't done it.*

Si hubiéramos llamado más temprano ayer, habríamos cerrado el trato.

If we had called earlier yesterday, we would have closed the deal.

As in English, past participles can also function as adjectives.

el idioma escrito — *the written language*

las ropas lavadas — *the washed (pieces of) clothing*

los libros más vendidos — *the highest-selling books, the most-sold books*

30.3. IRREGULAR PARTICIPLES

The following are some of the most common verbs with irregular present and past participles. Blanks indicate a regular form.

	Present Participle	Past Participle
abrir (*to open*)		abierto
caer (*to fall*)	cayendo	caído
creer (*to believe*)	creyendo	creído
cubrir (*to cover*)		cubierto
decir (*to say*)	diciendo	dicho
despedirse (*to say good-bye*)	despidiéndose	
dormir (*to sleep*)	durmiendo	dormido
escribir (*to write*)		escrito
hacer (*to do, to make*)	haciendo	hecho
ir (*to go*)	yendo	

	Present Participle	Past Participle
leer (*to read*)	leyendo	leído
morir (*to die*)	muriendo	muerto
oír (*to hear*)	oyendo	
pedir (*to ask for*)	pidiendo	
poder (*to be able to*)	pudiendo	podido
poner (*to put*)	poniendo	puesto
seguir (*to follow*)	siguiendo	
sentir (*to feel*)	sintiendo	
traer (*to bring*)	trayendo	traído
venir (*to come*)	viniendo	
ver (*to see*)	viendo	visto
volver (*to return*)	volviendo	vuelto

31. PROGRESSIVE TENSES

The Spanish progressive tenses are formed with the auxiliary *estar* and the present participle of the main verb. As in English, they denote an action that is happening at the time of speech, or that was or will be happening at a given point of reference in the past or present.

Estoy trabajando aquí.	*I'm working here.*
Estábamos leyendo un periódico.	*We were reading a newspaper.*
Estoy divirtiéndome.	*I'm having a good time.*
Está hablando.	*He's speaking.*
Estaba esperándome.	*He was waiting for me.*

32. THE PASSIVE VOICE

The passive voice is formed with the auxiliary *ser* and the past participle of the main verb. The past participle must agree with the subject.

La carta fue escrita por ella.   *The letter was written by her.*

El edificio será construido el   *The building will be built next month.*
mes próximo.

The passive is used as in English. Very often, however, Spanish uses the reflexive *se* where English uses the passive.

Aquí se habla inglés.   *English is spoken here.*

Se dice que este libro es   *It's said that this book is very*
muy interesante.   *interesting.*

33. TO BE
33.1. FORMS OF *SER* AND *ESTAR*

There are two verbs in Spanish that mean "to be": *ser* and *estar*. Here are the present tense forms of *ser* and *estar*.

ser	estar	
yo soy	yo estoy	*I am*
tú eres	tú estás	*you are*
usted es	usted está	*you are*
él es	él está	*he is*
ella es	ella está	*she is*
nosotros somos	nosotros estamos	*we are*
nosotras somos	nosotras estamos	*we are*
vosotros sois	vosotros estáis	*you are*
vosotras sois	vosotras estáis	*you are*

ser	estar	
ustedes son	ustedes están	*you are*
ellos son	ellos están	*they are*
ellas son	ellas están	*they are*

33.2. USES OF *SER*

a. To indicate a characteristic that is unlikely to change:

Mi hermano es alto.   *My brother is tall.*
Son muy inteligentes.   *They're very intelligent.*

b. With a predicate noun or pronoun, in which case it links two equal things:

Él es médico.   *He is a doctor.*
Él es escritor.   *He's a writer.*
Él es español.   *He's Spanish (a Spaniard).*
Soy yo.   *It's me.*

c. With an adjective, to indicate an inherent quality:

El libro es rojo.   *The book is red.*
Ella es joven.   *She's young.*
El hielo es frío.   *Ice is cold.*
Es encantadora.   *She's charming.*

d. To indicate origin, source, or material:

¿De dónde es Ud.?   *Where are you from?*
Soy de España.   *I'm from Spain.*
Es de madera.   *It's made of wood.*
Es de plata.   *It's silver.*

e. To indicate possession:

¿De quién es esto?   *Whose is this?*
Los libros son del señor.   *The books belong to Mr. Díaz.*
Díaz.

f. To tell time:

Es la una.	*It's one o'clock.*
Son las dos.	*It's two o'clock.*
Son las nueve y diez.	*It's ten past nine.*

g. To indicate cost:

Son a noventa pesos la docena.	*They are ninety pesos a dozen.*
Son a nueve euros cada uno.	*They are nine euros each.*

h. In impersonal constructions:

Es tarde.	*It's late.*
Es temprano.	*It's early.*
Es necesario.	*It's necessary.*
Es una lástima.	*It's a pity.*
¿No es verdad?	*Isn't it?*

33.3. USES OF *ESTAR*

a. To express position or location:

Está allí.	*He's over there.*
Está en México.	*She's in Mexico.*
Nueva York está en los Estados Unidos.	*New York is in the United States.*
Los Andes están en Sudamérica.	*The Andes are in South America.*
El Canal está en Panamá.	*The Canal is in Panama.*
¿Dónde está el libro?	*Where's the book?*
Está sobre la mesa.	*It's on the table.*

b. To indicate a state or condition that may change:

Ella está contenta.	*She's glad.*
Estoy cansado.	*I'm tired.*
Estoy listo.	*I'm ready.*

El café está frío.	*The coffee's cold.*
Está claro.	*It's clear.*
La ventana está abierta.	*The window's open.*
La puerta está cerrada.	*The door's closed.*

c. To form the present progressive tense:

| Están hablando. | *They are talking.* |
| Estamos caminando. | *We're walking.* |

d. To ask about or describe states or conditions of physical or mental health:

¿Cómo está Ud.?	*How are you?*
¿Cómo están ellos?	*How are they?*
Estamos tristes.	*We're sad.*
Están muertos.	*They're dead.*
Estoy enojada.	*I'm angry.*

33.4. ADJECTIVES WITH *SER* OR *ESTAR*

Some adjectives may be used with either *ser* or *estar* with a difference in meaning.

Él es malo.	*He is bad (an evil person).*
Él está malo.	*He is sick.*
Ella es pálida.	*She has a pale complexion.*
Ella está pálida.	*She is pale (because she's sick).*

Other adjectives like this include:

	with *ser*	with *estar*
bueno	*good*	*well, in good health*
listo	*clever*	*ready, prepared*
cansado	*tiresome, tiring*	*tired*

34. REGULAR VERBS WITH SPELLING CHANGES

34.1. VERBS ENDING IN -CAR

In verbs ending in -*car*, such as *buscar* (to look for), *c* changes to *qu* when followed by *e*. This occurs in the first person singular of the preterite and all persons of the present subjunctive.

Preterite	Present Subjunctive
busqué	busque
buscaste	busques
buscó	busque
buscamos	busquemos
buscasteis	busquéis
buscaron	busquen

Verbs conjugated like *buscar*:

acercar (*to place near*)	sacrificar (*to sacrifice*)
educar (*to educate*)	secar (*to dry*)
explicar (*to explain*)	significar (*to signify, to mean*)
fabricar (*to manufacture*)	tocar (*to touch, to play music*)
indicar (*to indicate*)	verificar (*to verify*)
pecar (*to sin*)	sacar (*to take out*)

34.2. VERBS ENDING IN -GAR

In verbs ending in -*gar*, such as *pagar* (to pay), *g* changes to *gu* when followed by *e*. This occurs in the first person singular of the preterite indicative and all persons of the present subjunctive.

Preterite	Present Subjunctive
pagué	pague
pagaste	pagues
pagó	pague
pagamos	paguemos
pagasteis	paguéis
pagaron	paguen

Verbs conjugated like *pagar*:

ahogar (*to drown*)

apagar (*to extinguish*)

arriesgar (*to risk*)

cargar (*to load, to carry*)

castigar (*to punish*)

congregar (*to congregate*)

entregar (*to deliver*)

investigar (*to investigate*)

juzgar (*to judge*)

llegar (*to arrive*)

obligar (*to compel*)

otorgar (*to grant*)

pegar (*to hit*)

tragar (*to swallow*)

34.3. VERBS ENDING IN -*GUAR*

In verbs ending in -*guar*, such as *averiguar* (to ascertain, to investigate), *gu* changes to *gü* when followed by *e*. This occurs in the first person singular of the preterite indicative and all persons of the present subjunctive.

Preterite	Present Subjunctive
averigüé	averigüe
averiguaste	averigües
averiguó	averigüe

Preterite	Present Subjunctive
averiguamos	averigüemos
averiguasteis	averigüéis
averiguaron	averigüen

Verbs conjugated like *averiguar*:
aguar (*to water, to dilute*)   atestiguar (*to attest*)

34.4. Verbs Ending in -ZAR

In verbs ending in *-zar*, such as *gozar* (to enjoy), *z* changes to *c* when followed by *e*. This occurs in the first person singular of the preterite indicative and all persons of the present subjunctive.

Peterite	Present Subjunctive
gocé	goce
gozaste	goces
gozó	goce
gozamos	gocemos
gozasteis	gocéis
gozaron	gocen

Verbs conjugated like *gozar*:

abrazar (*to embrace*)   organizar (*to organize*)
alcanzar (*to reach*)   rechazar (*to reject*)
cruzar (*to cross*)   rezar (*to pray*)
enlazar (*to join*)   utilizar (*to utilize, to use*)

34.5. Verbs Ending in -GER

In verbs ending in *-ger,* such as *coger* (to catch), *g* changes to *j* when followed by *o* or *a*. This occurs in the first person singular of the present indicative and all persons of the present subjunctive.

Present	Present Subjunctive
cojo	coja
coges	cojas
coge	coja
cogemos	cojamos
cogéis	cojáis
cogen	cojan

Verbs conjugated like *coger*:
acoger (*to welcome*)   proteger (*to protect*)
escoger (*to choose, to select*)   recoger (*to gather*)

34.6. Verbs Ending in -GIR

In verbs ending in *-gir,* such as *dirigir* (to direct), *g* changes to *j* when followed by *o* or *a*. This occurs in the first person singular of the present indicative and all persons of the present subjunctive.

Present	Present Subjunctive
dirijo	dirija
diriges	dirijas
dirige	dirija
dirigimos	dirijamos

Present	Present Subjunctive
dirigís	dirijáis
dirigen	dirijan

Verbs conjugated like *dirigir*:
afligir (*to afflict*)   rugir (*to roar*)
erigir (*to erect*)   surgir (*to arise, to come up*)
exigir (*to demand*)

34.7. Verbs Ending in -*GUIR*

In verbs ending in -*guir*, such as *distinguir* (to distinguish), *gu* changes to *g* when followed by *o* or *a*. This occurs in the first person singular of the present indicative and all persons of the present subjunctive.

Present	Present Subjunctive
distingo	distinga
distingues	distingas
distingue	distinga
distinguimos	distingamos
distinguís	distingáis
distinguen	distingan

Verbs conjugated like *distinguir*:
conseguir (*to get, to obtain*)   perseguir (*to persecute*)
extinguir (*to extinguish*)   seguir (*to follow*)

34.8. Verbs Ending in -*CER* and -*CIR*

Verbs ending in a vowel followed by -*cer* or -*cir,* such as *conocer* (to know) and *lucir* (to shine), change *c* to *zc* before *o* or *a*. This occurs in the first person singular of the present indicative and all persons of the present subjunctive.

Present	Present Subjunctive	Present	Present Subjunctive
conozco	conozca	luzco	luzca
conoces	conozcas	luces	luzcas
conoce	conozca	luce	luzca
conocemos	conozcamos	lucimos	luzcamos
conocéis	conozcáis	lucís	luzcáis
conocen	conozcan	lucen	luzcan

Verbs conjugated like *conocer*:

aborrecer (*to hate*)
acaecer (*to happen*)
acontecer (*to happen*)
agradecer (*to be grateful*)
amanecer (*to dawn*)
anochecer (*to grow dark*)
aparecer (*to appear*)
carecer (*to lack*)
compadecer (*to pity*)
complacer (*to please*)
conducir (*to conduct, to drive*)
crecer (*to grow*)

embellecer (*to embellish*)
envejecer (*to grow old*)
fallecer (*to die*)
favorecer (*to favor*)
merecer (*to merit*)
nacer (*to be born*)
obedecer (*to obey*)
ofrecer (*to offer*)
oscurecer (*to grow dark*)
padecer (*to suffer*)
parecer (*to seem*)
permanecer (*to last*)

desaparecer (*to disappear*)   pertenecer (*to belong to*)
desobedecer (*to disobey*)   reconocer (*to recognize*)
desvanecer (*to vanish*)   traducir (*to translate*)

34.9. VERBS ENDING IN -*CER*

In verbs ending in a consonant followed by -*cer*, such as *vencer* (to conquer), *c* changes to *z* when followed by *o* or *a*. This occurs in the first person singular of the present indicative and all persons of the present subjunctive.

Present	Present Subjunctive
venzo	venza
vences	venzas
vence	venza
vencemos	venzamos
vencéis	venzáis
vencen	venzan

· Verbs conjugated like *vencer*:
convencer (*to convince*)   ejercer (*to exercise*)

34.10. VERBS ENDING IN -*UIR*

In verbs ending in -*uir* (but not -*guir* or -*quir*), such as *construir* (to build), *y* is added to the stem of the verb before *a*, *e*, or *o*. This occurs in all persons of the present indicative (except the first and second familiar persons plural), all persons of the present and imperfect subjunctive, the imperative second person singular familiar, and the third person singular and plural of the preterite.

Present	Present Subjunctive
construyo	construya
construyes	construyas
construye	construya
construimos	construyamos
construís	construyáis
construyen	construyan

Note that *i* between two other vowels changes to *y*.

Preterite	Imperfect Subjunctive	Imperative
construí	construyera (se)	
construiste	construyeras (ses)	construye
construyó	construyera (se)	
construimos	construyéramos (semos)	
construisteis	construyerais (seis)	construid
construyeron	construyeran (sen)	

Verbs conjugated like *construir*:

atribuir (*to attribute*)   huir (*to flee*)
constituir (*to constitute*)   influir (*to influence*)
contribuir (*to contribute*)   instruir (*to instruct*)
destituir (*to deprive*)   reconstruir (*to rebuild*)

destruir (*to destroy*)   restituir (*to restore*)
distribuir (*to distribute*)   substituir (*to substitute*)
excluir (*to exclude*)

34.11. VERBS WITH STEMS ENDING IN -ER

In verbs with stems ending in -*er*, such as *creer* (to believe), the *i* of the regular endings becomes *y* before -*e* and -*ó*. This occurs in the present participle (*creyendo*), the third person singular and plural of the preterite indicative, and both forms of the imperfect subjunctive.

Preterite	Imperfect Subjunctive
creí	creyera (se)
creíste	creyeras (ses)
creyó	creyera (se)
creímos	creyéramos (semos)
creísteis	creyerais (seis)
creyeron	creyeran (sen)

Verbs conjugated like *creer*:
caer (*to fall*)   leer (*to read*)
construir (*to build*)   poseer (*to possess*)

34.12. VERBS WITH STEMS ENDING IN -IR

In verbs with stems ending in -*ir*, such as *reír* (to laugh), the *i* of the regular endings -*ie* and -*ió* is dropped to avoid a second consecutive *i*. This occurs in the present participle (*riendo*), the third person singular and plural of the preterite indicative, and all persons of both forms of the imperfect subjunctive.

Preterite	Imperfect Subjunctive
reí	riera (se)
reíste	rieras (ses)
rió	riera (se)
reímos	riéramos (semos)
reísteis	rierais (seis)
rieron	rieran (sen)

Another verb conjugated like *reír* is *sonreír* (to smile).

34.13. **VERBS ENDING IN *-LLER*, *-LLIR*, *-ÑER*, AND *-ÑIR***

In verbs with stems ending in *ll* or *ñ*, such as *tañer* (to toll, to ring), the *i* of endings beginning with *-ie* or *-ió* is dropped. This occurs in the present participle (*tañendo*), the third person singular and plural of the preterite indicative, and all persons of both forms of the imperfect subjunctive.

Preterite	Imperfect Subjunctive
tañí	tañera (se)
tañiste	tañeras (ses)
tañó	tañera (se)
tañimos	tañéramos (semos)
tañisteis	tañerais (seis)
tañeron	tañeran (sen)

Verbs conjugated like *tañer*:
bullir (*to boil*)   gruñir (*to growl*)

34.14. Verbs Ending in *-IAR* and *-UAR*

Some verbs ending in *-iar* or *-uar*, such as *enviar* (to send) and *continuar* (to continue), take a written accent over the *i* or the *u* of the stem. This happens in all persons of the present indicative except the first plural and second plural familiar, in all persons of the present subjunctive except the first plural and the second plural familiar, and in the singular familiar of the imperative (*tú*).

Present	Present Subjunctive	Present	Present Subjunctive
envío	envíe	continúo	continúe
envías	envíes	continúas	continúes
envía	envíe	continúa	continúe
enviamos	enviemos	continuamos	continuemos
enviáis	enviéis	continuáis	continuéis
envían	envíen	continúan	continúen
Imperative			
envía (tú)	enviad (vosotros)	continúa (tú)	continuad (vosotros)

Verbs conjugated like *enviar*:

confiar (*to trust*)

criar (*to bring up*)

desafiar (*to challenge*)

desconfiar (*to distrust*)

fiar (*to give credit*)

guiar (*to guide*)

Verbs conjugated like *continuar*:

actuar (*to act*)

efectuar (*to carry out*)

evaluar (*to evaluate*)

perpetuar (*to perpetuate*)

35. THE CONJUGATION OF REGULAR VERBS

Infinitive	Pres. & Past Participles	Present Indicative	Imperfect	Preterite	Future	Conditional	Present Perfect	Pluperfect	Preterite Perfect
-ar ending	hablando	hablo	hablaba	hablé	hablaré	hablaría	he....	había....	hube....
hablar	hablado	hablas	hablabas	hablaste	hablarás	hablarías	has....	habías....	hubiste....
to speak		habla	hablaba	habló	hablará	hablaría	ha....	había....	hubo....
		hablamos	hablábamos	hablamos	hablaremos	hablaríamos	hemos....	habíamos....	hubimos....
		habláis	hablabais	hablasteis	hablaréis	hablaríais	habéis....	habíais....	hubisteis....
		hablan	hablaban	hablaron	hablarán	hablarían	han....	habían....	hubieron....
							..hablado	..hablado	..hablado
-er ending	comiendo	como	comía	comí	comeré	comería	he....	había....	hube....
comer	comido	comes	comías	comiste	comerás	comerías	has....	habías....	hubiste....
to eat		come	comía	comió	comerá	comería	ha....	había....	hubo....
		comemos	comíamos	comimos	comeremos	comeríamos	hemos....	habíamos....	hubimos....
		coméis	comíais	comisteis	comeréis	comeríais	habéis....	habíais....	hubisteis....
		comen	comían	comieron	comerán	comerían	han....	habían....	hubieron....
							..comido	..comido	..comido
-ir ending	viviendo	vivo	vivía	viví	viviré	viviría	he....	había....	hube....
vivir	vivido	vives	vivías	viviste	virirás	vivirías	has....	habías....	hubiste....
to live		vive	vivía	vivió	vivirá	viviría	ha....	había....	hubo....
		vivimos	vivíamos	vivimos	viviremos	viviríamos	hemos....	habíamos....	hubimos....
		vivís	vivíais	vivisteis	viviréis	viviríais	habéis....	habíais....	hubisteis....
		viven	vivían	vivieron	vivirán	vivirían	han....	habían....	hubieron....
							..vivido	..vivido	..vivido

hablar

Future Perfect	Conditional Perfect	Present Subjunctive	Imperfect Subjunctive (-ra)	Imperfect Subjunctive (-se)	Present Perfect Subjunctive	Pluperfect Subjunctive (-ra)	Pluperfect Subjunctive (-se)	Imperative
habré...	habría...	hable	hablara	hablase	haya...	hubiera...	hubiese...	
habrás...	habrías...	hables	hablaras	hablases	hayas...	hubieras...	hubieses...	¡Habla (tú)!
habrá...	habría...	hable	hablara	hablase	haya...	hubiera...	hubiese...	¡Hable (Ud.)!
habremos...	habríamos...	hablemos	habláramos	hablásemos	hayamos...	hubiéramos...	hubiésemos...	¡Hablemos (nosotros)!
habréis...	habríais...	habléis	hablarais	hablaseis	hayáis...	hubierais...	hubieseis...	¡Hablad (vosotros)!
habrán... hablado	habrían... hablado	hablen	hablaran	hablasen	hayan... hablado	hubieran... hablado	hubiesen... hablado	¡Hablen (Uds.)!

comer

Future Perfect	Conditional Perfect	Present Subjunctive	Imperfect Subjunctive (-ra)	Imperfect Subjunctive (-se)	Present Perfect Subjunctive	Pluperfect Subjunctive (-ra)	Pluperfect Subjunctive (-se)	Imperative
habré...	habría...	coma	comiera	comiese	haya...	hubiera...	hubiese...	
habrás...	habrías...	comas	comieras	comieses	hayas...	hubieras...	hubieses...	¡Come (tú)!
habrá...	habría...	coma	comiera	comiese	haya...	hubiera...	hubiese...	¡Coma (Ud.)!
habremos...	habríamos...	comamos	comiéramos	comiésemos	hayamos...	hubiéramos...	hubiésemos...	¡Comamos (nosotros)!
habréis...	habríais...	comáis	comierais	comieseis	hayáis...	hubierais...	hubieseis...	¡Comed (vosotros)!
habrán... comido	habrían... comido	coman	comieran	comiesen	hayan... comido	hubieran... comido	hubiesen... comido	¡Coman (Uds.)!

vivir

Future Perfect	Conditional Perfect	Present Subjunctive	Imperfect Subjunctive (-ra)	Imperfect Subjunctive (-se)	Present Perfect Subjunctive	Pluperfect Subjunctive (-ra)	Pluperfect Subjunctive (-se)	Imperative
habré...	habría...	viva	viviera	viviese	haya...	hubiera...	hubiese...	
habrás...	habrías...	vivas	vivieras	vivieses	hayas...	hubieras...	hubieses...	¡Vive (tú)!
habrá...	habría...	viva	viviera	viviese	haya...	hubiera...	hubiese...	¡Viva (Ud.)!
habremos...	habríamos...	vivamos	viviéramos	viviésemos	hayamos...	hubiéramos...	hubiésemos...	¡Vivamos (nosotros)!
habréis...	habríais...	viváis	vivierais	vivieseis	hayáis...	hubierais...	hubieseis...	¡Vivid (vosotros)!
habrán... vivido	habrían... vivido	vivan	vivieran	viviesen	hayan... vivido	hubieran... vivido	hubiesen... vivido	¡Vivan (Uds.)!

36. STEM-CHANGING VERBS

The following tables show verbs whose stems change in certain tenses. In all other tenses not shown, these verbs are conjugated as regular verbs, without any stem change.

36.1. GROUP 1: *-AR* AND *-ER* VERBS ONLY

The first group includes *-ar* verbs and *-er* verbs with two types of stem changes:

o → *ue* when the stress falls on the verb root in the conjugated forms, as in *contar* (to count, to tell) and *volver* (to return)

e → *ie* when the stress falls on the verb root in the conjugated forms, as in *pensar* (to think) and *perder* (to lose)

Infinitive	Present Indicative	Present Subjunctive	Imperative	Similarly Conjugated Verbs		
contar (o → ue) to count	cuento cuentas cuenta contamos contáis cuentan	cuente cuentes cuente contemos contéis cuenten	cuenta contad	acordar acordarse acostarse almorzar apostar aprobar	avergonzar avergonzarse colgar costar encontrar jugar (u → ue)	probar recordar recordarse sonar volar
volver (o → ue) to return	vuelvo vuelves vuelve volvemos volvéis vuelven	vuelva vuelvas vuelva volvamos volváis vuelvan	vuelve volved	devolver doler dolerse llover morder mover	oler soler	
pensar (e → ie) to think	pienso piensas piensa pensamos pensáis piensan	piense pienses piense pensemos penséis piensen	piensa pensad	acertar apretar calentar cerrar confesar despertar	empezar encerrar gobernar plegar quebrar sentarse	temblar tentar
perder (e → ie) to lose	pierdo pierdes pierde perdemos perdéis pierden	pierda pierdas pierda perdamos perdáis pierdan	pierde perded	ascender atender defender descender encender entender	extender tender	

36.2. GROUP 2: -*IR* VERBS ONLY

The second group includes -*ir* verbs with four types of stem changes:

o → *ue* when the stress falls on the verb root in the conjugated forms, as in *dormir* (to sleep)

o → *u* when the stress falls on the ending, as in the present subjunctive and the third person of the preterite of *dormir*

e → *ie* when the stress falls on the root, as in *sentir* (to feel, to be sorry)

e → *i* when the stress falls on the ending, as in the present subjunctive and third person of the preterite of *sentir*

Infinitive	Present Indicative	Present Subjunctive	Preterite	Imperative	Similarly Conjugated Verbs	
dormir to sleep	duermes duermo duerme dormimos dormís duermen	duerma duermas duerma durmamos durmáis duerman	dormí dormiste durmió dormimos dormisteis durmieron	duerme dormid	morir (past participle: *muerto*)	
sentir to feel	siento sientes siente sentimos sentís sienten	sienta sientas sienta sintamos sintáis sientan	sentí sentiste sintió sentimos sentisteis sintieron	siente sentid	advertir arrepentirse consentir convertir diferir divertir	herir mentir preferir presentir referir sugerir

36.3. GROUP 3: -IR VERBS ONLY

The third group includes -*ir* verbs with one type of stem change: $e \rightarrow i$ when the stress falls on the verb root in the conjugated forms, and in the third person forms of the preterite, as in *pedir* (to ask for)

Infinitive	Present Indicative	Present Subjunctive	Preterite Indicative	Imperfect Subjunctive	Imperative	Similarly Conjugated Verbs
pedir to ask	pido pides pide pedimos pedís piden	pida pidas pida pidamos pidáis pidan	pedí pediste pidió pedimos pedisteis pidieron	pidiera (se) pidieras (ses) pidiera (se) pidiéramos (semos) pidiérais (seis) pidieran (sen)	pide pedid	competir conseguir corregir despedir despedirse elegir expedir reír repetir seguir servir vestir

37. COMMON IRREGULAR VERBS

The following chart includes the most common irregular verbs in the most important simple tenses. To form the compound tenses, use the appropriate form of the auxiliary *haber* along with the past participle. To form the progressive tenses, use the appropriate form of the auxiliary *estar* along with the present participle. Both of these auxiliaries are included below.

Infinitive Present and Past Participles	Present Indicative	Present Subjunctive	Imperfect	Preterite	Future	Conditional	Imperative
andar to walk / *andando* / *andado*	ando andas anda andamos andáis andan	ande andes ande andemos andéis anden	andaba andabas andaba andábamos andabais andaban	anduve anduviste anduvo anduvimos anduvisteis anduvieron	andaré andarás andará andaremos andaréis andarán	andaría andarías andaría andaríamos andaríais andarían	anda andad
caber to fit, to be contained in / *cabiendo* / *cabido*	quepo cabes cabe cabemos cabéis caben	quepa quepas quepa quepamos quepáis quepan	cabía cabías cabía cabíamos cabíais cabían	cupe cupiste cupo cupimos cupisteis cupieron	cabré cabrás cabrá cabremos cabréis cabrán	cabría cabrías cabría cabríamos cabríais cabrían	cabe cabed
caer to fall / *cayendo* / *caído*	caigo caes cae caemos caéis caen	caiga caigas caiga caigamos caigáis caigan	caía caías caía caíamos caíais caían	caí caíste cayó caímos caísteis cayeron	caeré caerás caerá caeremos caeréis caerán	caería caerías caería caeríamos caeríais caerían	cae caed
conducir to lead, to drive / *conduciendo* / *conducido*	conduzco conduces conduce conducimos conducís conducen	conduzca conduzcas conduzca conduzcamos conduzcáis conduzcan	conducía conducías conducía conducíamos conducíais conducían	conduje condujiste condujo condujimos condujisteis condujeron	conduciré conducirás conducirá conduciremos conduciréis conducirán	conduciría conducirías conduciría conduciríamos conduciríais conducirían	conduce conducid

Infinitive Present and Past Participles	Present Indicative	Present Subjunctive	Imperfect	Preterite	Future	Conditional	Imperative
dar to give	doy	dé	daba	di	daré	daría	da
	das	des	dabas	diste	darás	darías	dad
dando	da	dé	daba	dio	dará	daría	
dado	damos	demos	dábamos	dimos	daremos	daríamos	
	dais	deis	dabais	disteis	daréis	daríais	
	dan	den	daban	dieron	darán	darían	
decir to say, to tell	digo	diga	decía	dije	diré	diría	di
	dices	digas	decías	dijiste	dirás	dirías	decid
diciendo	dice	diga	decía	dijo	dirá	diría	
dicho	decimos	digamos	decíamos	dijimos	diremos	diríamos	
	decís	digáis	decíais	dijisteis	diréis	diríais	
	dicen	digan	decían	dijeron	dirán	dirían	
estar to be	estoy	esté	estaba	estuve	estaré	estaría	está
	estás	estés	estabas	estuviste	estarás	estarías	estad
estando	está	esté	estaba	estuvo	estará	estaría	
estado	estamos	estemos	estábamos	estuvimos	estaremos	estaríamos	
	estáis	estéis	estabais	estuvisteis	estaréis	estaríais	
	están	estén	estaban	estuvieron	estarán	estarían	
haber to have (auxiliary)	he	haya	había	hube	habré	habría	
	has	hayas	habías	hubiste	habrás	habrías	
habiendo	ha	haya	había	hubo	habrá	habría	
habido	hemos	hayamos	habíamos	hubimos	habremos	habríamos	
	habéis	hayáis	habíais	hubisteis	habréis	habríais	
	han	hayan	habían	hubieron	habrán	habrían	

Infinitive Present and Past Participles	Present Indicative	Present Subjunctive	Imperfect	Preterite	Future	Conditional	Imperative
hacer to do, to make	hago	haga	hacía	hice	haré	haría	haz
	haces	hagas	hacías	hiciste	harás	harías	haced
	hace	haga	hacía	hizo	hará	haría	
haciendo	hacemos	hagamos	hacíamos	hicimos	haremos	haríamos	
hecho	hacéis	hagáis	hacíais	hicisteis	haréis	haríais	
	hacen	hagan	hacían	hicieron	harán	harían	
ir to go	voy	vaya	iba	fui	iré	iría	ve
	vas	vayas	ibas	fuiste	irás	irías	id
	va	vaya	iba	fue	irá	iría	
yendo	vamos	vayamos	íbamos	fuimos	iremos	iríamos	
ido	vais	vayáis	ibais	fuisteis	iréis	iríais	
	van	vayan	iban	fueron	irán	irían	
oír to hear	oigo	oiga	oía	oí	oiré	oiría	oye
	oyes	oigas	oías	oíste	oirás	oirías	oíd
	oye	oiga	oía	oyó	oirá	oiría	
oyendo	oímos	oigamos	oíamos	oímos	oiremos	oiríamos	
oído	oís	oigáis	oíais	oísteis	oiréis	oiríais	
	oyen	oigan	oían	oyeron	oirán	oirían	
poder to be able, can	puedo	pueda	podía	pude	podré	podría	puede
	puedes	puedas	podías	pudiste	podrás	podrías	poded
	puede	pueda	podía	pudo	podrá	podría	
pudiendo	podemos	podamos	podíamos	pudimos	podremos	podríamos	
podido	podéis	podáis	podíais	pudisteis	podréis	podríais	
	pueden	puedan	podían	pudieron	podrán	podrían	

Infinitive Present and Past Participles	Present Indicative	Present Subjunctive	Imperfect	Preterite	Future	Conditional	Imperative
poner to put, to place *poniendo* *puesto*	pongo pones pone ponemos ponéis ponen	ponga pongas ponga pongamos pongáis pongan	ponía ponías ponía poníamos poníais ponían	puse pusiste puso pusimos pusisteis pusieron	pondré pondrás pondrá pondremos pondréis pondrán	pondría pondrías pondría pondríamos pondríais pondrían	pon poned
querer to want, to love *queriendo* *querido*	quiero quieres quiere queremos queréis quieren	quiera quieras quiera queramos queráis quieran	quería querías quería queríamos queríais querían	quise quisiste quiso quisimos quisisteis quisieron	querré querrás querrá querremos querréis querrán	querría querrías querría querríamos querríais querrían	quiere quered
reír to laugh *riendo* *reído*	río ríes ríe reímos reís ríen	ría rías ría riamos riáis rían	reía reías reía reíamos reíais reían	reí reíste rió reímos reísteis rieron	reiré reirás reirá reiremos reiréis reirán	reiría reirías reiría reiríamos reiríais reirían	ríe reíd
saber to know *sabiendo* *sabido*	sé sabes sabe sabemos sabéis saben	sepa sepas sepa sepamos sepáis sepan	sabía sabías sabía sabíamos sabíais sabían	supe supiste supo supimos supisteis supieron	sabré sabrás sabra sabremos sabréis sabrán	sabría sabrías sabría sabríamos sabrías sabrían	sabe sabed

Infinitive Present and Past Participles	Present Indicative	Present Subjunctive	Imperfect	Preterite	Future	Conditional	Imperative
salir to go out, to leave *saliendo* *salido*	salgo sales sale salimos salís salen	salga salgas salga salgamos salgáis salgan	salía salías salía salíamos salíais salían	salí saliste salió salimos salisteis salieron	saldré saldrás saldrá saldremos saldréis saldrán	saldría saldrías saldría saldríamos saldríais saldrían	sal salid
ser to be *siendo* *sido*	soy eres es somos sois son	sea seas sea seamos seáis sean	era eras era éramos erais eran	fui fuiste fue fuimos fuisteis fueron	seré serás será seremos seréis serán	sería serías sería seríamos seríais serían	sé sed
tener to have *teniendo* *tenido*	tengo tienes tiene tenemos tenéis tienen	tenga tengas tenga tengamos tengáis tengan	tenía tenías tenía teníamos teníais tenían	tuve tuviste tuvo tuvimos tuvisteis tuvieron	tendré tendrás tendrá tendremos tendréis tendrán	tendría tendrías tendría tendríamos tendríais tendrían	ten tened
traer to bring *trayendo* *traído*	traigo traes trae traemos traéis traen	traiga traigas traiga traigamos traigáis traigan	traía traías traía traíamos traíais traían	traje trajiste trajo trajimos trajisteis trajeron	traeré traerás traerá traeremos traeréis traerán	traería traerías traería traeríamos traeríais traerían	trae traed

Infinitive Present and Past Participles	Present Indicative	Present Subjunctive	Imperfect	Preterite	Future	Conditional	Imperative
valer to be worth, to cost *valiendo* *valido*	valgo vales vale valemos valéis valen	valga valgas valga valgamos valgáis valgan	valía valías valía valíamos valíais valían	valí valiste valió valimos valisteis valieron	valdré valdrás valdrá valdremos valdréis valdrán	valdría valdrías valdría valdríamos valdríais valdrían	val valed
venir to come *viniendo* *venido*	vengo vienes viene venimos venís vienen	venga vengas venga vengamos vengáis vengan	venía venías venía veníamos veníais venían	vine viniste vino vinimos vinisteis vinieron	vendré vendrás vendrá vendremos vendréis vendrán	vendría vendrías vendría vendríamos vendríais vendrían	ven venid
ver to see *viendo* *visto*	veo ves ve vemos veis ven	vea veas vea veamos veáis vean	veía veías veía veíamos veíais veían	vi viste vio vimos visteis vieron	veré verás verá veremos veréis verán	vería verías vería veríamos veríais verían	ve ved